DISCOURSES OF EDUCATION IN THE AGE
OF NEW IMPERIALISM

Discourses of Education in the Age of New Imperialism

edited by Jerome Satterthwaite
and Elizabeth Atkinson

Trentham Books
Stoke on Trent, UK and Sterling, USA

Trentham Books Limited
Westview House   22883 Quicksilver Drive
734 London Road   Sterling
Oakhill   VA 20166-2012
Stoke on Trent   USA
Staffordshire
England ST4 5NP

First published 2005

British Library Cataloguing-in-Publication Data
A catalogue record for this book is available from the British Library

ISBN-13: 978-1-85856-357-2
ISBN-10: 1-85856-357-7

Designed and typeset by Trentham Print Design Ltd., Chester and printed in Great Britain by Cromwell Press Ltd, Wiltshire.

Contents

PART TWO
PRAXIS: THINKING AND DOING

Discourse Power Resistance Series

SERIES EDITORS:
JEROME SATTERTHWAITE AND ELIZABETH ATKINSON

A brief account of the emergence of the Discourse, Power, Resistance Series is offered in the Introduction to this book. The series is intended for students, teachers, trainers, lecturers, researchers and those responsible for shaping educational policy. The series aims to promote a radical rethinking of educational theory and practice, to offer a sustained and thoughtful challenge to the status quo in education and to put forward positive alternatives.

Previous titles in the series are:

Discourse, Power, Resistance: Challenging the Rhetoric of Contemporary Education (2003), edited by Jerome Satterthwaite, Elizabeth Atkinson and Ken Gale

The Disciplining of Education: New Languages of Power and Resistance (2004) edited by Jerome Satterthwaite, Elizabeth Atkinson and Wendy Martin

Educational Counter-Cultures: Confrontations, Images, Vision (2004) edited by Jerome Satterthwaite, Elizabeth Atkinson and Wendy Martin.

Introduction

JEROME SATTERTHWAITE

Abbreviations:

DPR1   Satterthwaite, J, Atkinson, E and Gale, K (eds) (2003)
        Discourse, Power, Resistance: Challenging the Rhetoric of ⟵
        Contemporary Education. Stoke-on-Trent: Trentham

DPR2   Satterthwaite, J, Atkinson, E and Martin, M (eds) (2004)
        *The Disciplining of Education: New Languages of Power and
        Resistance.* Stoke-on-Trent: Trentham

DPR3   Satterthwaite, J, Atkinson, E and Martin, W (eds) (2004)
        Educational Counter-Cultures: Confrontations, Images, Vision.
        Stoke-on-Trent: Trentham

Discourse, Power, Resistance

This is the fourth volume in the series *Discourse, Power, Resistance*
(DPR). The first came out in 2003, following the first DPR conference
held in the University of Plymouth, UK, in the spring of 2002. The
conference was oversubscribed; delegates had to be turned away. The
atmosphere of the conference was electric. One after another, in
papers, workshops and seminars, delegates opened up debate about
what was going on in education world-wide; and, by and large, the
news was bad. Since then there have been two more conferences. Each
has been filled to capacity, made up of delegates from universities, colleges, schools and policy-making groups, mostly from the UK, but
increasingly from other parts of the world; a major contribution has
been made each year by delegates from the United States. Some people
are beginning to think and talk about DPR as a new movement in
education. Others resist this way of understanding DPR, worried that
we may be on the way to forming a recognisable pressure group,
developing an us-and-them bravado; or perhaps they fear that DPR,

under the influence of the kind of centripetal force associated with people clinging together as an old ship sinks, may begin to think of themselves as members of a disappearing élite. Probably a more useful way of thinking of DPR is simply as a forum where issues of urgent importance to all of us engaged in education can be debated and critically examined.

It is worth pausing, on the threshold of this new DPR publication, to consider briefly some of the issues which have dominated our discussions over the past four years and to suggest what may be the major concerns which have emerged.

Education and Government

One message from the DPR conferences and publications has been that, wherever you look, education is becoming an instrument of government. Governments are themselves obeying the demands of business, whose requirements have to do with the training of a workforce equipped with the skills to compete effectively in world markets. Education is being directed this way through the mechanisms of inspection, which are coupled with funding: if providers pass their inspection, the funds flow; if not, funding is switched elsewhere to promote rival (more compliant) providers. Everyone has agreed this is bad; strategies for resistance have been put forward. But the debates about education and government have not all been as straightforward as this. Stephen Rowland (DPR1:15), in a keynote paper, spelling out his more nuanced understanding of the right relationship between education and government, expressed a view that will have commanded wide consent amongst conference delegates and readers:

> ..... the role of the academy has always been to critique existing knowledge and contest the assumptions and the social forces that shape people's ways of thinking. It is through reason, careful observation and critical analysis that universities contribute to freeing society from the forces of unreason and prejudice. The role of the university, from this point of view, is not to serve the needs of the powerful, but to liberate us through the power of critical reasoning.

In terms of what it says and the way it says it, this is a measured statement; and rightly so: the cool formulation expects a thoughtful response from audiences and readers alike. Rowland, inviting us to think carefully and setting out that expectation with a steady attention to the grace and flow of good syntax, maintains a tone which has characterised a range of DPR papers. The eloquence is assured, mindful of rules. Resistance in education is shown as thoughtful, principled, grown-up.

Other voices within DPR have offered a no less thoughtful but a different voice. Atkinson (DPR1:5) established early on a more irreverent style for the articulation of deeply theorised and wholly serious critique. For her, ridicule is a powerful rejoinder of the educational postmodernist, confronted by the ponderous absurdities of the discourse of authority and power:

> How often have you laughed in recent staff meetings, as you've incorporated the latest government initiative into your own particular field of education? And how often do you laugh as you try to reconcile those initiatives with the counter-discourses of your own thinking? Maybe laughing would be a *good* start. Maybe a bit of Carnival is what we need. Why not shout O *le le* to the policy makers? Turn all the norms upside down? Take to the streets and proclaim that the Emperor has no clothes? Why not stand up and be counted?

Laughter is appropriate for what is ludicrous, absurd. Carnivalesque delight, frivolity, the ludic parade of witty irreverence, mock in this passage the solemnities of officialdom. This is another voice which has become familiar to DPR delegates and readers: the quick rhetoric of a studied and principled disrespect.

Criticism of government and other powerful corporate interventions in education has been at its most forceful in some of the contributions from colleagues in the United States. Hursh (DPR1:43) has analysed the destructive effect of testing; Apple (DPR3:3) has exposed the influence of powerful conservative groups on education in the USA, giving a chilling account of the ruthless drive to align educational provision with vested interests both corporate and ideological. Here is a single example of what Apple *sees as a powerful statement of the re-integration of educational policy and practice into the ideological agenda of neo-liberalism* (Apple, DPR3:7):

> I am referring here to Channel One, a for-profit television network that is now being broadcast into schools enrolling over 40% of all

middle and secondary school students in the nation ... In this reform, schools are offered a free satellite dish, two VCRs, and television monitors for each of their classrooms by a private media corporation. They are also offered a free news broadcast for these students. In return for the equipment and the news, all participating schools must sign a three-five year contract guaranteeing that their students will watch Channel One every day.

Here we are confronted by just one example of the brute, unsubtle penetration of education by business interests. Lather (DPR2:21), in a tour-de-force account of the same forces, has exposed their roots in a stony patriarchy; and she has spelled out the grim consequences for research. In the present volume both McLaren and Pinar address the issues raised for education by American imperialism, leaving us in no doubt about the impact of contemporary US government policy on the shaping of educational provision in the United States and internationally.

Learning

Although DPR is not a movement and has no defined position, there are signs of an emerging consensus. An example is that there has been little enthusiasm for the kind of complaining which is merely a way for aggrieved professionals to console themselves that the bad news is not their fault. Relentlessly, DPR conference papers, and the chapters in the books that followed, have directed critical attention to the provision itself – to the learning and teaching content, delivery and methods of assessment which make up the student experience of contemporary education. What has emerged from this critique has been a range of complex and stubborn problems, not primarily attributable to outside intervention, but rather deriving from the theories and practices of contemporary education itself, which have been shown to contribute to a systematic oppression of the learners. How is it that professional educators, overwhelmingly committed to offering the best possible educational experience to the learners, have found – to their great dismay – that many of the learners are not suited, not thriving, not learning, but rather experiencing frustration and anxiety, dropping out or failing? DPR has looked carefully at this, and has uncovered a range of contributing factors. The discourses of learning, teaching and assessment have been critically examined (Satterthwaite, DPR1:103; Nichols, DPR1:135, Burn and Finnigan, DPR1: 115), uncovering disquieting assumptions and prejudices on the part of educators, as they build up the pressure on learners to conform to academic conventions not always clearly relating to worthwhile learning; a pressure which explains, for example, why mature students

> ...assume a rhetoric of personal inadequacy to explain events invariably linked to processes and structures beyond their personal control (Reay *et al*, cited Evans and Martin, DPR2: 154).

Epistemology and Research

Not least amongst the issues which cause difficulty, for learners and teachers alike, in the delivery of learning has been what can only be thought of as an intellectual crisis: the sagging and eventual collapse of confidence in the body of knowledge which it had been thought was the remit of educators to pass on. Debates around epistemology and research have been amongst the most penetrating and incisive of the papers and chapters emerging from DPR (see, for example, Clegg and Ashworth, DPR2:53, Cole, DPR3:19, Bleakley, DPR3:149). They have, as is to be expected, hovered uncertainly over what may be thought of as the empirical/hermeneutic divide. There have been bold affirmations reminding us that empiricism claims to know there is a world out there, and to know that, with care and patience and the steady application of minds trained in the rigorous disciplines of objective enquiry, that world can be known and described for the benefit of other minds. Other voices have rejoined that hermeneutics problematises this claim, aware that minds themselves are irretrievably inscribing their particular distortions. On this view, the business of interpretation tells me – for what it is worth – merely how things seem to me. How things seem to me is, of course, something I can grasp with confidence: I cannot easily misunderstand my own point of view. The sadness though – if it is a sadness – is that I find myself telling myself – and anyone else who is listening or reading – only about myself: the world beyond my mind is not captured in the account I give. Attempts to resolve this dilemma have argued that both points of view are extreme, and to that extent both wrong; and that the attentive analysis of the thinking self, disclosed in publication, is to be valued as a means through which other minds arrive at their own self-recognitions: that, strangely, solipsisms can be shared.

Teaching

Although it has been normal for some time in education circles to dismiss the view that education is a process of passing on knowledge, this traditional understanding has been difficult to set aside. It is not only traditional-minded educators who have raised the plaintive question: *if we are not passing on knowledge, then what are we doing?* (see, for example, Harrison *et al*, DPR1:57, Atkinson, DPR3:55). One alternative pedagogy that has been considered is that education coaxes to the surface, codifies and renders systematic the knowledge the learner already owns deep down. This view has seemed implausible to most people interested in the philosophy of education: learning as recollection seems too close for comfort to Plato's *anamnesis*, relying on the improbable belief that each of us knows everything already. Words like 'intuition' and 'experience' have had to be worked hard to support this view, and have become deformed under the pressure. Other DPR papers (eg, Ecclestone, DPR2:117) have criticised the closely related view that learning may be thought of as self-actualisation, the learner becoming what she or he already is. Uneasiness with this view has focussed on the problem of making any sense of it: critics have argued that to claim that I become myself through the processes of education is to propose so soft a learning outcome as to be hardly an outcome at all, and that this line of argument prepares us for the surprising conclusion that we should avoid learning outcomes altogether, and think of learning as a process from which nothing in particular is to be expected.

Creativity

Learning to be myself is quite boring, unless that project is brought alive by the challenges of self-making. DPR has offered a forum for exciting investigations of the possibilities for being and doing, focused on the thunder-and-lightning affirmation, tracing its lineage through Heidegger and Nietsche back to Goethe and beyond, that being is doing (and doing is being). *In the beginning was the deed* is a brave claim, since it exposes to scrutiny those selves, those who-am-I-being constructions through which I offer myself to others to be known. If what I do, what I make, declares who I am, then the exposure is courageous. Exhibition is holding out, offering, what I have (a view, an insight, a self). Exhibiting, then, is creative, bringing into being the maker with the made and involving the viewer as active participant in the making. It is in the creative moment when selves express their being confronted by a world, that we are brought to recognise one another. Gale (DPR1:165) has shown the connection between creativity and resistance; Danvers (DPR3:165) has struggled to transcend in words and images the limits of representation; Perselli (DPR3:183, and again in the present volume) has looked from a distance at the intimate portraiture of selving, wondering at who may be disclosed.

Where do we go from here?

The brief survey outlined above has done less than justice to the range and complexity of the issues debated within the DPR forum. The issues highlighted have been selected to prepare us for the arguments put forward in this book, which are intended to be unsettling both in form and content. The book opens with the unashamed ranting of McLaren, abandoning conventional restraint, deploying sarcasm, ridicule and bombast to force the reader to notice the brutalities of contemporary American politics and the impact of those politics on education, which is rendered servile, harnessed to the service of the international corporations. McLaren's style is itself an act of discursive resistance. We are discomfited by the exposure to a passionate, principled anger, expressed with disregard for convention and decorum: what place have these quaint manners, the writing asks, when the savagery of cultural and economic imperialism confronts us?

Pinar follows, developing the connection with education.. 'The school in the US is a skill-and-knowledge factory... an accountant's concept'; worse, the knowledge conveyed in the curriculum is derived from the self-absorption of an imperial culture which is profoundly narcissistic, lost in itself, sustained by a deep-seated anti-intellectualism. Pinar develops the horrific account of US education put forward by Apple (DPR3:3) and developed by McLaren, as 'righteous victimhood', 'wounded and vengeful nationalism', and appeals for concerted work by educationalists world-wide to recover the creativity and individuality which he associates with the true curriculum. Turning to education in the United Kingdom, Cole presents the Marxist case that the blatant racism of education in the age of the British Empire, which everywhere promoted ideas of racial superiority, is matched in contemporary education by the uncritical assertion of US/Western racial and cultural supremacy; and Isherwood identifies the origin and legitimation of the imperial sense of racial and cultural superiority in the controlling tenets of patriarchal Christian dogma. Atkinson, clinching the arguments of the first part of the book, deploys the concept of otherness to account for the brutal insensitivities of the imperialist project.

After the sweep of part 1, it is appropriate to take stock, look carefully, think specifically. After all, we are trying to make practical changes in a real world where people are learning, or failing to learn, or learning badly, or learning what is worthless or what is pernicious. We are trying to change things for the better. How should we do this and how can we be sure we are doing so, rather than making things worse? These are difficult question both at the level of theory – where what we think is worthwhile may simply express a mindless prejudice – or at the level of practice, where our good ideas may fail in their practical application. The opening chapters of part two take the sort of care that is needed, if we are going to do things right; and show a way of making the kind of discriminating judgements which alone justify changing practice. These chapters are cool. They suggest how the passionate anger so powerfully evoked in part one can be deployed to make the changes we need. We are dealing here with what Haggis refers to as the 'epistemology of the close-up', and what Clegg describes as 'the practical wisdom of professional practice'.

We need to make sure, as best we can (and bearing in mind the difficulties referred to above about knowledge, certainty and intellectual confidence) that we know what we are talking about and what we are doing, so that we understand one another and get things right. One of the issues confronting practitioners and researchers trying to understand their practice is the difficulty of negotiating between opposing or divergent discourses: we do not all mean the same thing, or talk the same language. Boag-Munroe looks at this Babel-like breakdown in communication between disparate discursive communities: policymakers, inspectors and practitioners. Education, she suggests, will be incoherent until we recognise each other's languages. Ollin takes this further, spotting the positive value of wilful discursive misunderstanding. We are returning here to the celebration of the ludic, to the role of laughter in the construction of professional teacher identity. Ollin argues that, whilst large scale organised resistance has its place, the subversions practised daily by educators reformulating and reinterpreting managerial directives constitute a powerful and effective strategy by which learners and educators manage to put their own principles into practice within the framework of apparent compliance. Hermeneutics lives on, and is here deployed to good effect!

In the chapters of both parts of this book we follow an argument, from the rhetoric of political outrage, through the careful analysis of ways of knowing and doing, that has brought us to a threshold where the practice of education, the learning and teaching, the what and the how, can be scrutinised, and changes and developments considered. Instead, and disconcertingly, in the final chapters Perselli and Lambert change the subject; and not only the subject, but the tone, the discourse, switching to one of intensely serious play. There are daring refusals here, transgressions which highlight the normal boundaries of educational discourse. By simply ignoring 'more of the same' these chapters show the blinkered vision of much educational debate, and suggest exciting and radical possibilities for new, more inclusive vision.

The book began with a rant and ends with images and a poem, performance rounding out the argument. The challenge of the book is here brought into sharp focus: has the argument brought us to the point where playful gesture, laughter, fun, are the only recourse? Are we faced with the bitter recognition that, in the last analysis, education is in the grip of powerful forces which can be mocked but not seriously resisted? Or can we see, in the principled, careful and caring repositioning which is celebrated here, a personal and collective way forward for learners, teachers, policy-makers and regulatory bodies, who have been taking themselves too seriously and understanding their work too narrowly and too coldly by far? Lambert's poem ends appropriately for the argument of the book as a whole:

> and in this parting we are optimistic   are we
> can our optimism sit with the pain of recognition
> that the small and large injustices
> are all part of the same horrendous game
>
> but the state we are in is process
>
> and we are not standing still

PART ONE
GLOBAL IMPERIALISM AND TERROR: THE THEORY AND PRACTICE OF OTHERING

1

Critical pedagogy in the age of global empire: dispatches from headquarters

PETER McLAREN

Peter McLaren is furiously angry and he wants us to know this. This chapter opens with a bitter attack on the Bush administration, which, in McLaren's view, is extending its empire world-wide and making us all consumers of the American way of life, with its emphasis on consumerism, the Christian God, and so forth. McLaren sets aside the conventions of polite, cool, academic discourse, to attack what he sees as the most terrible (because it is the most powerful) oppression on earth. And then he tells us what won't work as a way of countering this oppression; and concludes by showing us what will. As his argument drives forward, we begin to see the role of education as he conceives it: critical revolutionary pedagogy. This chapter prepares us for Mike Cole's, which looks at the state of contemporary education in the UK; and for Lisa Isherwood's which explores the connection with traditional Christian theology.

When I was a child growing up in Canada in the 1950s, I shared a fear similar to that of some of my neighbourhood friends: that one day all the mannequins in the downtown department stores (the now defunct Eatons and Simpsons) would come to life and take over the world. It seems, half a century later, that my fear was duly justified. The department store mannequins have indeed taken over the world.

3

They captured the Bush Jr. White House in 2000 and seem to comprise almost half of the American electorate, that grim-faced, tight-jawed group that call themselves Republicans. Having convinced a large segment of the American population that they are the only ones capable of looking after the security and well-being of the United States citizenry, the Bush Jr junta took advantage of a tragic terrorist attack on the country to create a climate of fear that could facilitate their thirst for revenge and empire-building. Then the boy emperor and his handlers proceeded to unleash the most powerful military force in the world against the ragtag armies of much weaker sovereign countries. United States imperialism has garrisoned capitalism for the benefit of the transnational ruling elite, headquartered in Washington, and is kept in place by a humvee pedagogy of authoritarian populism and militarism. Here the curriculum is underwritten by a commitment to capital's worldwide exponential escalation of its capacity to produce and stabilised by the belief that it is more profitable for capital intergenerationally to produce and reproduce poverty than to end poverty around the globe. If you look closely enough behind Bush Jr's trademark impish smirk and the beady, bloodshot eyes of his closest advisors, you'll find Leo Strauss, J Edgar Hoover, Joe McCarthy, Roy Cohn and William McKinley staring at you. This chapter is an attempt to stare back at them.

We have entered a reality-zone already captured by its opposite. It is a world where order has given way to disorder, where reason has given way to unreason, where guilt is presumed over innocence, where the once noble search for explanations has been replaced by a dizzying vortex of plastic flags, stars and stripes rhinestone belts, coffee klatch war strategists, Sunday barbecue patrioteering, militant denunciations of war protestors, a generalised fear of whatever lies ahead, xenophobic hostility, and point-blank outrage.

Once the war on terror was in full throttle, some doyens of the establishment right must have been so thrilled at the prospect of limitless political and military opportunity that they were driven mad, especially after the consent of the public was secured, federal dragnets for rounding up suspicious Arabs were launched across the nation, wiretapping without warrants was put into effect, efforts were made to destabilise the UN convention against torture (in order to keep foreign observers out of the Guantanamo Bay prison camp), and a

Peter McLaren

move to reverse a decades-old ban on government assassination signed by Gerald Ford in 1976 was floated by the Bush administration through Congress so that now the US government 'has permitted CIA hit squads to recommence covert operations of the kind that included, in the past, the assassination of foreign heads of state.' Here the contradiction we face vastly exceeds the simple choice 'between mullahs and the mall, between the hegemony of religious absolutism and the hegemony of market determinism.' (Barber, 2002:17). Capitalism is irretrievably contradictory in its own self-constitution, predicated upon a failure to realise its truth in practice. It is a constitutive impossibility for capitalism to create equal access to education, to feed and clothe the poor and to provide medical assistance to those who are ill. Denys Turner remarks that

> Capitalism has to live its own morality ideologically, that is to say, it can sustain its moral convictions only as a way of recognising the fact that it installs the very conditions under which those convictions are unrealisable. It cannot abandon the moral language it cannot live. (1983:151)

In this era of casino capitalism, the house always wins.

At this particular historical moment, democracy seems acutely perishable. Its contradictions have become as difficult to ignore as sand rubbed in the eyes. Although dressed up as a promise, democracy has functioned more as a threat. Spurred on by feelings of 'righteous victimhood' and by a 'wounded and vengeful nationalism' (Lieven, 2003) that has arisen in the wake of the attacks of September 11, and pushing its wars on terrorism to the far reaches of the globe (with what Terry Eagleton calls a 'world-hating hubris' [2003:227], the United States is shamelessly defining its global empire as an extension of its democratic project. The US National Security Strategy of 2002 states that the United States will not hesitate to act alone and will 'preemptively' attack 'terrorists' who threaten its national interests at home or abroad.

One of its national interests is to bring free-market democracy to the rest of the world. What used to be called gunboat diplomacy is being rewritten as a diplomatic gunning down of any and all opposition to the unfettered movement of finance capital in and out of new markets. Sidestepping the inconvenient possibility that Iraq had no

5

connection to al Qaeda, the Pentagon hawks swept through the streets of Baghdad and arrived at the near culmination of their civilising mission by enacting a negation as one-sided as the positivity they oppose. It was the aftermath of shock and awe. On this topic Paul Brennan (2003, pp. 1-2) probes America's heart of darkness:

> Shock and Awe – and, indeed, the whole Bush idea that flexing our high-tech military might in the Middle East will remake the wicked everywhere into models of democratic values – sounds like nothing so much as Mr Kurtz's report to the International Society for the Suppression of Savage Customs (the Victorian equivalent of the Project of the New American Century), which Marlowe recounts for his listeners in Chapter 2 [of Joseph Conrad's *Heart of Darkness*]: He began with the argument that we whites, from the point of view of development we had arrived at, 'must necessarily appear to them [savages] in the nature of supernatural beings – we approach them with the might as of a deity,' and so on and so on. 'By the simple example of our will, we can exert a power for good practically unbounded,' etc, etc.

But Marlowe says the report was missing something:

> *There was no practical hint to interrupt the magic current of phrases, unless a kind of note at the foot of the last page, scrawled evidently much later, in an unsteady hand, may be regarded as the exposition of a method. It was very simple, and at the end of that moving appeal to every altruistic sentiment it blazed at you, luminous and terrifying, like a flash of lightning in a serene sky: 'Exterminate all the brutes!'*

Meanwhile, at home, we are witnessing a general intensification of labour by the over-extension of the working day, cutbacks in resources and social programmes combined with tax breaks for the very rich, relentless violations of laws by corporate executives, and the lack of waged work, all under the banner of the preferred euphemism for imperialism: fighting terrorism and bringing about free market democracy. It is hard to put pen to paper without feeling like Sisyphus with his block of stone toiling in the realm of the dead.

Recently Americans celebrated the 212th anniversary of the ratification of the Bill of Rights, yet we are all presumed guilty until proven innocent. And since now we can be denied the opportunity to prove our innocence, then guilt and innocence lose their meaning. In fact, by becoming their opposite they cancel each other out. They cease to exist. Only Sauron's eye of the security state remains. Inside, we all wear the hoods that the US military places over the heads of its prisoners. We all wait to be sent to Guantanamo Bay. We all are forced to stand for hours with our hands raised over our heads. We are all forced to listen to tapes of rabbits being slaughtered.

In the security state, lies are now 'creative omissions' or 'misstatements' while truth is whatever it needs to be to secure the strategic interests of the US. Global prosperity means tearing up the Kyoto treaty; preventing nuclear threats by rogue nations means threatening to use nuclear weapons in 'pre-emptive' strikes; creating global support against terrorism means blocking a UN investigation of the Israeli assault on the Jenin refugee camp; bringing war criminals to justice means preventing the establishment of an international criminal court. Today, the preferred choice of Bush policy makers is deceit and deception. It is important to recognise that, increasingly within the security state, nothing carries the aura of truth as much as deception; nothing is as real today as that which is fake. Naomi Klein captures this phenomenon – hardly restricted to the United States – in the following description:

> The blacklisting of the almanac was a fitting end for 2003, a year that waged open war on truth and facts and celebrated fakes and forgeries of all kinds. This was the year when fakeness ruled: fake rationales for war, a fake President dressed as a fake soldier declaring a fake end to combat and then holding up a fake turkey. An action movie star became governor and the government started making its own action movies, casting real soldiers like Jessica Lynch as fake combat heroes and dressing up embedded journalists as fake soldiers. Saddam Hussein even got a part in the big show: he played himself being captured by American troops. This is the fake of the year, if you believe the *Sunday Herald* in Scotland, as well as several other news agencies, which reported that he was actually captured by a Kurdish special forces unit.

What is most frightening is the chillingly preordained character of the Bush plutocracy given supernatural ballast by Bush's claim to be a special envoy of God. That he has asserted with clairvoyant confidence that God has appointed him president, and has called on him to lay waste to the evil-doers of the world (at least those evil-doers who sit on both untapped and fully operational oil reserves) has, for many God-fearing Christian Americans, given Bush the moral authority to turn the carnage inflicted by the world's most fearsome military machine into sacred wrath. With his ideological twin, Tony Blair, playing Lord Curzon, the Bush/Blair alliance does not bode well for peoples the world over who worship 'false' prophets (ie, who are non-Christian).

With the mighty chains of this Christian faith, Bush has hoisted his conscience onto the biblical back of God, to whose wrath he has faithfully committed himself and his armies of invasion. Bush wraps his depleted uranium shells in the 'divine right of kings' and the doctrine of the US Manifest Destiny before hurling them into the theatre of war with the deftness of a Super Bowl quarter-back. As US weapons of mass destruction effortlessly saw through tendon and bone, blast apart organs, and incinerate flesh with a vengeful fury, Bush sleeps as soundly as the 10,000 innocent Iraqi civilians that he has recently killed, but remains oblivious to the wails and shrieks of the countless numbers that he has left orphaned and crippled. After his routine three-mile jog and bedtime prayers, the former governor of Texas, who set the record for most executions by any governor in American history, has learned to unburden his heart by invoking the Lord for help in directing the nation's foreign policy. His mind unmercifully devoid of functioning synapses and unencumbered by the power of analysis, Bush unhesitatingly made his decision to invade and occupy Iraq 'because he believes, he truly believes, that God squats in his brainpan and tells him what to do' (Floyd, 2003:4). The Israeli newspaper *Haaretz* was given transcripts of a negotiating session between Palestinian prime minister Mahmoud Abbas and faction leaders from Hamas and other militant groups. In these transcripts, Abbas described his recent summit with Ariel Sharon and Bush. During the summit, Bush allegedly told Abbas:

> God told me to strike at *al-Quaida* and I struck them, and then He instructed me to strike at Saddam, which I did, and now I am determined to solve the problem in the Middle East. If you help me I will act, and if not, the elections will come and I will have to focus on them. (Regular, 2003, p1)

When, on the freshly mopped deck of the carrier, *USS Abraham Lincoln*, the US warrior president emerged in a snug-fitting flight suit from an S-3B Viking aircraft, his trademark swagger and petulant grin were greeted by patriotic cheers from throngs of wild-eyed officers and sailors. Appearing topside before a bold banner that announced 'Mission Accomplished', our boy emperor declared the 'battle of Iraq' a 'victory' in the ongoing 'war on terror'. This event was carefully choreographed by Bush's team of seasoned image-makers that included a former ABC producer, a former FOX News producer, and a former NBC cameraman paid for out of an annual budget of $3.7 million that Bush allots for his media co-ordinators. Bush's speech on the carrier paraphrased Chapter 61 of Isaiah, the very book that Jesus used when proclaiming that Isaiah's prophecies of the Messiah had come true, suggesting perhaps that Bush believes the Second Coming has begun (Pitt, 2003) and that his war on terror is playing an important role in this Biblical prophecy. Leftist commentators have noted that the Pentagon's 'Shock and Awe' bombing strategy was copied from the Nazi strategy of *Blitzkrieg* (lightning war) and the Luftwaffe's doctrine of *Schrecklichkeit* aimed at terrorising a population into surrender, and that the Bush Doctrine of preventive war mirrors the rationale behind Hitler's march into Poland (Hitler had claimed Poland was an immediate threat to the safety of the Reich). And while Bush *padre's* vow to establish a New World Order and Hitler's vow to create a *Neue Ordung* have to be seen in their historical and contextual specificity, the comparison of the Bush dynasty to the Third Reich does extend beyond fascist aesthetics, media spectacle, and the police state tactics of the Office of Homeland Security. It can be seen in the machinations of capital and the role of the military-industrial complex in imperialist acts of aggression disguised as 'freedom'.

Bush will continue to represent those loyal minions who were outraged by Janet Jackson's exposed breast at the Super Bowl, but sat down with their families to watch with patriotic pride the Shock and Awe bombing of Baghdad spectacle on CNN.

The hawks around Bush genuflect at the intellectual altar of the late philosopher-king and University of Chicago classicist, Leo Strauss, who maintained that only an elite few in the government warrant the sacred custodianship of the truth and are thereby charged with using 'noble lies' to keep the truth from the unwashed masses by preoccupying everyday citizens not only with real or perceived external threats to the nation but also with the task of developing nationalist or militantly religious sentiments fanatical enough to ensure their willingness to die for the nation.

Straussians are first and foremost pragmatists who will resort to whatever works best to secure control. Karl Rove, the president's political adviser, not only puts Straussian strategy to work, he is also reported to 'reread Machiavelli the way the devout study their Bibles' (Maertens, 2004). As Tom Maertens (2004) asserts:

> It was the Bush-Rove team that deployed the scurrilous push-pull techniques against Senator John McCain in the 2000 South Carolina primary. (Sample question: 'Would you be more likely or less likely to vote for John McCain for president if you knew he had fathered an illegitimate black child?' In reality, the brown-skinned child with McCain was his adopted Bangladeshi daughter, but the race-baiting worked and McCain was defeated.)

The new Orwellian ambience in the US can be sniffed in the words of prominent right-wing journalist Charles Krauthammer: 'America is no mere international citizen. It is the dominant power in the world, more dominant than any since Rome. Accordingly, America is in a position to reshape norms – How? By unapologetic and implacable demonstrations of will' (cited in John McMurtry, 2001). Sound Nietzschean? Readers who are fans of *Zarathustra* might be emboldened by the words uttered by David Rockefeller at the June 1991 Bilderberg meeting in Baden, Germany: a 'supranational sovereignty of an intellectual elite and world bankers ... is surely preferable to the national autodetermination practiced in past centuries' (cited in John McMurtry, 2001). When you put Krauthammer and Rockefeller together, you complete the circuit of totalitarian logic involving 'full-spectrum dominance' set in train by the juggernaut of globalised capital.

The following characterisation of the United States by John Bellamy Foster (2001) may be unsettling to some, but it is certainly not far-fetched to anyone acquainted with the United States Cold War history over the past half century: 'By any objective standard, the United States is the most destructive nation on earth. It has killed and terrorised more populations around the globe than any other nation since the Second World War' (p8). It is precisely this question that critical educators need to engage, as morally repellent as it may be to some. As US tanks roll over the dead and dying in Baghdad and other

Iraqi cities, we assert that one of the principle contradictions today is between the criminal ruling class of US imperialism, and the exploited and oppressed peoples, nations around the world, on the other. Regardless of the recent so-called Shock and Awe 'victory' of Bush and his quislings in Iraq, we argue that the working out of this contradiction constitutes one of the major forms of motion that will eventually determine human history and geography.

Liberal Capitalist Democracy

It is my profound conviction that capitalism is not something that can be fixed, or humanised, because, as Dave Hill, Mike Cole, Paula Allman and Glenn Rikowski have argued, its very value form is premised on the exploitation of human labour. Yet, even in progressive circles, scholars on the Anglo-American left have dismissed Marxist educators calling for a socialist democracy as extremists or juvenile leftists. Consequently, critical revolutionary educators need to pose to their progressive liberal counterparts some searching questions. Can liberal reformers – even World Bank dissenters such as Jeff Sachs, George Soros and former Senior Vice-President and chief economist of the World Bank and Nobel Prize recipient, Joseph Stiglitz (2002) – rebuild and redirect the capitalist financial system in the interests of the poor and powerless? Can they prevent the rationality of financial capital – which is more interested in short term profits than investing in fixed capital and long-term technological progress – from prevailing over what is rational from the standpoint of society as a whole? Can they prevent the suffering of workers due to the dismantling of protectionist trade barriers? Can they stop privatisation from resulting in oligopolies and monopolies? Can they stop the IMF from bailing out international investors and granting elites the opportunity to protect their financial assets by massive capital flight, while placing the burden of repaying loans, in the words of Tony Smith (2002), 'on the very group that benefited least from them, working men and women'? Do they have the power to prevent the gangster capitalists of Russia, for instance, from buying up most of the privatised assets and natural resources of the country? Can they stop the multilateral agencies from advancing the particular interests of the United States? Can they prevent new nation state-driven racisms that follow in the wake of the new US phallomilitary warrior nationalism currently providing ideological ballast for its practices of primitive accumulation via cluster bombing Iraq? Can they transcend the creation of pluto-cratic political subjectivities from above in order to combat the uneven development of epidemics such as AIDS and SARS in the equal opportunity inevitability of death? Can they reverse the systematic tendencies to crises of over-accumulation and financial collapse or the structural mechanisms generating uneven develop-ment? Can they prevent speculative bubbles from expanding and bursting? Can the balance of power in capital/wage labour relations shift in favour of labour? Can the fundamental dynamic of capitalist property relations be challenged? Questions such as these cut to the roots of the capitalist system. From the perspective of our analysis, honest answers to these questions will lead to a resounding 'no'. Liberal capitalist reformers in the main fail to comprehend 'that money is the alien form of appearance of abstract labour' and they refuse to challenge the money fetish as the master trope of capitalist social relations (Smith, 2002). Of course, liberal reform efforts to make global capitalism more 'humane' are welcome, but it still remains the case that in the last instance they cannot prevent financial disaster from being visited upon developing countries or the poor in general because these problems are inherent in the system of property and productive relations that constitute the very blood and gristle of the capitalist system (Smith, 2002).

Let me offer a Lacanian inspired description of the liberal democracy that I have been describing.

The key point is that liberal capitalist democracy sustains the alibi that the corrupt behaviour of corporate bosses is an aberration and not the 'spectral double' of law abiding business leaders; it sustains the myth that the real American corporate leader is a church-going philanthropist who wants to contribute to making the United States a better place for working men and women. Liberal democracy oc-cludes the fact that violence (of corporate leaders, police, criminals) is a symptom of liberal democracy's failure to respond to the suffering of others (Zizek, 2002). If we see liberal democracy as a totality then we can recognise it as a dialectical unity of itself and its other. The notion that we live in a meritocracy is the form of appearance of its very opposite: the absence of equality in a society divided by race and class. Liberal democracy, as a master signifier of 'America', con-stitutes an imaginary supplement or, in Lacanian terms, a 'big Other' that acts on behalf of all citizens, an excess that serves ideologically to justify all acts in its name on the basis that it is ultimately for the common good of humanity. This supplement enables US citizens to endure America's unbearable contradictions such as its lack of medical insurance for the poor, its growing homeless population, its corporate scandals, its institutionalised forms of racism, its torture training centre at the School of the Americas in Fort Benning, Georgia, its support in the past of a long list of fascist dictatorships in Guatemala, El Salvador, Iran, Indonesia and Chile, its past funding and training of the Contra terrorists, its invasions of Panama and Grenada, and its recent role in the coup attempt in Venezuela, not to mention financial and military aid to the ruthless Colombian regime.

The seemingly inexorable advance of capitalism, against which workers and their school-aged children have little, if any, redress, has led many educators to despair. Few educational critics would deny that the last several decades of school reform have not had their professed effect and that working-class and ethnic minority students for the most part are faring badly in standardised tests and in securing any jobs at all, let alone what could be described as decent work. Much contemporary educational criticism on the left is postmodernist in orientation and disposition; and while we would be wise not to characterise this work as mere flummery, even the best of it has, nevertheless, signalled a discernible shift 'from politics to culture' (Eagleton, 2003:12) and in the main such criticism has had a nugatory effect overall on educational change. The failure of the political order is embodied in the desperate lives of the world's suffering and homeless populations. As Eagleton notes:

> The dispossessed are a living sign of the truth that the only enduring power is one anchored in an acknowledgement of failure. Any power which fails to recognise this fact will be enfeebled in a different sense, fearfully defending itself against the victims of its own arrogance'. (2003:176)

My own position within the anti-capitalist and Marxist humanist alliance falls within the purview of *socialist anti-capitalism*. To this end I have tried to develop a re-materialised approach to critical pedagogy that Paul Allman (1999, 2001) has named *revolutionary critical pedagogy*. Such an approach to pedagogy insists on understanding social life from the standpoint of the strategic centrality of class and class struggle. This contrasts with the post-modernised cultural studies approach that is fixated on discourse and power.

The Politics of Difference

An historical materialist approach that drives the critique offered by revolutionary critical pedagogy understands that categories of difference are social/political constructs that are often encoded in dominant ideological formations and that they often play a role in moral and legal state-mediated forms of ruling. It also acknowledges the material force of ideologies – particularly racist ideologies – that assign separate cultural and/or biological essences to different segments of the population which, in turn, serve to reinforce and rationalise existing relations of power. But more than this, an historical materialist understanding foregrounds the manner in which difference is central to the exploitative production/reproduction dialectic of capital, its labour organisation and processes, and in the way labour is valued and remunerated.

The real problem is the internal or dialectical relation that exists between capital and labour within the capitalist production process itself – a social relation in which capitalism is intransigently rooted. This social relation – essential to the production of abstract labour – deals with how already existing value is preserved and new value (surplus value) is created (Allman, 2001). The process of actual exploitation and the accumulation of surplus value is best understood as a state of constant manipulation and as a realisation process of concrete labour in actual labour time – within a given cost-production system and a labour market. Difference (racial as well as gender difference) is encapsulated in the production/reproduction dialectic of capital. It is this relationship that is mainly responsible for the inequitable and unjust distribution of resources. A deepened understanding of this phenomenon is essential for understanding the emergence of a polarised labour market and the fact that disproportionately high percentages of people of colour are trapped in the lower rungs of the domestic and global labour market (McLaren and Farahmandpur, 1999). Difference in the era of global capitalism is crucial to the workings, movements and profit levels of multinational corporations; but these types of complex relations cannot be mapped out by using truncated ways in which people of colour (and, more specifically, women of colour) provide capital with its superexploited labour pools – a phenomenon that is on the rise all over the world. Most social relations constitutive of radicalised differences are considerably shaped by the relations of production and there is undoubtedly a racialised and gendered division of labour whose severity and function vary depending on where one is situated in the capitalist global economy (Meyerson, 2000).

In stating this, we need to include an important caveat that differentiates our approach from those invoking the well-worn race/ class/gender triplet which can sound, to the uninitiated, both radical and vaguely Marxian. It is not. Race, class and gender, while they invariably intersect and interact, are not co-primary. This triplet approximates what the philosophers might call a 'category mistake.' On the surface the triplet may be convincing – some people are oppressed because of their race, others as a result of their gender, yet others because of their class – but this is grossly misleading, for, as Eagleton points out (Eagleton, 1998:289)

> It is not that some individuals manifest certain characteristics known as 'class' which then results in their oppression; on the contrary, to be a member of a social class just is to be oppressed.

and in this regard class is a wholly social category. Furthermore, even though class is usually invoked as part of the aforementioned and much vaunted triptych, it is usually gutted of its practical, social dimension or treated solely as a cultural phenomenon – as just another form of difference. In these instances, class is transformed from an economic and, indeed, social category to an exclusively cultural or discursive one or one in which class merely signifies a subject position. Class is therefore cut off from the political economy of capitalism and class power severed from exploitation and a power structure *in which those who control collectively produced resources only do so because of the value generated by those who do not* (Hennessy and Ingraham, 1997, p2).

Socialism is not a discredited dream. It is a current that runs through periods such as the menacing present and is animated by and in struggle against all forms of oppression and exploitation. Whilst the anti-war movement will undoubtedly have to overcome certain internal problems to grow much larger and to curb future wars in Syria,

Iran or Venezuela, what we are seeing today is the emergence of a completely new quality of social consciousness that could provide the concrete basis for an internationalist political movement. What matters here is that against the backdrop of US imperialism, the only way students are ever going to win lasting 'peace' or the right to a decent education or job is through the linking of their struggles with all the victims of the vicious ruling class, including workers whose blood, sweat and toil is the living fuel that makes the economy run.

In creating the conditions for social change, then, the best pedagogy recognises the limits of traditional reformist pedagogical practice by prioritising the need to question the deeper problems, particularly the violent contradictions (eg, the gap between racism and the American Dream), under which students are forced to live. Critical revolutionary pedagogy raises the question: do we know whose hands ground the capitalist lenses through which we comprehend the world and do we know from whence came the bloodstains on the lens grinder's workbench?

Against tremendous odds, the challenge over the last several decades has been to humanise the classroom environment and to create pedagogical spaces for linking education to social justice initiatives and to that end we are indebted to critical pedagogy. Yet, faced with the urgency for change, approaching social transformation through the optic of revolutionary critical pedagogy ratchets up the struggle ahead. Revolutionary critical pedagogy dilates the aperture that critical pedagogy has struggled to provide for teachers and students over the last several decades by further opening up the pedagogical encounter to its embeddedness in globalised social relations of exploitation, and also to the revolutionary potential of a transnational, gender-balanced, multiracial, anti-imperialist struggle. A revolutionary critical pedagogy raises the following questions for consideration by teachers, students, and other cultural workers: how can we liberate the use-value of human beings from their subordination to exchange-value? How can we convert what is least functional about ourselves as far as the abstract utilitarian logic of capitalist society is concerned – our self-realising, sensuous, species-being – into our major instrument of self-definition? How can we make what we represent to capital – replaceable commodities – subordinate to who we have also become as critical social agents of history? How can we make critical self-reflexivity a demarcating principle of who we are and critical global citizenship the substance of what we want to become? How can we make the cultivation of a politics of hope a radical end in itself? How can we de-commodify our subjectivities? How can we materialise our self-activity as a revolutionary force and struggle for the self-determination of free and equal citizens in a just system of appropriation and distribution of social wealth? How can we make and remake our own nature within the historically specific conventions of capitalist society so that we can make this self-activity a revolutionary force to dismantle capitalism itself and create the conditions for the development of our full human potential? How can we confront our producers (ie, the social relations of production, the corporate media, cultural formations and institutional structures) as an independent power?

Completely revolutionising education does not depend upon the great white men that capitalist education teaches us are our presidents, heroes and role models. It relies upon the broad masses of people recognising that the whole system must be transformed to reflect their interests. This is the strength of a revolutionary critical pedagogy, that it is fighting for the interests of the multi-racial, gendered working class and indigenous peoples all the way through. It seeks to transform schools into political and cultural centres, where crucial questions – from international affairs to education policy – are debated and struggled over openly. It is a pedagogy that not only conjures up the audacious urges of the oppressed but also enables them to fight back against the system's repeated attacks by raising people's understanding of their political opponents and developing their organisation and fighting position. It is a call to battle, a challenge to change this monstrous system that wages permanent warfare against the world and the planet, from state terror in the homeland to the dumping of toxic chemicals on Native American lands and communities of colour and devastating bombing campaigns against sovereign nations. It is a pedagogy of hope that is grounded in the unfashionable reality, history, and in the optimism of oppressed peoples and nations everywhere.

Critical pedagogy is secured by the most effective of revolutionary tools: critique. It is focused not only on the practice of critique but also on the critique of pedagogical practice. Unfortunately, many resisting subjects and agents mistake discursive empowerment for social and economic enablement. Their coming to voice and the politics of self-affirmation and self-identity fails to challenge the gross materiality of exploitation. Certainly the question of developing voice and the politics of self-assertion are fundamentally important but often the autonomous individual of bourgeois ideology is misrecognised as the voice of the organic intellectual.

The practice of discursive democracy that equates democracy with the affirmation of voice substitutes verbal empowerment and individual expression for material democracy – for the equal access of all to social and economic resources through collective social struggle to transform existing social relations.

According to Teresa Ebert:

> Critique is that knowledge-practice that historically situates the condition of possibility of what empirically exists under patriarchal-imperialist-capitalist labour relations and, more importantly, points to what is suppressed by the empirically existing: what could be (instead of what actually is). Critique indicates that what is, is not necessarily the real/true but rather only the existing actuality, which is transformable...
>
> ...Quite simply then, critique is a mode of knowing that inquires into what is not said, into the silences and the suppressed or missing, in order to uncover the concealed operations of power and underlying socioeconomic relations connecting the myriad details and seemingly disparate events and representations of our lives. In sum, materialist critique disrupts that which represents itself as what is, as natural, as inevitable, as the way things are, and exposes the way 'what is' is historically and socially produced out of social contradictions and how it supports inequality. Critique enables us to not only explain how class, race, gender and imperialist oppression operate so we can change it, but also to collectively build the emancipatory subjectivities we need to carry out the revolutionary struggle.

Critique is often difficult to execute and requires the development of historical material analysis of one's own self-constitution as a social agent within the totality of capitalist social relations. We often fail to recognise our responsibility to others because we are preoccupied with the others' relations to us. We forget our network of obligations.

Peter McLaren

Insofar as we, in the words of E. San Juan (2003:5), *claim to live in a community of singular persons who alternatively occupy the positions of speakers and listeners, I's and you's, and who have obligations to one another, and reciprocal accountabilities,* we mistake the struggle for liberation with the pursuit of subjective, autonomous self-identity, failing to realise that subjective self-identity is impossible outside our relation to the Other, and that we can never be free of our obligations to others.

As long as capitalism is not dead, neither is the heart of Marxism and class struggle. But at the same time we must remember that socialists work not for Marxism as a theory, but for socialism – Marxism is a tool, not an end in itself. It is, however, an essential tool in attempting to conceive of capitalism and its attendant forms of oppression as a whole. That is not to say that everything Marx said or anticipated has come true. That is certainly not the case. But Marx did provide us with fundamental insights into class society that have held true to this day. Rather than jettisoning Marx and decentring the role of capitalism in creating misery around the globe and discrediting socialist struggle, there is a need to challenge vigorously the assumptions that have come to constitute the core of contemporary radical theory, pedagogy and politics.

To defeat capitalist globalisation and the accumulation of corporate profits by private owners means developing a philosophy that can help us to organise praxis to this end. Our position as revolutionary critical educators is to support continent-wide mobilisations against the neo-liberal offensive and the Washington consensus, whose objective is to turn back all the social rights achieved over the past half-century. We advocate a gender-balanced, multiracial opposition to imperialism, to war, to capitalist globalisation, to the law-and-order policies that have made a mockery of our democratic freedoms and that institutionalise violence against the most vulnerable groups in our society. We challenge the productivist model of development that puts the future of humanity at risk, and we demand democratic control over choices of development and of production. In doing so, we steadfastly refuse to submit to social liberalism, which controls the institutions of the state in the interests of the minority who own all the wealth, and we work toward a socialist alternative to capitalism so that social needs are satisfied. Here we advocate the politics of inter-

19

nationalism, especially in light of the rise in power of social movements and continental social forums. We refer to diverse groups that include the *piqueteros* in Argentina, the *cocaleros* in Bolivia, the landless workers in Brazil, the Packakutik indigenous movement in Ecuador, the Zapatistas in Mexico and the Bolivarian Circles in Venezuela. The convergences necessary to give a true credibility to the conviction that another world is possible will not just happen on their own, they must be struggled for and guided by all of our efforts. This is the challenge of researchers, scholars, and activists working together for global justice and peace.

Marx's new society based on being rather than having, creating rather than controlling, relating rather than dominating will neither emerge from endless negation nor the spontaneous activities of the multitude, but, as Peter Hudis notes, will require an articulation of a positive vision of the new, a competing vision of a future alternative to capitalism. This means taking seriously the notion of praxis, and recognising that theory is more than the trajectory of ideas moving from theoreticians to the masses. It also means recognising that movements from practice by the masses are also forms of theory. As Marx (1978) wrote in *The German Ideology*, historical materialism *does not explain practice from the idea but explains the formation of ideas from material practice*. For Marx, 'not criticism but revolution is the driving force of history' (*ibid*:164). While it is surely true that activists who have warmed their political hands on the urban bonfires of Spanish Harlem winters have never read Hegel's *Philosophy of Right*, they nevertheless are theoreticians implicitly.

History needs a more powerful ally than the left-liberalism of today's postmodernised academic left. Left unreconciled, capital propels progress to a higher level of disunity. We do not seek an imageless metaphysical truth where thought thinks itself, we seek transformation of the conditions of social reproduction where the struggle preserves yet overcomes past struggles, to emerge at a point where a new social universe can be imagined and a new vision of the future can be won where the corporate walls of oppression and the ramshackle edifice of capital crumble into dust.

What has become clear is that the real threat to the security state is not terrorism but the struggle for socialism and democracy. For it is the self-movement and self-management of working people struggling for socialism and democracy that poses the greatest challenge to the transnational robber barons who administer the security state and who have acquired an unquenchable vampire-like thirst for finance capital.

Critical revolutionary pedagogy can serve the important purpose of generating new ways of thinking about the state and its relationship to the production of and possibilities for human agency, both now and in the crucial years ahead of us. Humans are conditioned by structures and social relations just as humans create and transform those structures and relations. Everything in human history passes through the realm of subjectivity and it is through this dance of the dialectic that we create our future. The democracy in which we live is indeed at a tragic crossroads, and we must fiercely question its present historical course in order to outlast despair and hold on to the vision that first brought this worthy concept into existence.

(Note: This chapter borrows from a number of writings over the past several years, all of which can be found together in one volume in Peter McLaren, *Capitalists and Conquerors: Critical Pedagogy Against Empire*. Rowman and Littlefield, in press.)

References

Allman, P (1999) *Revolutionary Social Transformation: Democratic Hopes, Political Possibilities and Critical Education*. Westport, CT: Bergin and Garvey

Allman, P (2001) *Critical Education Against Global Capitalism: Karl Marx and Revolutionary Critical Education*. Westport, CT: Bergin and Garvey

Barber, B (2002) *Beyond Jihad vs. McWorld: On Terrorism and the New Democratic Realism. The Nation*, 274(2, January 21) : 11-18

Bennett, W (2002) *Why We Fight: Moral Clarity and the War on Terrorism*. New York: Doubleday

Brennan, P (2003) *Mistah Kurtz's New Job: America's Heart of Darkness. OC Weekly*, vol. 8, no. 31 (April). As retrieved from: http://www.ocweekly.com/ink/03/31/books-brennan.php

Cole M, Hill D, Rikowski G, McLaren P (2000) *Red Chalk: On schooling, capitalism and politics*. London: The Tufnell Press

Eagleton, T (1996) *The Illusions of Postmodernism*. Cambridge, Massachusetts: Blackwell

Eagleton, T (1998) Defending the Free World, in: Regan, S (Ed.) *The Eagleton Reader*. Malden, Massachusetts: Blackwell

Eagleton, T (2003) *After Theory*. New York: Basic Books

Ebert, R (2004) Less is Moore in Subdued, Effective '9/11'. *Chicago Sun-Times*. May 18, Retrieved from: http://www.suntimes.com/output/eb-feature/cst-ftr-cannes18.html

Ebert, T (n.d.) *Subalternity and Feminism in the Moment of the (Post)Modern: The Materialist Re-Turn.* As retrieved from: http://www.geocities.com/ CapitolHill/Lobby/ 2072/AOVol3-3Subalterity.html

Floyd, C (2003) The Revelation of St. George. *Counterpunch* (June 30). http:// www.counter punch.org/floyd06302003.html December 20

Foster, J B (2001) Imperialism and 'Empire', *Monthly Review,* (December). As retrieved from: http://www.monthlyreview.org/1201jbf.htm

Hennessy, R and Ingraham, C (Eds.) (1997) Introduction: Reclaiming Anti-capitalist Feminism, in: *Material Feminism: A Reader in Class, Difference, and Women's Lives.* New York and London: Routledge

Hudis, P (2003) Report to National Plenum of News and Letters Committees, August 30, 2003. Organizational Responsibility for Marxist-Humanism in Light of War, Resistance, and the Need for a New Alternative

Klein, Naomi The Year of the Fake, *The Nation,* 278(3): 10

Landau, S (2004) Is Venezuela Next?, *Progreso Weekly,* March 25. As retrieved from: http:// www.progresoweekly.com/index.php?progreso=Landauand otherweek=1080194400

Lind, M (2004). Churchill for Dummies, *The Spectator,* (April 24). As retrieved from: http:// www.antiwar.com/spectator/spec280.html

Lieven, A (2003) The Empire Strikes Back, *The Nation,* (June 19) http://www. thenation.com/doc.mhtml?i=20030707ands=lieven

Maertens, T (2004) Clarke's Public Service, *Star Tribune,* (Sunday 28 March). As retrieved from: http://www.truthout.org/docs_04/033004B.shtml

Marx, K (1978) The German Ideology, Part One, in: Tucker, R C (Ed.) *The Marx-Engels Reader* (2nd edition: 146-200). New York. W W Norton

McLaren, P and Farahmandpur, R (1999a) Critical Pedagogy, Postmodernism, and the Retreat from Class: Towards a Contraband Pedagogy, *Theoria,* 93: 83-115

McLaren, P and Farahmandpur, R (1999b) Critical Multiculturalism and Globalization. Some Implications for a Politics of Resistance, *Journal of Curriculum Theorizing,* 15(3): 27-46

McMurtry, J (2001) Why is There a War in Afghanistan? *Opening Address, Science for Peace Forum and Teach-in,* University of Toronto, December 9, 1-13

Meyerson, G (2000) Rethinking Black Marxism: Reflections on Cedric Robinson and Others, *Cultural Critique,* 3(2). As retrieved from: http://eserver.org/ clogic/3-1%262/ meyerson.html

Pitt, W (2003) 'George W Christ?' *Truthout* (May 5). Found at http://www. truthout. org/docs_03/050503A.shtml.

Regular, A (2003) 'Road Map is a Life Saver for us,' PM Abbas tells Hamas, Haaron, Monday, August 11. http://www.haaretz.com/hasen/pages/ ShArt. jhtml?itemNo=310788andcontrassID=2andsubContrassID=1and sbSubContrassID=0 andlistSrc=Y

San Juan, Jr E (2003) US War on Terrorism and the Filipino Struggle for National Liberation. *Dialogue and Initiative.* (Fall), pp. 2-6.

Smith, T (2002) An Assessment of Joseph Stiglitz's *Globalization and Its Discontents,* Department Seminar, Philosophy Department, Iowa State University, October 29, 2002; Teach-in sponsored by Alliance for Global Justice, Ames, October 16, 2002. Available at: http://www.public.iastate. edu/~tonys/Stiglitz.html

Stiglitz, J (2002) The Roaring Nineties. *The Atlantic Monthly* (October). As retrieved from: http://www.theatlantic.com/issues/2002/10/stiglitz.htm

Tabb, W (2001) Globalization and Education as a Commodity. Available at: http://www.psc-cuny.org/jcglobalization.htm

Turner, D (1983) *Marxism and Christianity*. Oxford: Basil Blackwell

Wilden, A (1980) *The Imaginary Canadian: An Examination for Discovery*. Vancouver, Canada: Pulp Press

Zavarzadeh, M and Morton, D (1994) *Theory as Resistance: Politics and Culture after (Post) Structuralism*. New York: The Guilford Press

Zizek, S (2002) *Revolution at the Gates: Selected Writings of Lenin from 1917*. London and New York: Verso

2

Curriculum studies and the politics of educational reform

WILLIAM F PINAR

In this chapter, William Pinar offers a psychoanalytical perspective on the state of curriculum studies – and curriculum control – in the US today, a state which will be recognised elsewhere in the Anglophone world. Pinar contrasts the dangers of narcissism – the retreat into presentistic self-absorption (prevalent since 9/11 but, he argues, by no means a new phenomenon in American culture) – with the benefits of a focus on subjectivity. He urges a mobilisation of educators' consciousness in order to create spaces of intellectual freedom and professional autonomy 'behind enemy lines', and explores the potential of an internationalisation of curriculum studies which will enable us not only to take a wider perspective on the shaping of curriculum but also to bring a greater understanding to our own practices and constraints. Pinar's analysis echoes the concerns of McLaren, Cole and Atkinson over the foundations of current political and educational moves, and foreshadows Isherwood's analysis of the place of self in policy analysis.

There was a time, not so long ago, when internationalism was a key component of proletarian struggles and progressive politics in general. (Michael Hardt and Antonio Negri, 2000:49)

In many colleges and schools of education in the US, research is focused on teaching or, as many prefer, instruction. The dominant interest is in learning *how* to teach more effectively, so that students can learn more quickly, as measured on standardised examinations. Such educational research is a form of social and behaviour science. While hardly disinterested in questions of pedagogy, the interdisciplinary field of curriculum studies attends to *what* knowledge is worth knowing. More influenced by scholarship in the humanities and the arts than by research in the social and behavioural sciences, the field studies the cultural, historical, and political questions that surround and inform the central curriculum question: what knowledge is of most worth?

Like the humanities and the arts, the academic field of curriculum studies is embedded in national culture, a fact underscored in the first *International Handbook of Curriculum Research* (Pinar, ed, 2003). Because school curriculum and curriculum research are embedded in their respective national cultures, in the political present (a different present in different nations and regions), in cultural questions represented in various curricula as well as in curriculum research, and in those public debates and policies surrounding those curricula and research, studying the academic field of curriculum studies locally and globally (as each is embedded in the other) enables scholars to strengthen and make more sophisticated their critical and intellectual distance from their respective cultures and from those processes of cultural standardisation and economic exploitation which the phenomenon of globalisation threatens.

Because contemporary curriculum studies are, in part, about the relations among academic knowledge, subjective meaning, and social significance, the field is (again, in part) a kind of cultural criticism. Because the field is very embedded in national culture, it is the US I study. The cultural problem of American narcissism, painfully and violently obvious in the aftermath of the 9/11 attacks, has occupied me for decades. Today is not the occasion to trace how my early work in autobiography was, in part, an effort to grapple with American narcissism, including, of course, my own (Pinar, 1994). Today I cite it to introduce my discussion – in which I hope you will participate – of the internationalisation of curriculum studies.

One of my motives for participating in internationalisation is to contest the sometimes unbelievable self-involvement of American curriculum studies. One way US curriculum studies scholars can work through that cultural problem is to become more aware, in fact regard it as part of our professional responsibility, to keep track of what others interested in the concept of curriculum (or its equivalent) are doing around the world. It was toward this end that my co-director of LSU's Curriculum Theory Project – Bill Doll – and I organised a 1999 conference on the relations between philosophy of education and curriculum studies worldwide, followed in 2000 by a much larger conference on the internationalisation of curriculum studies (Trueit *et al*, 2003). It was toward that end that, at that second meeting, I initiated the process that resulted in the establishment of the International Association for the Advancement of Curriculum Studies (www.IAACS.org) and its US affiliate, the American Association for the Advancement of Curriculum Studies (http://aaacs.info). It was toward that end that I edited the first international handbook of curriculum research (Pinar, ed, 2003).

British readers will not be surprised to learn that progress is slow, and not only (but especially) in the United States. Relatively few senior scholars participate in AAACS meetings – of course, we are obligated to too many meetings already, but I think narcissism is also at play – and relatively few Americans attended the first triennial meeting of the IAACS in Shanghai last October.[1] The nightmarish political situation in the US does not help, of course. As Christopher Lasch (1978, 1984) appreciated, narcissism is a byproduct of self-devaluation, not old-fashioned (that is, pre-Freudian) egoism.

> *The Pressure Upon Us:*
> *Comments on the American Scene*
>
> Fellow educators – are we not lost?
> Do we know where we are,
> remember where we have been,
> or foresee where we are going?
> (Dwayne E. Huebner, 1999: 231)

Of course, there is no way for me to escape being an American, and my definition of curriculum as a 'complicated conversation' (Pinar *et al*, 1995:848) is thoroughly (although hardly exclusively: see, for instance, Oakeshott, 1959) an American idea. In the paradigm shift that occurred in American curriculum studies almost thirty years ago, we left a more narrowly institutional (some would say bureaucratic) conception of our work as curriculum development to a more scholarly effort to understand curriculum (Pinar *et al*, 1995, chapter

4; Pinar, ed 1999). By enlarging and complicating our conception of curriculum – yes, it still includes objectives, course syllabi, etc. but it is now as well a highly symbolic concept in which curriculum debates are understood, for instance, as debates over the identity of the nation – we hope to protect, at least conceptually, American teachers' still shrinking space of intellectual freedom, professional autonomy and personal creativity and, in so doing, support the intellectual freedom and creativity of the students they teach.

The discursive reformulation of our work as curriculum theorists from *curriculum development to understanding curriculum* represents, in part, a sober acknowledgement of the triumph in the schools of the business model – an insistence that educational achievement be quantified and that all engaged in the process of education must focus on the bottom line: in other words, test scores (Pinar *et al*, 1995). We in the university are left trying to protect and create spaces of intellectual freedom and professional autonomy behind enemy lines, as it were. Given the right-wing authoritarianism of the Bush Administration, now in its second term, many Americans feel they are behind enemy lines.

The pressure upon us is enormous. Students, teachers, administrators and, yes, education professors are pressed to work harder, to achieve more, to raise those test scores. While accompanying this political pressure are sometimes calls for increased teacher autonomy, such autonomy is always relative, performed in the shadow of standardised examinations. By test scores schools will be compared; those that fail are threatened with closure. What is operative today in the politics of American school reform is an accountant's concept of education, higher figures (i.e. higher test scores) indicating the accumulation of knowledge, which presumably translates into increased gross national product.

That the US school reform movement is dominated by business thinking and is thereby obsessed with the bottom line comes as no surprise to any serious student of US curriculum history. Despite progressive fantasies of the school as a laboratory for democracy (Dewey, 1916), the truth is that the American public schools[2] were established to make immigrants into Americans and to prepare all citizens for jobs in an industrial economy (Spring, 1972). The private sector did not want to pay for this job preparation and so it persuaded the public sector to pay. On this issue, little has changed in the last 100 years. The schools are still assumed to exist for the sake of job preparation, despite continuing, if largely empty, rhetoric linking education with democracy and a politically-engaged citizenry.

While the point of the American public schools has not changed much, the economy they were designed to support has. The consensus view is that the American economy is less and less industrial and more and more service-oriented, strongly information-based, increasingly organised around technological developments, including the internet. It is said to be international or global in character. Rather than the assembly line of the early automobile factory, the major mode of economic production today is semiotic (i.e. production of signs, symbols, and other information), and it occurs not in factories but in committees and in front of computer screens in corporate offices. Most American schools, however, still tend to be modelled after the assembly-line factory. Modelling schools after contemporary corporations *would* represent an improvement. Even in the corporate model, however, the economic function of schools remains unchallenged, and the modes of cognition appropriate to even corporate schools are fewer and narrower than intelligence more broadly understood.

The school in the US is a skill-and-knowledge factory (or corporation); the education professoriate is being reduced to the status of supervisory personnel. As the great curriculum theorist Dwayne E. Huebner recognised over twenty-five years ago, we educators are lost in roles created by others. As his comment quoted earlier suggests, many of us seem to have forgotten the past, and we are unable to imagine the future. This submergence in the present is not unique to educators; Christopher Lasch (1978:5) argued that Americans generally have become so presentistic, so self-involved in surviving the present that, for us: 'To live for the moment is the prevailing passion – to live for yourself, not for our predecessors or posterity.'

While Lasch's (1978) portrait of what he termed the culture of narcissism is overdrawn it is, in my judgment, largely accurate. Retreating from a public sphere that no longer seems meaningful and worthy of their investment, Americans retreat into the apparent safety of private life where, they discover, there is no safety either. 'On the contrary,' Lasch (1978:27) notes, 'private life takes on the very qualities of the anarchic social order from which it is supposed to provide a refuge.'

With no place to hide, Americans retreat into – and, Lasch argues, become lost in – themselves. The psychoanalytic term for this personality disturbance is narcissism, not to be confused with egoism or selfishness (see Lasch, 1984:18). Recoiling from meaningful engagement in the world, the privatised self atrophies – Lasch (1984) uses the term *minimal* to denote that contraction of the self which narcissism necessitates – and becomes unable to distinguish between self and other, let alone participate meaningfully in the public sphere. The past and future disappear in individualistic obsession with psychic survival in the present. As Lasch (1978:xvi) suggests: 'The narcissist has no interest in the future because, in part, he has so little interest in the past.'

Because the public sphere in the US – including the school classroom – has become so predatory for so many, not a few teachers have retreated into the (apparent) safety of their own subjectivities. But in so doing, they have abdicated their professional authority and ethical responsibility for the curriculum they teach. They have been *forced* to abdicate this authority by the bureaucratic protocols that presumably hold them accountable but which, in fact, render them unable to teach. (Instead, they are supposed to 'manage learning.') As a field, traditional curriculum studies in the US – in the past too often a support system for the school bureaucracy – was complicit with this presentistic capitulation to the reform *du jour*. As the distinguished curriculum historian Herbert Kliebard (1970) made clear, the ahistorical and atheoretical character of traditional curriculum studies disabled teachers from understanding the history of their present circumstances.

My work has emphasised the significance of subjectivity to teaching, to study, to the process of education (Pinar, 1994). The significance of subjectivity is not as a solipsistic retreat from the public sphere. As Lasch (1978:9) points out, subjectivity can be no refuge in an era when '[t]he possibility of genuine privacy recedes'. The significance of subjectivity is, in part, that it is inseparable from the social; it is only when we – together and in solitude – reconstruct the relation between the two that we can begin to restore our 'shattered faith in the regeneration of life' (Lasch, 1978:207) and cultivate the 'moral discipline ... indispensable to the task of building a new order' (Lasch 1978:235-236). Today, our educational labour is, I am suggesting, simultaneously subjective and political. To undertake this project of social and subjective reconstruction, we (and not only in the US, I suspect) must remember the past and imagine the future, however unpleasant this labour may be. Not only intellectually but in our character structure we must become *temporal*, living simultaneously in the past, present and future. In the autobiographical method I have devised, returning to the past (the regressive) and imagining the future (the progressive) must be understood (the analytic) for the self to become expanded (in contrast to being made minimal in Lasch's schema) and complicated then, finally, mobilised (in the synthetical moment). Such an autobiographical sequence of ourselves as individuals and as educators might enable us to awaken from the nightmare we are living in the present (see Pinar, 2004).

The first step we can take toward reconstructing education in the US is acknowledging frankly the historical present. The historical present – in which educators have little control over the curriculum, the very organisational and intellectual centre of schooling – has several markers, prominent among them accountability, an apparently commonsensical idea that makes teachers, rather than students and their parents, responsible for students' educational accomplishment. Is it not obvious that education is an opportunity offered, not a (business) service rendered?

To help us understand the present, I invoke the psychoanalytic notion of *deferred action* (*Nachträglichkeit*), a term Freud employed to explain how the experience of trauma is deferred – and, I would add, displaced – into other subjective and social spheres, where it is often no longer readily recognisable. I argue that the trauma of the Cold War in the 1950s and the 1954 US Supreme Court decision to desegregate the public schools (coupled with the primacy of students in 1960s civil rights struggles) was displaced and deferred onto public education. In the aftermath of these traumas, public education was racialised and gendered in the American popular imagination. Bluntly stated, we can understand the nightmare that is our subjugation in the present only if we appreciate that we teachers are the victims of displaced and deferred misogyny and racism.

In arguing that racism and misogyny have been deferred and displaced into public education in the US, I am not suggesting that they have been absorbed there. Racism and misogyny remain pervasive in

America today, and while teachers also suffer from deferred and displaced versions of them, white racism remains corrosive and endemic, especially (but not only) in the American South, now the political epicentre of American presidential politics (Black and Black, 1992). Indeed, my argument here regarding the deferred and displaced action of racism and misogyny underlines how these forms of social hatred and prejudice intensify as they mutate.

Nor am I arguing that the subjugation of US public school teachers is only racialised and gendered. It is classed as well. In contrast to elite professions such as medicine and, less so, law, public school teaching in the US has long been associated with the lower-middle class, and not only in salary. Public school teaching has historically required a shorter and less rigorous credentialing period. Moreover, many teachers have been – in the popular imagination if not always in fact – the first members of their families to complete higher education. (One hundred years ago, public school teaching rarely required a college degree.) The political problems of public education are, in part, class-based, but they are, I suggest, straightforwardly so. There is little that is deferred and displaced about the class-based character of the political subjugation of the teaching profession.

Moreover, teachers' present subjugation – its peculiar intensity and irrationality – cannot be grasped by class analysis alone. While class conflict in the United States has produced strong right-wing reaction, it has not tended to produce the vicious contempt teachers and *their* teachers – the education professoriate – have encountered. To grasp this overdetermined reaction, one must invoke models of racial prejudice and misogyny, wherein complex and convoluted psychological structures and processes intensify emotion well beyond rhyme or reason. We must move to the sphere of psychopathology to grasp the history of the present of public education in the United States.

We can glimpse this phenomenon of deferral and displacement in the Kennedy administration's educational response to the Cold War (intensifying with the Sputnik satellite launch in 1957 and the Cuban missile crisis in 1962), specifically its embrace of physical fitness in 1960 and 1961 and, during this same period, its initiation of a National Curriculum Reform Movement. This Movement was dedicated to aligning the secondary school subjects with the academic disciplines as they existed at the university and, in so doing, establish academic – to parallel physical – rigour in the schools. To accomplish this curricular alignment, the control of curriculum had to be taken from teachers. The continuing legacy of Cold War curriculum politics structures the deplorable situation in which we teachers find ourselves today. Starting in the early 1960s, then, US educators began to lose all control over the curriculum, including the means by which students' study of it is assessed.[3]

While 1960s curriculum reform was gendered (female teachers had allowed young male bodies to go soft: see Griswold, 1998), it was profoundly racialised as well. It was 1954 when the US Supreme Court ruled that public schools must be desegregated, but in the South this did not occur until the late 1960s and early 1970s. (Desegregation never occurred in the North of the US, as primarily white suburban school districts ring primarily black urban ones.)

As schools became racial battlegrounds and the pretext for white flight, and as college students fought to desegregate other public spaces (perhaps most famously lunch counters and public transportation), racial anxiety began to intensify among European Americans, an anxiety right-wing Republican presidential candidate Barry Goldwater worked to exploit in his 1964 campaign against Democratic President Lyndon B Johnson. It is the same white racism Alabama Governor George Wallace tried to exploit in his 1968 and 1972 presidential campaigns (Black and Black, 1992).

While this pervasive and intensifying (white) anxiety – not limited to the American South – was focused upon the public schools, it echoed through the culture at large, as broader issues of racial justice and, indeed, of the American identity itself (was this still, or even primarily, an European nation?) were stimulated by the desegregation of the nation's schools. Public education – in the North especially in the urban centres, in the South everywhere – became racialised.

The political problem of US teachers today – their scapegoating by politicians and by uninformed parents, their loss of academic freedom (the very prerequisite for professional practice) – cannot be understood apart from right-wing politicians' manipulation of public education as a political issue. This political manipulation was first successfully employed in the 1960 Kennedy presidential campaign. In subsequent campaigns, the tactic was appropriated by the right, enabled all along by white reactionaries in the Deep South (Black and Black, 1992).

From this evocation of the past in the present, let us focus for a moment on futuristic conceptions of American education. These attempt to sidestep history and culture; they are primarily technological in nature. In fantasies of the future, screens – television, film, and, especially, computer screens – seem everywhere, prosthetic extensions of our enfleshed bodies, dispersing our subjectivities outward, far from our concrete everyday communities into abstract cyberspace and a 'global village'. In this prosthetic extension of the everyday ego we took ourselves to be, the self seems to evaporate. Subjectivity itself mutates, and the self which autobiography purports to identify and express distends into hypertextual personae, ever-changing cyborg identities. New forms of subjectivity and sexuality appear as the natural world threatens to become virtual. In today's politics of public miseducation, the computer becomes the latest technological fantasy of educational utopia, a fantasy of teacher-proof curriculum, a fantasy of going where no man has gone before.

As curriculum theorists have long appreciated, the exchange and acquisition of information is not education. Being informed is not equivalent to erudition. Information must be tempered with intellectual judgement, critical thinking, ethics, and self-reflexivity. The complicated conversation that is the curriculum requires each of these. This is not a recipe for high test scores, but a common faith in the possibility of self-realisation and democratisation, twin projects of social and subjective reconstruction.

After considering for a moment the future in the present, I turn now to an analytic moment. In this phase I face the facts comprising the present, namely the profoundly anti-intellectual conditions of our professional labour in the US. These are conditions both internal and external to the schools and to the university-based academic fields of curriculum studies and teacher education. The challenge of education in this profoundly anti-intellectual historical moment is made, contrary to expectation, *more* difficult by our situation in the US university, where many arts and sciences colleagues – as we term them more hopefully than accurately – too often mistake academic vocationalism and their own budgetary self-interest for interdisciplinary, socially critical, subjectively-engaged education (see, for instance, Hofstadter,[4] 1962).

34

Due to the anti-intellectualism of American culture generally, due to the deferral and displacement of racism and misogyny onto public education more specifically, and due to reactionary (white) southern culture and history now politically hegemonic in the US, the field of education has (understandably) remained underdeveloped intellectually. But there are, as well, reasons internal to the field, reasons for which we are responsible, that American educators and education professors suffer political subjugation today. Americans cannot begin to respond to the displaced and deferred racism and misogyny which I have identified until we face the internalised consequences of our decades-long subjugation, namely a pervasive and crippling anti-intellectualism (see Pinar, 2004, chapter 7).

Whatever our fate in the US – and given our betrayal by government, the future is not bright – we curriculum studies scholars must carry on, our dignity intact. We must renew our commitment to the intellectual character of our professional labour. We can do so, first, by engaging in frank and sustained self-criticism. There is, in the US, a deep-seated and pervasive anti-intellectualism within the academic field of education, obvious in teacher education, but expressed in the anti-theoretical vocationalism found not only in that field. The problem we face in the US is hardly helped by the hostility of some arts and sciences colleagues, and it is only intensified by the scapegoating of public schools and the education professoriate by (especially right-wing) politicians. Despite these assaults on the profession, we cannot retreat into a defensive posture that keeps us from facing frankly the anti-intellectualism built into the field and from taking steps, both individually and as a professional collectivity, to correct it (see Pinar, 2004).

After these brief moments of reflection on the past and the future in the present and that self-understanding which self-reflexive analysis invites, I dwell in a synthetic moment, a moment during which we might mobilise ourselves, both as individuals and as a profession. After the shattering (or evaporation) of the ego that regression to the past and contemplation of the future invites, we return to the present, to become mobilised for pedagogical engagement in the reconstruction of the private and public spheres in curriculum and teaching. Public education structures self-formation and social reconstruction while, in many of its present forms, it blocks both. Teachers ought not to be only school-subject specialists; I suggest that they become private-and-public intellectuals who understand that self-reflexivity, intellectuality, interdisciplinarity and erudition are as inseparable as are the subjective and the social spheres themselves (Pinar, 2004).

In the US, it is long past time for us to confront those politicians, parents, and school and university administrators who misunderstand the education of the public as a business. Mobilised, we must enter into the public arena and teach our fellow citizens – including un-comprehending colleagues and self-aggrandising administrators – what is at stake in the education of children, an education in which creativity and individuality, not test-taking skills, are primary. In our time, to be intellectual requires political activism, as Peter McLaren, for one (see chapter 1 of this volume), has long understood.

Within our profession, we must repudiate those legislative actions by government – such as the Bush administration's *No Child Left Behind* legislation – that destroy the very possibility of education by mis-construing it as a business. While we struggle as intellectuals recon-structing the private and public spheres of curriculum and teaching in schools, we must, especially among ourselves, keep hope alive. We can recapture the curriculum, someday. Without reclaiming our academic – intellectual – freedom we cannot teach. Without intel-lectual freedom, education ends; students are indoctrinated, forced to learn what the test-makers declare to be important.

Organisational, Administrative, and Intellectual Next Steps

> After a new theory of value, then, a new theory of subjectivity must be formulated that operates primarily through knowledge, com-munication, and language. (Hardt and Negri, 2000:29)

That is a brief review of the current situation in the US. I offer this commentary on the American scene to suggest one way an inter-national curriculum studies conversation might begin, one value it might have. In explaining to colleagues outside our specific national situations, we are encouraged to distance ourselves from our situa-tions, enabling us to reflect more critically upon them and what they demand of us. Links among various curriculum inquiries in various national settings might be elaborated; differences clarified and ex-plored. These are evident in the *International Handbook of Curri-culum Research*, about which I will comment now, concluding with what I perceive to be next steps in the internationalisation of curriculum studies.

Several points became clarified during the editing of the *International Handbook of Curriculum Research*. As I suspected, the curriculum field is very much embedded in national cultures and regional settings. Much curriculum work – research and curriculum development initiatives – functions in the service of school reform, stimulated and sometimes stipulated by governmental policy initiatives, including legislation. As Angel Diaz Barriga (2003a, 443) notes in his review of curriculum studies in Mexico, 'the field of curriculum is an outstandingly practical domain'. In British curriculum studies this seemed very much the case, exemplified, perhaps, in the work of Lawrence Stenhouse (1971).⁵

In the US at present, the practical is too often a cover for bureaucratic surveillance and intervention, instrumental rationality in the service of the bottom line and test scores. Considerable curriculum scholarship worldwide is critical of this business rhetoric of school reform; from this fact we can conclude that the field is not merely a conceptual extension of the state's political and bureaucratic apparatus. There is a relative intellectual independence in most but not all countries. This last point is heartening to those of us committed to an intellectually autonomous, vibrant, scholarly field of curriculum studies worldwide. However, it cannot be taken for granted, as politicians' manipulation of the political rhetoric of school reform represents an ongoing threat to the relative intellectual autonomy and academic freedom of curriculum scholars, not to mention public school teachers.

It is also clear from studying the *Handbook* that, to a considerable extent, the internationalisation of curriculum studies has already occurred, except perhaps in the US. Intellectual influences from the US and the UK, especially in the area of critical curriculum thought (related to 1970s scholarship, characterised then as the new sociology of education), are evident in a number of Latin American fields, for instance (see Moreira, 2003). These influences do not seem to have been imported, in general, uncritically, but rather adopted somewhat self-consciously, and for specific and local purposes (although this may not have been the case with earlier waves of conceptual imports, especially US empirical research). Indeed, in his review of Brazilian curriculum studies, Antonio Moreira (2003, 171) concludes that the importation of 'foreign material' involves 'interactions and resistances, whose intensity and whose potential 'subversiveness' vary according to international and local circumstances'.

In the case of Canadian scholarship in phenomenology and hermeneutics (see Chambers, 2003), it is the US which has been the importing nation (see Pinar et. al., 1995, chapter 8). With the establishment of the International Association for the Advancement of Curriculum Studies and the publication of several international collections, including the *Handbook,* the internationalisation of the field will no doubt continue, perhaps at an accelerated rate. This possibility asks scholars worldwide to become knowledgeable, more critical, more self-conscious and selective regarding the appropriation of scholarship from sources outside one's homeland, as there are intellectual as well as, in some countries, political complexities in such appropriation.

Understanding curriculum is today simultaneously an international (global) phenomenon and a local, situated practice. Attention to the local means not only attention to current, usually politically instigated, waves of school reform. In order to resist the danger of submergence in political rhetoric and over-zealous governmental participation in the intellectual and psycho-social life of schools, curriculum studies as a field must labour to remain, and/or become, more intellectually independent. As Mariano Palamidessi and Daniel Feldman (2003, 119) point out in their essay on curriculum studies in Argentina, there can be 'little distinction between the intellectual field ... and the activities of official agencies'.

To advance the field, I submit, such distinction must be cultivated. Indeed, vigorous debate and differences in point of view – not only among ourselves but also from politicians and government officials – must be articulated and supported. Curriculum scholars, I suggest, must become intellectuals (and, especially, public intellectuals) as well as technical specialists with bureaucratic expertise that governments and their agencies can employ (Pinar, 2004). A sophisticated field of curriculum studies would occupy, it seems to me, a broad spectrum of scholarship and professional activity, from the theoretical to the institutional, from the global to the local, from the university to the school.

We might think of our scholarly effort to understand curriculum locally as well as globally as supporting the horizontality of the field. But it is clear to me, from the studies published in the handbook, for the field to advance or mature (to employ Antonio Moreira's formulation, 2003:171), the field must support verticality as well. That is to say, in each nation or region, as well as worldwide, the field needs historical studies and, as well, future-oriented studies. Historical studies might enable us to understand and work through the specificities of our national cultures and the embeddedness of curriculum theory and practice within them. Moreover, historical studies may enable us to resist any uncritical acceptance of globalisation. Within our specific national and regional cultures, historical scholarship means that we are less vulnerable to political slogans (such as the privatisation and marketisation of public education), and to the discursive and material manipulations by specific regimes of reason and power. While internationalisation supports transnational communication, it is important for each nation (and/or region) to cultivate its own indigenous and conceptually independent curriculum theorising, inquiry, and research.

In asserting this, I realise I am drawing upon strands of critical thought that have sought to establish sites of resistance founded both on the individual identities of social subjects and the collective identities of national and regional groups, structuring such subjective sites in terms of local struggles. In this tradition I myself have constructed curriculum in terms of *place*, and, specifically, the American South (i.e., the former slave states), in order to refocus and reanimate struggles of resistance to racism, classism, and misogyny (see Pinar, 2004). Internationally, place-based movements have been set up against the apparently 'undifferentiated and homogeneous space of global networks' (Hardt and Negri, 2000:44).

At other times, Michael Hardt and Antonio Negri point out, such political arguments have emerged from long-standing traditions of leftists in which nationalism and the nation is posited as the site of resistance against the domination of foreign and/or global capital. If capitalist domination is now globalised, this reasoning went, then resistances must seize upon the local and there construct barriers to global capital's accelerating flows. 'What needs to be addressed, instead,' Hardt and Negri (2000:45) assert, is precisely the production of locality, that is, the social machines that create and recreate the identities and differences that are understood as the local. The differences of locality are neither pre-existing nor natural but rather effects of a regime of production. Globality similarly should not be understood in terms of cultural, political, or economic *homogenization*. Globalization, like localization, should be understood instead as a regime of the production of identity and difference, or really of homogenization and heterogenization.

If Hardt and Negri are right, then, the historicisation and theorisation of curriculum do not guarantee help *contra* globalisation and, specifically, the marketisation of education. What they can do, at least for those of us working where these phenemona are well advanced, is to enable us to help our colleauges in the schools *understand* what is happening to them and to the children in their charge. That is a rather different project from bureaucratic intervention, especially intervention based upon governmental and other political initiatives.

I make this point because it is clear from the *Handbook* that the field remains very much focused on school improvement. We are less focused on the intellectual project of understanding. While the two are, of course, intertwined and synergistic, in the near term, at least, advancement might mean, certainly in the US context, a certain shift in the centre of gravity of the field: from an exclusive and often bureaucratic preoccupation with instrumental interventions in the school-as-institution to the intellectual project of understanding. While hardly abandoning bureaucratic protocols aimed at institutional improvement, some segment of the field, it seems to me, must be devoted to curriculum theory and history, i.e. scholarly efforts to *understand* curriculum, including curriculum development, implementation and evaluation.

In doing so there are, as several essays in the *Handbook* make clear, important ethical and political dimensions to the labour of curriculum development and scholarship. We cannot pretend, as mainstream social science once did, to be neutral. Especially in those nations in reconstruction after emancipation from colonial regimes, ethical and political dimensions are explicit, as indicated in Rivera's (2003) essay on the Philippines, Malaysia, and Thailand, in Jansen's (2003) essay on Zimbabwe and Namibia, and in Pandey and Moorad's (2003) essay on Botswana.

Not only are those engaged in decolonisation engaged ethically and politically. Wherever we are located 'in the non-place of Empire' (Hardt and Negri 2000, 208), we all are politically and ethically engaged, and in local and global ways that can be usefully articulated and elaborated in our research. For those of us facing and resisting the privatisation and marketisation of public education, we are forced to negotiate among complex and often conflicting professional responsibilities, themselves structured and animated by ethical obligations and political commitments.

Conclusion

> Internationalization [is]...tantamount to global ethics and
> solidarity. (Bengt Thelin, 1992: 10)

> Freedom in this sense means not only the task of resistance
> to multiple forms of domination but also the creation
> of new modes of being, eroticism, social relations, and,
> ultimately, new models of democracy.
> (Ewa Plonowska Ziarek 2001, 219)

The accelerating and expanding complexity of our work as curriculum scholars – what the Mexican scholar Frida Diaz Barriga (2003b, 457) so nicely characterises as the polysemic character of the field – calls upon us to continue to make scholarly efforts toward the self-conscious understanding of our work and the curriculum work of teachers and students in the schools, all of us situated culturally, historically, and now, as we are acutely clear, globally.

From the essays in the *International Handbook*, it is clear that there are conditions – perhaps *especially* in the English-speaking world – that render such work difficult. The business logic characterising educational reform, not only but especially in the US, creates anti-intellectual conditions (both internal and external to the field) in which to work. In such conditions, it is, I believe, incumbent upon us to build intellectual and organisational infrastructure if the intellectual and political projects of resistance and understanding are to continue.

In this time of assault from government, of compromised academic – intellectual – freedom (especially for teachers in the schools), it is imperative to create discourse that, as Ziarek suggests, enables us to resist that assault and to create new models of democracy, not ultimately but immediately. Such organisational structures, of which the Discourse -Power Resistance Conference might be one example, support us in creating not only discursive forms of resistance to power, but discursive forms *of* power that enable us, and our colleagues in schools, to understand and, thereby, advance from the present.

References

Black, E and Black, M (1992) *The Vital South: How Presidents are Elected*. Cambridge, MA: Harvard University Press.

Chambers, C (2003) 'As Canadian as Possible under the Circumstances': A view of contemporary curriculum discourses in Canada, in: Pinar, W (ed) *International Handbook of Curriculum Research*. Mahwah, N J: Lawrence Erlbaum:

Dewey, J (1916) *Democracy and Education*. New York: Macmillan

Diaz, Barriga, A (2003a) Curriculum Research: Evolution and Outlook in México, in: Pinar, W (ed) *International Handbook of Curriculum Research*. Mahwah, N J: Lawrence Erlbaum: 443 – 456

Diaz, Barriga, A (2003b) Main Trends of Curriculum Research in México, in: Pinar, W (ed) *International Handbook of Curriculum Research*. Mahwah, NJ: Lawrence Erlbaum: 457 – 469

Furlong, J (2002) Ideology and reform in teacher education in England, *Educational Researcher*, 31(6): 23 – 25

Goodson, I F (1983) *School Subjects and Curriculum Change*. London: Falmer. (2nd edition: 1987; 3rd edition: 1993, with foreword by Peter McLaren.)

Goodson, I F (1988a) *International Perspectives in Curriculum History*. Boston, MA: Routledge and Kegan Paul

Goodson, I F (1988b) *The Making of Curriculum: Collected essays*. Philadelphia, PA: Falmer

Goodson, I F (1989) Curriculum reform and curriculum theory: a case of historical amnesia, *Cambridge Journal of Education*, 19(2): 131-141

Goodson, I F (1997) *Subject Knowledge: Readings for the study of school subjects*. New York: RoutledgeFalmer

Goodson, I F and Ball, S (eds) (1984) *Defining the Curriculum: Histories and Ethnographies*. London: Falmer

Goodson, I F and Hargreaves, A (eds) (1996) *Teachers' Professional Lives*. New York: RoutledgeFalmer

Goodson, I F and Walker, R (1991) *Biography, Identity and Schooling: Episodes in educational research*. London: Falmer

Goodson, I F, Knobel, M, Lankshear, C and Mangan, J M (2002) *Cyber Spaces/ Social Spaces: culture clash in computerized classrooms*. New York: Palgrave Macmillan

Griswold, R L (1998) The 'flabby American,' the body, and the cold war, McCall, L and Yacovone, D (eds), *A Shared Experience: Men, women, and the history of gender*. New York: New York University Press: 323 – 348

Hamilton, D (1976) *Curriculum Evaluation*. London: Open Books
Hamilton, D (1990) *Curriculum history*. Geelong, Victoria, Australia: Deakin University Press
Hardt, M and Negri, A (2000) *Empire*. Cambridge, MA: Harvard University Press
Hofstadter, R (1962) *Anti-intellectualism in American life*. New York: Vintage
Huebner, D E (1999) *The Lure of the Transcendent*. Mahwah, NJ: Lawrence Erlbaum
Jansen, J D (2003).What education scholars write about curriculum in Namibia and Zimbabwe, in: Pinar, W (ed) *International Handbook of Curriculum Research*. Mahwah, NJ: Lawrence Erlbaum: 471 – 478
Kliebard, H M (1970) Persistent issues in historical perspective, *Educational Comment*: 31 – 41 (Also in Pinar, F (ed) (1975a), *Curriculum Theorizing: the Reconceptualists*. Berkeley: McCutchan: 39 – 50. Reissued in 2000 as *Curriculum Theorizing: The Reconceptualization*. Troy, NY: Educator's International Press.)
Lasch, C (1978) *The Culture of Narcissism: American life in an age of diminishing expectations*. New York: Norton
Lasch, C (1984) *The Minimal Self: Psychic survival in troubled times*. New York: Norton
McClintock, R (1971) Toward a place for study in a world of instruction, *Teachers College Record*, 73(20): 161 – 205
Moreira, A F B (2003) The curriculum field in Brazil: emergence and consolidation, in: Pinar, W (ed) *International Handbook of Curriculum Research*. Mahwah, NJ: Lawrence Erlbaum:171 – 184
Oakeshott, M (1959) *The Voice of Poetry in the Conversation of Mankind*. London: Bowes and Bowes
Palamidessi, M and Feldman, D (2003) The development of curriculum thought in Argentina, in: Pinar, W (ed) *International Handbook of Curriculum Research*. Mahwah, NJ: Lawrence Erlbaum: 109 – 122
Pandey, S N and Moorad, F R (2003) The decolonization of curriculum in Botswana, in: Pinar, W (ed) *International Handbook of Curriculum Research*. Mahwah, NJ: Lawrence Erlbaum: 143 – 170
Pinar, W F (1994) *Autobiography, Politics, and Sexuality: Essays in curriculum theory 1972-1992*. New York: Peter Lang
Pinar, W F. (ed) (1999) *Contemporary Curriculum Discourses: Twenty years of JCT*. New York: Peter Lang
Pinar, W F. (ed) (2003) *International Handbook of Curriculum Research*. Mahwah, NJ: Lawrence Erlbaum
Pinar, W F (2004) *What is Curriculum Theory?* Mahwah, NJ: Lawrence Erlbaum
Pinar, W F, Reynolds, W, Slattery, P and Taubman, P (1995) *Understanding Curriculum*. New York: Peter Lang
Reid, W A (1978) *Thinking About the Curriculum*. London: Routledge and Kegan Paul
Reid, W A (1980) Rationalism or humanism? The future of curriculum studies, *JCT*, 2(1): 93 – 108

Reid, W A (1984) Curriculum, community, and liberal education: a response to the Practical 4, *Curriculum Inquiry*, 14(1): 103 – 111

Reid, W A (1994) *The Pursuit of Curriculum: Schooling and the public interest.* Albex

Reid, W A (1998) Systems and structures or myths and fables? A cross-cultural perspective on curriculum content, in: Gundem, B B and Hopmann, S (eds) *Didaktik and/or Curriculum: An International Dialogue.* New York: Peter Lang

Reid, W A (1999) *Curriculum as Institution and Practice: Essays in the deliberative tradition.* Mahwah, NJ: Lawrence Erlbaum

Rivera, F D (2003) In Southeast Asia: Philippines, Malaysia, and Thailand: conjunctions and collision in the global cultural economy, in: Pinar, W (ed) *International Handbook of Curriculum Research.* Mahwah, NJ: Lawrence Erlbaum: 553 – 574

Spring, J (1972) *Education and the Rise of the Corporate State.* Boston, MA: Beacon Press

Stenhouse, L (1971) The humanities project: the rationale, *Theory Into Practice*, 10: 154-162

Stenhouse, L (1975) *An Introduction to Curriculum Research and Development.* London: Heinemann

Stenhouse, L (1979) *Curriculum Research and Development in Action.* London: Heinemann

Stenhouse, Lawrence (1982) *Teaching About Race Relations.* London: Routledge and Kegan Paul

Stenhouse, L (1983) *Authority, Education and Emancipation.* London: Heinemann

Stenhouse, L (1995) *An education that empowers: a collection of lectures in memory of Lawrence Stenhouse.* London: Multilingual Matters

Thelin, B (1992) Education for global survival: Reflections based on some Swedish experiences and examples. Paper presented at the annual meeting of the American Educational Research Association, San Francisco, April

Trueit, D, Wang, H, Doll, Jr., W E and Pinar, W F (eds) (2003) *The Internationalization of Curriculum Studies.* New York: Peter Lang

Ziarek, E P (2001) *An Ethics of Dissensus: Postmodernity, feminism, and the politics of radical democracy.* Stanford, CA: Stanford University Press

Notes

1   The 2006 meeting will be held in Europe, in Finland. For information visit the Association's website: www.iaacs.org.

2   For 'public schools' in the US, read 'state schools' in the UK. By a strange quirk of language, the term 'public school' in the UK refers to a private school, as does the term 'private school'.

3   For the centrality of 'study' – not teaching or instruction or pedagogy (even the critical kind), see McClintock (1971).

4   Relying on John Furlong's study of ideology and teacher education reform in England, I surmise the situation here has not been altogether different. Furlong (2002) reports that in the late 1960s in Britain the 'Black Papers' were published, a series of well-pub-

licised critiques of progressive education made mostly by arts and sciences professors. It was not, Furlong continues, until 1979 and the election of Margaret Thatcher that those supporting the Black Papers enjoyed influence. At that time attention became focused on teacher education, mishandled by what was then characterised as the 'liberal education elite' (quoted in Furlong, 2002:23). In the US, it is the 'education establishment' which has been scapegoated by the right-wing as responsible for low test scores.

5   Laying the foundation for the reemergence of the British curriculum field would involve, it seems to me, historical scholarship, recovering the work of past scholars like Laurence Stenhouse (1971, 1975, 1979, 1982, 1983, 1995) and reintegrating the work of contemporary scholars like Ivor Goodson, 1983, 1988a, b, 1989, 1997; Goodson and Walker, 1991; Goodson and Ball, 1984; Goodson and Hargreaves, 1996; Goodson, Knobel, Lankshear and Mangan, 2002), David Hamilton (1976, 1990), and William Reid (1978, 1980, 1984, 1994, 1998, 1999).

3

Empires old and new: a Marxist analysis of the teaching of imperialism, actual and potential, in the Engish school curriculum

MIKE COLE

Mike Cole takes seriously in this chapter the suggestion made recently by Prince Charles that history teaching in UK schools should reinstate the history of the British Empire. Cole goes further, arguing that not only should UK schoolchildren learn about British imperialism, they should also encounter the ugly mixture of racisms through which the understanding of British Imperialism has been mediated in the past. That, Cole argues, is itself a historical phenomenon we need to confront. Cole's impatience with postmodernism is rehearsed in this chapter, as is his insistence, derived from mainstream Marxism, that the bottom line is class, and that class struggle is the way to understand what is at stake in contemporary historical controversy.

Introduction

At the Prince of Wales summer school for English and history specialists in July 2003, calls were made from the prince himself, along with historian, Professor Niall Ferguson and Scott Harrison, history advisers to Ofsted (the official schools' watchdog in Britain), for the history of Britain's imperial past to be reinstated at the core of the secondary school curriculum (Pike, 2003). Ferguson presented a TV programme on the British Empire watched by more than 2 million people in Britain. I will argue that Marxists should endorse these calls, in the pursuit of an education which examines imperialisms, past and present, and which puts economic, social and political analysis of everyday life at the centre of the curriculum.[1]

Racism

In order to understand imperialism, it is necessary to have a conceptual awareness of the concepts of racism and racialisation. Elsewhere (e.g. Cole, 2004b; Cole and Stuart, 2005) I have suggested that in order to encompass the multifaceted nature of contemporary racism, it is important to adopt a broad concept of racism. I defined racism as including intentional as well as unintentional racism, biological as well as cultural racism that is seemingly positive as well as obvious negative racism, dominative racism (direct and oppressive) as opposed to aversive racism (exclusion and cold-shouldering) (Kovel, 1988) and overt as well as covert racism. All of these forms of racism can be individual or personal as well as institutional and there can, of course, be permutations among them (Cole, 2004b:37-38; Cole and Stuart, 2005).

I have also argued elsewhere that racism in British society may be viewed as a continuous process from the origins of the Welfare State up to the present, both in general terms (Cole, 1992; Cole, 2004a; Cole and Virdee, 2005) and with particular respect to education (Cole 1992; Cole 2004a, 2004b; Cole and Blair, 2005).

Racialisation and Common Sense

The concept of racialisation is useful to understand this process. Robert Miles has defined racialisation as an ideological process[2] that accompanies the exploitation of labour power (the capacity to labour), where people are categorized into the scientifically defunct notion of distinct races. As Miles puts it, the processes are not *explained* by the fact of capitalist development (a functionalist position). However 'the process of racialisation cannot be adequately understood without a conception of, and explanation for, the complex interplay of different modes of production and, in particular, of the social relations necessarily established in the course of material production' (1987:7). It is this interconnection which makes the concept of racialisation inherently Marxist.[3]

48

For Marxists, any discourse is a product of the society in which it is formulated. In other words, 'our thoughts are the reflection of political, social and economic conflicts and racist discourses are no exception' (Camara, 2002:88). Dominant discourses (e.g. those of the Government, of Big Business, of large sections of the media, of the hierarchy of some trade unions) tend to directly reflect the interests of the ruling class, rather than the general public. The way in which racialisation connects with popular consciousness, however, is via common sense. Common sense is generally used to denote a down-to-earth good sense and is thought to represent the distilled truths of centuries of practical experience, so that to say that an idea or practice is 'only common sense' is to claim precedence over the arguments of left intellectuals and, in effect, to foreclose discussion (Lawrence, 1982:48). As Diana Coben (2002:285) has noted, Gramsci's distinction between good sense and common sense 'has been revealed as multifaceted and complex'. For, common sense

> is not a single unique conception, identical in time and space. It is the 'folklore' of philosophy, and, like folklore, it takes countless different forms. Its most fundamental characteristic is that it is ... fragmentary, incoherent and inconsequential (Gramsci, 1978:419)

The rhetoric of the purveyors of dominant discourses aims to shape common sense discourse into formats which serve their interests.

British Imperialism and the School Curriculum
Racialisation is historically and geographically specific. Thus, in the British colonial era, implicit in the rhetoric of imperialism was a racialised concept of 'nation'. British capitalism had to be regenerated in the context of competition from other countries and amid fears that sparsely settled British colonies might be overrun by other European races.

Thus, an imperial race was needed to defend the nation and the colonies (Miles, 1993: 69). Intentional and overt institutional racism was rampant in all the major institutions of society: in the Government, the TUC and, of course, at the heart of capitalism itself. By the end of the nineteenth century, the ideology of the superiority of the British race and the inferiority of Britain's colonial subjects was available to all through popular culture (Cole, 1992; Cole and Virdee, 2005). It had become common sense to view the world in this way.

Britain had become a dominative and overtly institutionally racist society.

Racism was institutionalised in popular culture in the British Imperial era in many ways, in popular fiction (Miles, 1982:110 and 119), in missionary work, in music hall, in popular art (Cole, 1992; Cole and Virdee, 2005); and in education (Cole, 2004b; Cole and Blair, 2005).

The primacy of the Bible and religion was replaced by the growing influence of imperialism which was central in shaping the changing school syllabus, especially from the 1900s onwards[4].The addition of subjects like history, domestic science and games to the elementary school curriculum was conceived and justified by reference to their contribution to national strength, efficiency (Humphries 1981:40) and, of course, the Empire. Thus many English readers, for example, contained passages glorifying the monarchy and celebrating Britain's commercial wealth and progress, and English teachers were increasingly encouraged to give instruction in the duties of citizenship. More specifically, the introduction of Domestic Science subjects was directly related to the fear of race degeneracy, since the intention was to teach working class mothers how to manage their homes efficiently (*ibid*). As Humphries puts it, following Dyhouse and Davin:

> Subjects such as home economics, laundry work, cookery and needlework aimed to instruct working-class girls in the correct performance of their future duties of motherhood, housework and domestic service, thereby promoting the reinvigoration of the nation and Empire through a sexist division of labour (*ibid*)

Similarly, he goes on, the inclusion of games and sports in the school curriculum was justified in terms of encouraging a corporate spirit and developing the physical strength and moral fibre of [male] working class youth – a direct transplant of elements of the public school ethos to state elementary schools to foster the development of imperial warriors.

Geography texts were prime conveyors of racialisation. The transmission of overt biological racism was facilitated by the portrayal of adult colonial subjects as degenerate children. The nineteenth century vision of Africans as children sunk in tropical abundance was perpetuated into the twentieth century. In Nelson's *The World and its Peoples* (published circa 1907) the African was described as an overgrown child, vain, self-indulgent, and fond of idleness. Life is so easy to him in his native home that he has never developed the qualities of industry, self-denial and forethought (*ibid*)

In this text, it was explained that the 'Dark Continent' was thus described because of the 'barbarous condition of its inhabitants' (*ibid*). And, as if to prove the point, the Chambers' *Geographical Reader* repeated the old canard that '[m]any of the Central African tribes are so savage as still to be cannibals' (*ibid*), while '[t]he wretched bushmen [were] the lowest most debased human beings on the face of the globe' (Nelson's *The World and its Peoples*, cited in *ibid*, 185). In the same book, Asia was similarly denigrated as a continent of dying nations rapidly falling back in civilisation (cited in *ibid*, 184). Australian Aboriginals were:

among the most miserable of men [sic]. They roamed nearly naked, and were ignorant of everything except the chase. The explanation of their degraded condition lies in the arid climate of Australia ... Their great poverty led them to practise vices like cannibalism and the murder of the sick and helpless (Herbertson's *Man and his Work*, cited in *ibid*, 185)

It was perhaps history, however, that was the most important subject so far as the instilling of nationalism, patriotism and imperialism was concerned. As Humphries puts it:

History was widely viewed as a source of moral examples, good and bad, the study of which would encourage children to develop a sense of duty and loyalty towards national institutions. As a consequence, the history syllabus focused attention on military victories and imperial power, while history textbooks described a heroic national stereotype that was compared with stereotypes of inferior races and frequently contained homilies on the need for patriotic duty (Humphries, 1981:40)

As Chancellor explains, the Black Hole of Calcutta, in which a party of English people was imprisoned, the result being that most of them died from suffocation, is reported widely in textbooks. There are many accounts of how the victims trampled each other down 'amid the laughter of the guards' (Edwards' *A School History of England*, cited in *ibid*:122) and how they heard their cries for mercy savagely mocked (Holborn's *Historical Studies*, cited in *ibid*). In reality, survivors' eye witness accounts inform us not that the guards laughed, but that they did their utmost to bring the prisoners water (*ibid*). Later the Indian Mutiny was used as yet another example of Indian cruelty. Nana Sahib was described by several writers as 'a fiend in human shape' or as 'a monster' (Jack's *Historical Readers,* cited in *ibid*). One author commented: 'and truly the barbarous cruelty with which they had executed this massacre, presented a tale of unheard of horror' (Tegg's, *First Book of English History,* cited in *ibid*). Chancellor does note, however, that 'a significant minority' do refer to 'the equal brutality of the English in the suppression of disorder in the Indian sub-continent' (*ibid*).

While there was some criticism of British rule in the eighteenth century, the textbook orthodoxy was that Indians were lucky to be ruled by the British (*ibid*:123). The author of the *Pitman's Reader* described the native response to Lawrence during his period as Viceroy: '[u]nder his able guidance the natives soon learned to recognize the justice and sound sense of their conquerors and gradually settled down to peaceful work in the rice-fields' (cited in *ibid*). And the author of the *Warwick Readers* described Indians as sensible enough to recognise that they needed firm rule, although they were incapable of providing it themselves (cited in *ibid*:123-4). As s/he put it, '[t]he people of India see that we desire their welfare and they know it is only our rule which keeps them at peace with one another' (cited in *ibid*:124). Little praise was afforded the fighting qualities of the Indians save when they were under British command; then tribute was paid to 'the devotion and gallantry with which the Indian troops obeyed their British officers' during the mutiny (*Warwick Readers,* cited in *ibid*).

The peoples of Africa were treated in a similar fashion. Commenting on the Boer War, one author wrote:

> [t]he people within the Queen's dominions were determined that the paramount power in South Africa should be Great Britain, and that the white races south of the Zambesi should have equal rights (Hassall's *A Class-book of English History,* cited in *ibid*).

Meanwhile in Fletcher and Kipling's *A School History of England* there is a description of the freed slave in the West Indies, indicating his need to be looked after by his 'colonial masters':

> Lazy, vicious and incapable of any serious improvement or of work except under compulsion. In such a climate a few bananas will sus-

tain the life of a negro quite sufficiently; why should he work to get more than this. He is quite happy and quite useless and spends any extra wages which he may earn upon finery (cited in *ibid*)

The English, by way of contrast, were portrayed as brave and honest, with one writer asserting that '[y]ou must be truthful if you would be truly English' (Laurie's *English History Simplified*, cited in Chancellor, 1970:118) and another claiming that '[t]hey all show the bold, frank, sturdy character which so strongly marks out the Anglo-Saxon race' (Livesey's *Granville History Readers*, cited in *ibid*:118).

Thus in the Imperial era, in order to justify the continuance of 'the strong arm and brave spirit' of the British Empire (Pitman's *King Edward History Readers* [for Juniors] 1901:5-6, cited in Chancellor, 1970:127-8), and the ongoing and relentless pursuit of expanding capital accumulation, the subjects of the colonies were racialised in school textbooks as fierce, brutal, lazy children.

The New Imperialism: a Postmodern Fantasy

I have argued at length elsewhere about the dangers of post-modernism (in academia), specifically about the way in which it acts as an ideological support for global capitalism (e.g. Cole and Hill 2002; Cole, 2003, 2004d, 2004e). Now firmly in the public as well as the academic domain (and therefore more dangerous), post-modernism is particularly pernicious in its protagonists' advocacy of 'the New Imperialism'. Thus Cooper (2002:5: http://fpc. org.uk/articles/169 accessed: 11/08/04) argues that what is needed is a new kind of imperialism, one which is acceptable to what he refers to as 'a world of human rights and cosmopolitan values'; an imperialism 'which, like all imperialism, aims to bring order and organisation' [he does not mention exploitation and oppression] 'but which rests today on the voluntary principle'.

Postmodern imperialism, he argues, takes two forms. First the voluntary imperialism of the global economy, where institutions like the IMF and the World Bank provide help to states 'wishing to find their way back into the global economy and into the virtuous circle of investment and prosperity' (*ibid*). If states wish to benefit, he goes on 'they must open themselves up to the *interference* of international organisations and foreign states' (*ibid*) (my emphasis).

The second form of postmodern imperialism Cooper calls 'the imperialism of neighbours', where instability 'in your neighbourhood poses threats which no state can ignore'. It is not merely soldiers that come from the international community, he argues, 'it is police, judges, prison officers, *central bankers* and others' (my emphasis). 'Elections are organised and monitored by the Organisation for Security and Cooperation in Europe (OSCE). Local police are financed and trained by the UN' (*ibid*). Cooper has in mind the European Union, which is, of course, engaged in a programme which will eventually lead to massive enlargement. If this process is a kind of voluntary imperialism, Cooper suggests, 'the end state might be described [sic] as a cooperative empire. 'Commonwealth' might indeed not be a bad name' (*ibid*). He concludes that '[t]hat perhaps is the vision, but, in the context of 'the secret race to acquire nuclear weapons' and.... the growth of organised crime, including international terrorism, there may not be much time left [for the establishment of this empire]' (*ibid*: 6.)

While '[w]ithin the postmodern world, there are no security threats ... that is to say, its members do not consider invading each other' (*ibid*:3), that world, according to Cooper has a right to invade others. The postmodern world has a right to pre-emptive attack, deception and whatever else is necessary. As he puts it:

> Among ourselves we operate on the basis of laws and open cooperative security. But when dealing with more old-fashioned kinds of states outside the continent of Europe, we need to revert to the rougher methods of an earlier era – force, pre-emptive attack, deception, whatever is necessary to deal with those who still live in the nineteenth century world of every state for itself. Among ourselves, we keep the law but when we are operating in the jungle, we must also use the laws of the jungle (*ibid*:3-4).

So what is the background of this leading advocate of postmodern new imperialism; of the legitimacy of a 'pre-emptive attack' on 'old-fashioned' non-European states? Between 1999 and 2001, he was Tony Blair's Head of the Defence and Overseas Secretariat, in the British Cabinet Office. Now posted to Brussels in the capacity of what the *Daily Telegraph* (25 October 2003) describes as 'right-hand man to Javier Solana, Europe's foreign and security policy supremo', 'he retains close links with Downing Street, where his ideas are held in great respect.'(http://www.derechos.org/nizkor/excep/cooper.html).

Blair is, of course known for his belief in a benign globalisation (for a critique of this position, see, for example, Cole, 2005). However, while Blair is widely known to work 'hand in glove' with President Bush, he does not, openly at least, advocate (postmodern) new imperialism.

Julie Hyland (2002:4) has argued that Cooper's thesis is fundamentally flawed. This is because central to it is an insistence that that there is no longer any real conflict of interests between the major powers. While Cooper places certain reservations with respect to the United States and Japan, he is confident that they all have a vested interest in collectively policing the world. Hyland cites Lenin (1975: 111) who argued that all alliances between the major powers 'are *inevitably* nothing more than a 'truce' in periods between wars'. As Lenin put it:

> Peaceful alliances prepare the grounds for wars, and in their turn grow out of wars; the one conditions the other, producing alternating forms of peaceful and non-peaceful struggle on one and the same basis of imperialist connections and relations within world economics and world politics (Lenin, 1975, cited in Hyland, 2002: 4)

Hyland shows that Cooper argues throughout as if the major powers can simply decide to set aside their differences in order to pursue a common political agenda. However, in reality, imperialism is not a policy, but 'a complex set of economic and social relations characterised by an objective conflict between the major powers over who controls the world's markets and resources' (*ibid*:5). She concludes that the struggle for oil, the source of power, has not only been the major factor in Western imperial intervention, but is likely to be the key focus of potential conflict between the major powers (*ibid*).

That a conflict of interests remains firmly on the agenda is not merely the view of the Left. Leading historian of Empire, Dominic Lieven, for example, who believes that 'the ideology of US empire is democratic and egalitarian' (2004:25) cites 'bringing 1.25bn Chinese into the first world' as an indication that the 'the great game of empire is far from over' (*ibid*).

The New Imperialism: the US Reality

The key player in the New Imperialism is, of course, not the 'European Commonwealth', but the United States. US imperial hegemony is widely recognised in liberal as well as Marxist circles. Thus as *Guardian* columnist Hugo Young states unequivocally:

> the problem that Mr. Cooper ignores and that seems not to even trouble Mr. Blair any more is that the only [new world order] currently on offer is for the rest of the globe to be remade in America's image and in the interests of the security of the US and its corporations. If there is any such thing as an acceptable postmodern imperialism, this most certainly is not it (Young, 2002, cited in Hyland, 2002:8)

This statement underestimates (even in 2002) Blair's allegiance to US capitalism. In concluding that any new imperialist agenda needs to recognise that 'America is a threat to global order too' (*ibid*:8), Young also understates the real threat posed by the US to the continued existence of the world.

Epitomising the essence of the actually existing new Imperialism is the Project for the New American Century (http://www.newamerican century.org/). Proudly and openly Reaganite, its principles include, 'increasing defence spending'; 'challenging regimes'; 'promoting political and economic freedom' and 'extending an international order'. This makes it abundantly clear that as long as the New Imperialism continues to exist, so too will (imperialist) wars.

Globalisation and the US Empire

Globalisation is often used *ideologically* to justify the New Imperial Project. Globalisation is championed as the harbinger of free trade and is heralded by some as a new phenomenon. It is, in fact, as old as capitalism itself, but it is a phenomenon that alters its character through history (Cole, 1998)[5]. Ellen Meiksins Wood (2003:134) has captured succinctly its current manifestations:

> Actually existing globalization... means the opening of subordinate economies and their vulnerability to imperial capital, while the imperial economy remains sheltered as much as possible from the adverse effects. Globalization has nothing to do with free trade. On the contrary, it is about the careful control of trading conditions in the interest of imperial capital. (cited in McLaren and Farahmandpur, 2005)

The New Imperialism no longer seeks direct territorial control of the rest of the world, as did British Imperialism, but instead relies on puppet governments to do its bidding. This is because capital is now accumulated via the control of markets, rather than by sovereignty over territories. The New Imperialism does not require invading forces to stay for lengthy periods. It is therefore an imperialism *in absentia*. President Bush was thus partly right when he stated in his 2003 state of the union address that America seeks to 'exercise power without conquest'. He was right in the sense that America does not seek British Imperialist-type *long-term colonial conquest*. What it seeks is what Benjamin Zephaniah (2004:18) describes as 'cultural and financial imperialism'. This can involve sending in the troops in the short-term, or it can be done without armies[6]. As he puts it, 'they send in men in suits and they colonise the place financially' (*ibid*)[7].

Just as in the days of the British Empire there is an ideological requirement for racialisation. As Zephaniah states:

> when I come through the airport nowadays, in Britain and the US especially, they always question me on the Muslim part of my name. They are always on the verge of taking me away because they think converts are the dangerous ones (2004:19).

Islamophobia is a key component of racialisation connected to the New Imperialism. According to The Commission on British Muslims and Islamophobia (CBMI), Britain is 'institutionally Islamophobic', with hostility towards Islam permeating every part of British society (Doward and Hinsliff, 2004). The report produces a raft of evidence suggesting that since 9/11, there has been a sharp rise in attacks on followers of Islam. Ahmed Versi, editor of the Muslim News, who gave evidence, said:

> We have reported cases of mosques being firebombed, paint being thrown at mosques, mosques being covered in graffiti, threats made, women being spat upon, eggs being thrown. It is the visible symbols of Islam that are being attacked (*ibid*).

More than 35,000 Muslims were stopped and searched in 2003, with fewer than 50 charged (*ibid*).

Islamophobia, like other forms of racism, can be cultural or it can be biological, or it can be a mixture of both. Echoing the quote from the school textbooks cited above, where Asia was denigrated as 'a continent of dying nations rapidly falling back in civilisation' and where reference was made to 'the barbaric peoples of Asia', the former Archbishop of Canterbury recently defended a controversial speech in which he criticised Islam as a faith 'associated with violence throughout the world'. At the Gregorian University in Rome he said that Islam was resistant to modernity and Islamic societies had contributed little to world culture for hundreds of years http://www.timesonline.co.uk/article/0,,1-1052154,00.html .

A more biological Islamophobic racism is revealed by Jamal al-Harith, a British captive freed from Guantanamo Bay. He informed *The Daily Mirror* that his guards told him: 'You have no rights here'. Al-Harith went on,

> [a]fter a while, we stopped asking for human rights – we wanted animal rights. In Camp X-Ray my cage was right next to a kennel housing an Alsatian dog.
>
> He had a wooden house with air conditioning and green grass to exercise on. I said to the guards, 'I want his rights' and they replied, 'That dog is member of the US army'.
>
> (http://www.mirror.co.uk/news/allnews/content_objectid=
> 14042696_method=full_siteid=50143_headline=-MY-HELL-IN-
> CAMP-X-RAY-name_page.html9)

Whither Imperialist Education?

In contemporary societies, we are in many ways being globally *mis*-educated. The Bush and Blair administrations' propaganda war about weapons of mass destruction, aimed at masking new imperialist designs and capital's global quest for imperial hegemony and oil is an obvious example.

This is very much the case with schooling. Tied to the needs of global, corporate capital, education world-wide has been reduced to the creation of a flexible work-force, the openly acknowledged, indeed lauded (by both capitalists and politicians) requirement of today's global markets (Cole, 2005). Business is in schools, both in the sense of determining the curriculum and exercising burgeoning control of schools as businesses (Allen *et al*, 1999; McLaren and Farahmandpur, 1999a, 1999b; McLaren, 2003; McLaren and Farahmandpur, 2005).

An alternative vision of education is provided by McLaren. Education should, he argues (following Paulo Freire), put 'social and political analysis of everyday life at the centre of the curriculum' (McLaren 2003:xxix). If we are to return to the teaching of imperialism, past and present, with integrity in English schools, the syllabus must incorporate the following, *in addition* to a critical analysis of the actual events themselves.

First, there must be a thorough and critical analysis of theories of imperialism, classical, Keynesian, postmodern *and* Marxist (e.g. Barratt Brown, 1976). Second, there should be a discussion of the way in which British imperialism was taught in the past and why. Third, and allied to this, school students need the skills to deconstruct pro-imperialist and/or racist movies and/or TV series, still readily available in the age of multiple channel, digital TV. Fourth, at a national level, students need a critical awareness of how British Imperialism relates to and impacts on racism and racialisation, both historically and in the present (including the ability to make links with xenophobia, xenoracism and xeno-racialisation)[9]. Fifth, at a global level, students will need skills to evaluate the New Imperialism and the permanent war being waged by the US with the acquiescence of Britain. Boulangé (2004) argues that it is essential at this time, with the Bush/Blair war on terror and Islamophobia in many European cities reaching new heights, for teachers to show solidarity with Muslims in schools today. For 'this will strengthen the unity of all workers, whatever their religion' (p24), and this will have a powerful impact on the struggle against racism in all spheres of society, and schools in particular. In turn, this will strengthen the confidence of workers and students to fight on other issues.

I will conclude with a quote from Ferguson (2003):

> Empire is as 'cutting edge' as you could wish ... [It] has got every-thing: economic history, social history, cultural history, political history, military history and international history – not to mention contemporary politics (just turn on the latest news from Kabul). Yet it knits all these things together with ... a metanarrative

For Marxists, an understanding of the metanarrative of imperialism, past and present, does much more than this. It takes us to the crux of the trajectory of capitalism from its inception right up to the twenty-first century; and this is why Marxists should endorse its teaching. Of course, the role of education in general, and teaching about imperialism in schools in particular, has its limitations and young people are deeply affected by other influences such as the media and by peer culture. However, if we do not reintroduce an *honest* evaluation of imperialism in British schools, large numbers of people may continue to be enslaved by an ignorance of Britain's imperial past, rather than becoming empowered by an awareness of it.

With respect to the New Imperialism, it could either have been accepted as common sense, as inevitable, or even as benign, or it could be under constant challenge. Education, by default, might aid its progress, or it could contribute to a critical awareness of New Imperialism's manifestations; and, from a Marxist perspective, the need for its demise, and replacement with a new world order.

References

Allen, M, Benn, C, Chitty, C, Cole, M, Hatcher, R, Hirtt, N and Rikowski, G (1999) *Business, Business, Business: New Labour's Education Policy.* London: the Tufnell Press

Barratt Brown, M (1976) *The Economics of Imperialism.* Harmondsworth: Penguin

Boulangé, A (2004) The hijab, racism and the state, *International Socialism*, 102 (Spring): 3-26

Bunting, M (2004) Look past the hijab, *The Guardian*, May 10th : 15

Camara, B (2002) Ideologies of Race and Racism, in: P Zarembka (ed) *Confronting 9-11, Ideologies of Race, and Eminent Economists.* Oxford: Elsevier Science

Chancellor, V (1970) *History for their Masters.* Bath: Adams and Dart

Coben, D (2002) Metaphors for an Educative Politics: 'Common Sense,' 'Good Sense' and Educating Adults, in: Borg, C, Buttigieg, J and Mayo, P (eds) *Gramsci and Education.* Lanham, MD: Rowman and Littlefield

Cole, M (1986) Teaching and Learning about Racism: a critique of Multicultural Education in Britain, in: Modgil, S, Verma, G, Mallick, K and Modgil, C (eds) *Multicultural Education: the Interminable Debate.* Lewes: The Falmer Press

Cole, M (1992) Racism, History and Educational Policy: From the Origins of the Welfare State to the Rise of the Radical Right. Unpublished PhD. Thesis: University of Essex

Cole, M (1998) Globalisation, Modernisation and Competitiveness: a critique of the New Labour project in education, *International Studies in Sociology of Education*, 8(3): 315-332

Cole, M (2003) Might It Be in the Practice that It Fails to Succeed? A Marxist Critique of Claims for Postmodernism and Poststructuralism as Forces for Social Change and Social Justice, *British Journal of Sociology of Education*, 24(4): 487-500

Cole, M (2004a) Rule Britannia 'Rule Britannia' and the new American Empire: a Marxist analysis of the teaching of imperialism, actual and potential, in the English school curriculum, *Policy Futures in Education*, 2(3)

Cole, M (2004b) 'Brutal and Stinking' and 'Difficult to Handle': the historical and contemporary manifestations of racialisation, institutional racism, and schooling in Britain, *Race, Ethnicity and Education*, 7(10): 35-56

Cole, M (2004c) F*** you – human sewage: contemporary global capitalism and the xeno-racialisation of asylum seekers, *Contemporary Politics*, 10(2): ??

Cole, M (2004d) 'Fun, amusing, full of insights, but ultimately a reflection of anxious times: a critique of postmodernism as a force for resistance, social change and social justice', in: Atkinson, E, Martin, W and Satterthwaite, J (eds) *Educational Counter-Cultures: confrontations, images, vision*. Stoke-on-Trent: Trentham Books

Cole, M (2004e) The 'Ordeal of the Undecidable' vs. the 'Inevitability of Globalized Capital': a Marxist Critique, in: Pruyn, M and Huerta-Charles, L (eds) *Peter McLaren: paths of dissent*. New York: Peter Lang

Cole, M (2005) New Labour, Globalization and Social Justice: the role of education, in: Fischman, G, McLaren, P, Sunker, H and Lankshear, C (eds) *Critical Theories, Radical Pedagogies and Global Conflicts*. Lanham, Maryland: Rowman and Littlefield

Cole, M and Blair, M (2005) Racism and Education: from Empire to New Labour, in: Cole, M (ed) *Education, Equality and Human Rights 2nd Edition*. London: Routledge/Falmer

Cole, M and Hill, D (2002) Resistance Postmodernism: – Progressive Politics or Rhetorical Left Posturing, in: Hill, D, McLaren, P, Cole, M and Rikowski, G (eds) *Marxism Against Postmodernism in Educational Theory*. Lanham, Md: Lexington Books

Cole, M and Stuart, J S (2005) Do you ride on elephants' and 'never tell them you're German': the experiences of British Asian and black, and overseas student teachers in south-east England, *British Educational Research Journal*

Cole, M and Virdee, S (2005) 'Race', Racism And Resistance: from Empire to New Labour', in: Cole, M (ed) *Education, Equality and Human Rights: Issues of Gender, 'Race', Sexuality, Special Needs and Social Class*. 2nd Edition, London: Routledge/Falmer

Cooper, R (2002) Why we still need empires, *The Observer*, April 7th (http://observer.guardian.co.uk/worldview/story/0,11581,680117,00.html

Doward, J and Hinsliff, G (2004) British hostility to Muslims 'could trigger riots' (http://www.guardian.co.uk/race/story/0,11374,1227977,00.html)

Fekete, L (2001) 'The Emergence of Xeno-racism', Institute of Race Relations, (http://www.irr.org.uk/2001/september/ak000001.html)

Ferguson, N (2003) Prince and empire are the key to history, *The Sunday Times*, July 6th

Ferguson, N (2004) American empire – who benefits?, Empire and the dilemmas of liberal imperialism, CD accompanying *Prospect*, March, 2004

Gramsci, A (1978) *Selections from Prison Notebooks*. London: Lawrence and Wishart

Hall, S, Critcher, C, Jefferson, T, Clarke, J and Robert, B (1978) *Policing the crisis: mugging, the state and law and order.* London: Palgrave MacMillan

Hill, D (2001) Equality, Ideology and Education Policy, in: Hill, D and Cole, M (eds) *Schooling and Equality: Fact, Concept and Policy.* London: Kogan Page

Humphries, S (1981) *Hooligans or Rebels? An Oral History of Working-Class Childhood and Youth 1889-1939.* Oxford: Basil Blackwell

Hyland, J (2002) British foreign policy adviser calls for a new imperialism, World Socialist Web Site 27 April http://www.wsws.org/articles/2002/apr2002/coop-a27.shtml

Kovel, J (1988) *White Racism: A Psychohistory.* London: Free Association Books

Lawrence, E (1982) Just Plain Common Sense: the 'roots' of racism, in: Centre for Contemporary Cultural Studies (ed) *The Empire Strikes Back: race and racism in 70s Britain.* London: Hutchinson

Lieven, D (2004) Imperial History, CD accompanying *Prospect,* March, 2004

Lind, M (2004) debate: After the War, CD accompanying *Prospect,* March, 2004

McLaren, P (2003) Critical Pedagogy in the Age of Neoliberal Globalization: notes from history's underside, *Democracy and Nature,* 9(1): 65-90

McLaren, P and Farahmandpur, R (1999a) Critical Pedagogy, Postmodernism, and the Retreat from Class: Towards a Contraband Pedagogy, in: Hill, D, McLaren, P, Cole, M and Rikowski, G (eds) *Postmodern Excess in Educational Theory: Education and the Politics of Human Resistance.* London: Tufnell Press

McLaren, P and Farahmandpur, R (1999b) Critical Multiculturalism and the Globalization of Capital: Some Implications for a Politics of Resistance, *Journal of Curriculum Theorizing,* 15(4): 27-46

McLaren, P and Farahmandpur, R (2005) Who Will Educate the Educators?: Critical Pedagogy in the Age of Globalization, in: Dirlik, A (ed) ????

Miles, R (1982) *Racism and Migrant Labour.* London: Routledge and Kegan Paul

Miles, R (1987) *Capitalism and Unfree Labour: Anomaly or Necessity?* London: Tavistock

Miles, R (1993) *Racism After 'Race Relations'.* London: Routledge

Pike, N (2003) Schools Ignore it – but is it time for the empire to strike back? *The Guardian,* July 5th

Pilger, J (2004) Of the token hangers-on who make up the Anglo-America 'coalition of the willing', only Australia remains true to the *über*-sheriff in Washington, New Statesman, 5th April: 13-14

Project for the New American Century (http://www.newamericancentury.org/)

Purdy, J (2004) Universal Nation, CD accompanying *Prospect,* March, 2004

Zephaniah, B (2004) Rage of Empire, *Socialist Review,* 281(January): 18-20

Notes

1 This chapter draws on a longer paper (Cole, 2004a), which first appeared in the e journal, *Policy Futures in Education.*

2 As Hill (2001:8) points out, the influence of ideology can be overwhelming. He cites Terry Eagleton (1999 1:xiii) who has written: '[w]hat persuades men and women to mistake each other from time to time for gods or vermin is ideology'. The pertinence of this observation resonates throughout this chapter.

3   I am interested here in the utilisation of the Marxist concept of racialisation to under-
    stand racism over time, rather than with the relationship between racism and capitalism
    per se; e.g. the possible existence of racism in pre-capitalist or post-capitalist social
    formations.

4   Elsewhere (Cole, 1992, 2004a; Cole and Blair, 2005) I have examined imperialism and
    schooling more generally. Here I will concentrate on the curriculum.

5   Globalisation is also universally heralded as inevitable (Cole, 1998, 2004d, 2004e,
    2005). Thus Thomas Friedman, a New York Times writer who has become America's
    official explainer of globalisation, likes to compare the process to the dawn: there is no
    escaping it; objecting to it is futile; and it shines alike on the just and the unjust (Purdy,
    2004:28).

6   It seems that John Howard is pursuing the same policy in the South Pacific, sometimes
    with troops, sometimes without (Pilger, 2004:13-14).

7   This does not stop many neo-Conservatives in the United States, however, hankering
    after British Imperialism (and in particular the young Winston Churchill) as their model
    (Lind, 2004, p5), as does the aforementioned popular historian and TV presenter Niall
    Ferguson, for whom the British Empire was relatively benevolent. In a recent speech, he
    argued that the American Empire which 'has the potential to do great good' needs to
    learn from the lessons of the British Empire. First it needs to export capital and to invest
    in its colonies; second, people from the United States need to settle permanently in its
    colonies; third, there must be a commitment to imperialism; fourth there must be
    collaboration with local elites. Success can only come, he concludes, if the Americans
    are prepared to *stay* (Ferguson, 2004).

9. The term, 'xeno-racism' is Sivanandan's. As he puts it:

    It is a racism that is not just directed at those with darker skins, from the former
    colonial territories, but at the newer categories of the displaced, the dispossessed
    and the uprooted, who are beating at western Europe's doors, the Europe that
    helped to displace them in the first place. It is a racism, that is, that cannot be
    colour-coded, directed as it is at poor whites as well, and is therefore passed off
    as xenophobia, a 'natural' fear of strangers. But in the way it denigrates and reifies
    people before segregating and/or expelling them, it is a xenophobia that bears all
    the marks of the old racism. It is racism in substance, but 'xeno' in form. It is a
    racism that is meted out to impoverished strangers even if they are white. It is
    xeno-racism (A. Sivanandan, cited in Fekete, 2001

    Elsewhere, I have described the ongoing *process* of racialisation that accompanies this
    new form of racism as xeno-racialisation (Cole, 2004c).

4

Incarnation in times of terror: Christian theology and the challenge of September 11th

LISA ISHERWOOD

In this chapter Isherwood returns to McLaren's attack on Western (American) imperialism. No less savagely than McLaren, but from the standpoint of Liberation Theology, she confronts what she sees as the destructive influence of traditional Christian teaching which, with its patriarchy, its insistence on absolutes of power, authority and moral certainty, offers a metaphysical support for the imperial project of Western capitalism. She sees the events of 9/11 as a consequence of Western imperialist greed; and the Western response to those events as an extension of the imperialist project. If Christianity has been complicit in this project, it is because the central Christian insight of incarnation has been set aside. Isherwood reverses the traditional reading which has the Word made flesh; she argues for flesh to be made word: for the encounter, skin on skin, of human relationships at their simplest, to be the Christian praxis of redemption. This chapter, following the Marxist account in Cole's, demonstrates how Marxist and Christian insights – conventionally understood as mutually antagonistic – unite in their rejection of what both understand as the destructive hegemony of capitalism.

Now that we have had time to reflect and to see what happened next, it has become all too apparent that the events of September 11th – and those before and since – were truly shocking. The images of falling masonry and falling bodies played over and over again are meant to obliterate the events that led to such a seismic eruption and to justify the horrors since. These horrors take many forms, from the devastation of lives, homes and countries to the strengthening of the Imperial Monster and the rallying of theology to the assistance of that unleashed beast. These are crucial times; yet many in the world seem to be inert. I do not think that we felt unconcerned or even hardened to the plight of others before and after the events of September 11th – most of us felt and feel powerless: caught up in a web, not entirely of our making, of politics, economics , imperialism and the underpinning racism. Contrary to political mythology September 11th did not change everything, it merely accelerated global agendas and events and provided a pretext for the destruction of social democracy.

At the time that the Towers came down, Rowan Williams, the Archbishop of Canterbury, was delivering a lecture about spirituality in the close vicinity. There is a great deal of irony in this since the shock waves that were physically felt by the Archbishop have subsequently been felt throughout the theological world. Times of great terror and uncertainty are the ideal conditions for closing the theological borders, for narrowing the territory and providing answers and certainties for this life and the life to come. It is also the territory in which politics and right-wing religion carry out their most intimate dance of seduction. Many of the factors that were underlying causes of September 11th can find an environment in which to thrive in the abusive theology that is right-wing fundamentalism. Even as the dust was settling those opportunist men of religio/politcs, Pat Robinson and Jerry Falwell, were taking centre stage with their theology of retribution for a sinful nation: a theology that uses every misfortune to sound the same old divisive and bigoted diatribe – in short to remove and reduce the human rights of all those who they feel should be denied them. We know the list by now; and gradually we are beginning to see the politics behind what at first appears to be laughable theology. When George W wonders publicly whether atheists can be called American citizens as America is one nation under God, a God that atheists do not acknowledge, it is time for concern.

We are truly shocked by the blatant way in which the United States made a war out of an act of terrorism and further refused to allow Pakistan to extradite Bin Laden: a move that he had agreed to in order to stand before an international tribunal to see if there was a case to answer. Why did the United States refuse? They explained it was because it would bring about a premature collapse of the international effort to capture him! (Pilger, 2002:100) The truth perhaps was spoken by Colin Powell: 'America will have a continuing interest and presence in Central Asia of a kind that we could not have dreamed of before September 11th' (*ibid*:105).

The objective, then, is not the capturing of a terrorist but the conquest of a region, militarily but, most importantly, economically. With slick movements America made the link between *Al Quaida* and Iraq and the machine was in motion. We watched with disbelief as large corporations carved up the business interests in Iraq even before a shot was fired, and we heard the munitions magnates singing 'Oh what a lovely war' as each smart bomb shattered the lives and aspirations of thousands.

Despite the voices of millions raised in protest, the machine could not be halted; and as it cranked up, the human rights of many US citizens were suspended almost unnoticed. Indeed, the United States violated a range of conventions as it went around the world kidnapping citizens of many nations and transporting them to Guantanamo Bay where they still languish without trial and beyond the reach of law.

The events of September 11th and those that have followed act as a hermeneutic for Christian theology because they encapsulate the world we are in, the global economic and imperialist mess and the ways that Christian theology has become an ally rather than a judge of this destructive praxis. Those of us who explore the reality of enfleshed redemption are asked, in a deep and disturbing way, what can incarnation offer in these times of terror? Let me be clear here: the terror is that perpetuated by the brokers of advanced capitalism and its global agenda of greed based on the insistence that all that is distinctive in human cultures be reduced to nothingness (Ritzer, 2004). The acts of violent resistance that such a mindset provokes are almost glimpses of redemption, suggesting that the spirit is not dead. People are not so crushed by the hand of the Monster that they have no cause, no culture, no desire to be who they are – they have not been McDonaldised into oblivion! They have, however, been robbed of a voice and imaginative and creative ways to express their personhood – they are reduced to violence and we are reduced to stunned silence and impotent witnessing.

Carter Heyward remarks that the American people are grieving deeply for lost illusions as well as for lost loved ones. After September 11th they felt insecure, shaken to the core; they fled to churches where they worshipped icons of patriarchal power; and felt better. (Heyward, 2002:53) What they actually did was take part in the problem and set the circle in motion again – they rooted themselves deep in abstract power and the metaphysics that such a power requires, and in so doing they divided the world between good/bad, us/them, the righteous/the infidel.

As theologians we can take no comfort in the fact that this could happen. It is no mere accident that those who attend church can find both security and demons in their teachings. We are part of a system rooted in the safety of metaphysics and the betraying dualisms that spring from it. We are therefore a divided people – divided from one another and within our own skins. This I see as the root cause of our stunned silence, impotent witnessing and inability to resist – we are removed from the source of our imagination, we do not trust our embodied selves and we are cast adrift in the world of the market and its military servicing. In short, our theology has failed us; it has enabled us to be delivered up to the Monster and its service industries.

What are the challenges of September 11th? John Pilger has framed the question: 'Who will put aside the chessboard and explain that only when great grievances, injustice and insecurity are lifted from nations will terrorism recede?'(Pilger, 2002:157) He makes it plain that economics underpins the actions of the USA and its allies and that when the globalisation agenda is mentioned the reality is the globalisation of poverty, where the majority never have access to all that we call normal in a civilised society. There is no desire to include all peoples in developed standards of living; indeed, such an idea is seen as a threat. The First World still needs the rest, but only the sea, air, materials and space in which to dispose of its waste; it does not need the people. What the response to September 11th was really about was the advancement of savage capitalism, not the overcoming of a threat through the containment of terror. Indeed, the illusion of dire consequences and of the ever lurking terrorist are effective tools in the hands of those who wish to further diminish real politics through the reduction of democracy to a mere election ritual, where indistinguishable parties manage single ideology states (ibid:2) in the interests of the increase of wealth for the few at the expense of the many. When faced with this reality we have to dig deep to find a Christian theology that goes beyond the call to love each other more and to forgive our enemies. We have to be equipped to overcome the political oppression by rejecting the theology which supports it.

Carter Heyward was one of the first theologians to reflect on the events of September 11th. She demands that we wage peace, not war. In line with her Christological understanding she suggests that our response to the fear and uncertainty that we feel in this world of terror should be an embrace of vulnerability, a vulnerability that is Christic in nature, one that truly opens us to mutuality in relation and offers redemptive possibilities. Within the context of current world politics this translates as much more than letting down the psychological barriers. As with all Heyward's work there is an ethical edge; so waging peace through vulnerability involves engaging with social and economic injustice. (Heyward, 2002:79) Heyward suggests that we embrace vulnerability rather than look for assured safety through bombs and the enforcement of western economic systems. She points out that it was the desire by the USA for security through the acquisition of great wealth and control of resources that led to September 11th.

For Heyward, then, the questions raised by September 11th throw us back to addressing the pervasive problem of the greed that underpins savage capitalism and its politics of power and conquest. Heyward is also offering a challenge to those of the Christian Right who still operate from the notion of an imperial and conquering God who rewards the faithful with financial prosperity as well as riches in heaven. This God presides over the Bush government.

Heyward is not alone in this. Mary Grey, although not addressing the aftermath of September 11th, has much to say about conversion to the neighbour as a way of overcoming the greed of advanced capitalism. Remembering Gandhi, she asks us to think of the most marginalised and the poorest before we act, and to ask what will be the effect of our actions on their lives (Grey, 2003:199). This, she suggests, will lead to relationships based on justice. She acknowledges that this approach does not seem to have mass appeal; we prefer our own comforts to the wellbeing of others.

Grey moves her analysis further by suggesting that we are not, in fact, innately bad people, but rather people who have been worked on by the markets and their advertising gurus – we are an addictive society fascinated by the seduction of the markets. She is in agreement with Deleuze, who explains that capitalism does not just exert power by extracting labour and production but by capturing and distorting the fundamental human power of desire. Grey suggests that once this has happened we have no dreams that propel us beyond the mundanely material, and so no ability to resist the market. Indeed we have an almost obsessive need that the market should keep feeding us. Anthony Giddens has reminded us, in a parody of Marx, that we have nothing to lose but our mock Rolex watches. In practice, we do not even wish to lose them; they proclaim our non-identity and we are addicted to our oblivion, believing it to signal something of significance about a self we have trouble articulating. Our chains may continue to bind us but we stagger under their weight with joy, once we have the accoutrements of dreams adorning our ever more indistinguishable bodies.

Grey argues for the urgent recovery of desire. She wants us to know what we are for as much as what we are against. She puts forward as a theological task of great significance the reclaiming of the language of desire by theologians from the High Priests of the market. While we continue to long and yearn for the new car, the new house and all the goods that shine so brightly in them, we silence God. Salvation become an exchange economy with the blest showered with gifts in the super cathedrals of capitalism. This exchange economy is evident in some of the more bloody notions of atonement. The blameless Christ gives his life in exchange for the forgiveness of sinners; and the exchange is seen as fair and the sacrifice sufficient in order that the gift of salvation may be bestowed. The price has been paid and the sinners' redemption results. It is no accident that it tends to be fundamentalist Protestants who make the links between financial prosperity and salvation, blandly accommodating the suffering of others into their own blessed life.

Grey engages with the work of Tim Gorringe and Daniel Bell in order to come to a fuller understanding of what this process of recovering desire may involve. For Gorringe there is a need to develop a renewed theology of the senses which he sees as possible through a wider notion of sacramentality (*ibid*:194). He argues that a revaluation of the place of eros will enliven Christians to find alternatives in a world of bland sameness; this eros, he argues, is best situated within a eucharistic understanding and best celebrated within the same context. This is a narrow view: not all people attend church; and not all those who do find the liturgy to be a place for renewing and reviving the senses. Gorringe is attempting to confine the eros that Heyward has re-released into the Christian tradition, the raw power of dynamic connection that in her theology underpins and propels us to the vulnerability in mutual relations that she advocates as the way to wage peace. Gorringe's portrayal of eros tends to build boundaries and create us-and-them, rather than release us all into the dance of erotic connection of redemptive praxis.

Grey is critical of Bell, who suggests that desire is restless in consumerism because its true end is God. This is not a new suggestion. Its limitations are shown within the present world when he suggests that the best place to achieve this fulfilment of desire is in a monastery based on 12th century lines! He asserts that God is waiting to release the poor and oppressed from the excesses of capitalism through the therapy of forgiveness and not through demanding human rights. (Bell, 2001:166) Forgiveness, he argues, overcomes conflict based in claims to rights; and the terror of justice is warded off by the refusal to assert these rights. Desire, we are told, always gives and never acquires or possesses. At this point liberation theologians may wonder what ever happened to the last forty years of theology. What ever happened to the God of justice and how on earth can secular declarations regarding the end of history affect theology so negatively? It is true that Fukiyama was signalling the grip of savage capitalism when he declared that history has ended, that there is no space for development, only repetition and the spread of one ideology. But this is the ideology which theology is standing against, rather than supporting through the reaffirmation of dubious and disembodied theological musings. Bell is taken with Hinkelammert's assertion that we are in the grip of a 'mysticism of death' (*ibid*:12), a madness that in its destruction of people and nature amounts to collective suicide. He sees this as the opposite of the true and well directed mysticism of the monastery. He would do well to consider the requirements of much male mysticism: a death of the self which when held up as a spiritual goal actually kills genuine desire and any sense of self-determination. Traditional Christianity has contributed to our present predicament through precisely this negative theology and the great vacuum it leaves when it claims that the Christian believer has been filled by an external colonising, yet benevolent, God . This sounds uncomfortably like the descriptions one hears from those who have been abused by an authority figure. Just as people who have been repeatedly abused can find it hard to identify their edges and their own desires, so too the Christian who gives herself over to a battering by the 'three-personed God' (John Donne) in the name of love is offering herself to the world in a wounded state and one that can make decisive action difficult.

Grey suggests that it is the Spirit that, as she puts it, 'finds cracks in culture in order to give birth to alternative cultural expressions.'(Grey, 2003:110) The Spirit, she argues, finds a home at the edges of the personal and the non-personal from where it reawakens the power of dreaming and imagining. The Spirit is the power of life and space for living, vitality and energy, and connects us to all living systems. It draws us out into the unknown and sustains us in it. Grey is close here to Heyward; but the latter is describing the role and power of eros and the desire for erotic connection with all of creation that is our driving force and our birthright. For Grey, then, the Spirit appears to enter the world and us, while for Heyward the erotic lies within us and is called forth through the presence of others and the recognition of their erotic natures.

Michael Ignatieff comments:

> It is not a sense of radical difference that leads to conflict with others but the refusal to admit a moment of recognition. Violence must be done to the self before it can be done to others. Living tissue of connection and difference must be cauterised before a neighbour is reinvented as an enemy. (Grey, 2003: 115)

Christian theology with its insistence on dualism allows us to do the necessary damage to ourselves in order that we may make enemies and learn to hate. I am unconvinced that a Spirit theology can provide the required healing as this too remains one step removed. What is needed is engagement with raw/radical incarnation, the vulnerability and bravery to feel and to touch. We need skin on skin. I remember

Paul Simon saying that the black South African musicians who played with him on the Graceland album were bound together in strong bonds of friendship. However, when, after the first performance, he spontaneously embraced the lead singer, the singer burst into tears – this was the first time he had been touched by or had touched a white man. Nothing was the same from then on – they were humans to each other and hitherto unspoken and unacknowledged boundaries were exposed and gradually overcome. Thought alone cannot do this; abstract theology has clearly and constantly proved it cannot change the world when it fears to touch. Dualistic theology rips us from ourselves and cauterises us, enfeebling our judgement, our heart, our passion.

So where has this reflection on September 11th brought me? If the events are used as a hermeneutical tool they offer a sound critique of the world in which we live and the savage capitalism that roams within it. They also encourage some theologians to look again at the tradition and make bold attempts at renewing it in order that it may speak to our condition. Radical vulnerability of the kind that Heyward espouses is preferable to a barrage of bombs and a renewal of imperial aspirations. Grey is right to argue that desire has been misled and that if the market is to be contained it has to be confronted by people who are firmly rooted in other ways of desiring. The market does not listen to reason; it is led by consumer desire which it in turn derives from media and social pressure. A new Christian self-worth and self-direction is needed to stand unperturbed before that savage beast and confront it with the passionate spears of unrefined and uncluttered desires – desires that spring from the raw and mutual relationality of all living things. These are powerful truths; but the question remains: how we can transform desire when we have theologies that do not allow for insights beyond an ethereal and self-indulgent longing after God, a romantic and slightly sado-masochistic notion that we find no rest until we find it outside ourselves in the perfect divine? For me the question is again and unsurprisingly a Christological one – September 11th requires that I look again at what we claim about our incarnate God. How does incarnation stand in times of terror? Does it cauterise and deliver us, or does it root us in who we are and make us resisters?

Although we know very little about Jesus it is helpful to us that the redemptive tale we tell began in Galilee, a volatile political arena in which oppression and injustice, then as now, were the causes of civil unrest and the spur for a variety of religious responses. We may argue that the time is right to engage once again with incarnation in the raw as the response of the divine to times of terror. Our incarnate brother did not flee from politics even though he was offered the chance to rise above it all through a metaphysical engagement with his own divine nature. Is this not what the temptations of the devil were about: fly high, control nature, be a GOD? His response was a choice for life: to be involved in the real stuff of everyday living and to find and share the divine amongst his friends. I see this as a real rejection of the dualism involved in abstract metaphysics, and a challenge to those who would follow to be brave enough to grasp their own incarnation. I understand Jesus to be a comrade who through transgressive praxis made a hole – created a space, opened up a gap – in what was hitherto understood as reality, and invited others to make it bigger. There can be no better time than now to make it even bigger, to probe deep in one's own divine/human nature and find a way through the maze of misinformation, and to resist the temptation to rise above it all through consumption of the right products.

Incarnation in times of terror, now as then, cannot afford the luxury and get-out clause of the Word made flesh – that theological nicety that allows us to run and hide in preformed ideas and laid-out absolutes. Now is a time for dialogue not monologues, particularly divine monologue. I have argued in the past for an understanding of incarnation as the flesh becoming word, that is, the drawing out through engaged praxis, skin on skin, of our Christic natures, and the living out of what it is we prefer to project into the realm of metaphysics (Isherwood, 1999). The flesh made word enables us to find a voice and to make our desires known – we do not have to conform to agreed absolutes but rather discover where real power leads us. Further, our bodies and the bodies of others, far from being aliens to us through the basic dissociation that much Christian doctrine has required – and thus being prime targets for the market – become sites of moral imperatives. Those who are starving present themselves as challenges to redress the imbalances in food distribution, those who are poisoned by toxic waste challenge the ethics of business and profit and bring into focus the whole wellbeing of the planet as well as of people. Those who labour under the genocidal reality of advanced capitalism present in their bodies a moral challenge to find alternative economic systems. When the flesh is word these questions cannot be delayed or avoided by talk of reward in heaven. Those who have only violence left as a way to be heard shake us to the core and challenge our faith and courage. We are frightened; and frightened people shrink within their skins, wishing to be invisible and protected. Incarnation in times of terror demands that we flee from the temptation to hide in the comfort of metaphysics and that we commit to our flesh and the flesh of others as the sites through which redemptive praxis unfolds. This rooting of the divine within and between us is a foundational act of resistance to markets which take advantage of our uprooted desires; when Christ is in heaven we are removed from ourselves and uprooted enough to be vulnerable to manipulation through an engagement with delayed end-of-the-world scenarios and present partial satisfactions.

Committing to flesh is a risky business: there are any number of outcomes – a very frightening thought in these unstable times. However, risking embodiment is perfectly in line with a religion that has incarnation at the heart. Incarnation acknowledged as risk means that the kingdom – that is to say, our vision – is always on a knife-edge between the gloriously successful empowerment of ourselves and others, and the devastatingly wrong and mundanely unimaginative. If we are to break out of the hold that oppressive systems increasingly seem to have on the world then vision empowered by imagination is crucial. Our second act of resistance is then to be alive to counter-cultural possibilities, to living transgressively. We have to incarnate transgression; we have to play with existing categories and break boundaries. Living transgressively spurs us on to be limitless and without boundary; it requires that we face imaginatively those barriers erected in our own minds, cultures, religious systems and environments and overcome them through the power of intimate connection. This risk is what is required in these times of terror and apparent inevitability. The time is right, as both Grey and Heyward suggest, for the creative, imaginative and transgressive Christian to come alive. We have to think beyond boundaries; and we can do this best when we have also destabilised the Christ of ultimates and absolutes, the Christ who only leads to already decided answers which fail us.

Critics of this approach claim that I am making a crucial mistake by plunging into flesh and sidelining metaphysics. They argue that metaphysics give the space required to see things differently, to have another perspective. I do not accept this. It seems to me that using the same old system, whatever it is, will lead to the same old answers. Many of those who fled to church to be saved from their fear of impending doom have either backed the war, remained silent in the face of the re-emergence of an aggressive imperialist agenda or understood the conflict in terms of good against evil. Many have simply felt powerless. They have not faced the real questions of relationality but rather settled for a naïve problematising. The Christ who is stripped of metaphysics moves us away from easy palliatives to a place of living documents – back to ourselves – as the ongoing unfolding Christian narrative. If we take the risk of hearing the flesh we may indeed change the world. I would go so far as to say that those who choose to hide in the safety of the metaphysical Christ actually betray Christ incarnate.

A real issue that is raised here is that of power; the events of September 11th are a graphic illustration of this issue. The target was a symbol of the greatest disempowerer on the planet; the attackers those who felt there was nothing left to them if they were to be in control of their own destiny. The response has been to exert power over those who are powerless. The incarnate, enfleshed Christ shifts the axis of power dramatically from distanced power to empowerment through intimate connection. As Heyward has highlighted, this calls for a radically different response; it requires courage, which the dropping of SMART bombs does not, and a willingness to look your estranged bother/sister in the eye. It is from this connection that empowerment ensues: Heyward is right when she calls for an embrace of vulnerability. In this context that vulnerability is not simply about facing those who you feel may hurt you but also placing yourself differently in relation to the world's resources. The West needs to give up the safety of over-consumerism and face the psychological and physical demands of living lightly on the planet – no longer hiding in products and plentiful resources, but taking one's rightful place as a sharer in limited resources. We have to find anew who we are, enacting the dance of the seven veils – removing layers of false consciousness and comfort – as we move more deeply into our own

Christic natures to stand boldly in our naked humanness, as the only way to halt the advance of genocidal, savage capitalism.

Much of this has been said before although perhaps not in a way quite as critical of the basics of the Christian faith. However, what September 11th has highlighted for us is that we can no longer play at Christology in the head or even in the churches – we have to enflesh it deep in the marrow of who we are, stripped of the trappings of false and created identities, be they commercial or theological. The Christian Right is finding influence in places of power; they aim to reassert the imperial Christ who has had such devastating effects throughout history. This Christ was a destroyer of cultures and an obliterator of peoples; and he is not dead in their hands. Such Christo-fascism must be resisted; but we must be careful not to fall into the same hole of 'rightness' in attempting to resist it.

More than the Archbishop shook when the towers came tumbling down. He, after a period of some distress and disquietude, has recovered his equilibrium. I would hope that the theological world does not so easily recover, settling back into routines of thought and practice that enhance rather than solve the problems that terror faces us with. Now is the time to enflesh Christ; to stand firm in that embodied challenge. The walls have tumbled down; there are new vistas to behold. What we build again must be centred in *dunamis* (deep power) and not *exousia* (authority) and come from the knowledge that relationality enables the flourishing of humans, non-humans and the planet as a whole. This enfleshed knowing will oppose the deadening and divisive realities of advanced capitalism and empower us to find other, more life-affirming and whole ways of being.

Bibliography

Bell, D (2001) *Liberation Theology After the End of History: The Refusal to Cease Suffering.* London: Routledge

Grey, M (2003) *Sacred Longings: Ecofeminist Theology and Globalisation.* London: SCM

Heyward, C (2002) *God in the Balance: Christian Spirituality in Times of Terror.* Cleveland: Pilgrim Press

Isherwood, L (1999) *Liberating Christ. Exploring Christologies of Contemporary Liberation Movements.* Cleveland: Pilgrim Press

Pilger, J (2002) *The New Rulers of the World.* London: Verso

Ritzer, G (2004) *The Globalisation of Nothingness.* London: Pine Forge Press

5

Equality, diversity and othering: what happens to identity in a globalised world?

ELIZABETH ATKINSON

In this chapter, Elizabeth Atkinson explores some of the ways in which the process of Othering maintains its hold over contemporary social and political relations. Focusing in particular on US interventions in Afghanistan and Iraq post-9/11, her discussion echoes the concerns of McLaren and Isherwood in the earlier chapters in this section, and also links to the critiques of current affairs offered by Pinar and Cole. Drawing on a range of interpretive perspectives, Atkinson demonstrates how we create and perpetuate notions of the Other through language, image and action, and proposes a move towards policies and practices of the self which link the personal, the social and the political. She suggests that it is by interrogating our own individual practices of Othering, as well as those embedded in policy rhetoric, that we can provide local solutions which might have global effects.

Introduction: What on earth are we doing?

In a policy context where 'equality and diversity' are all the rage, and where the forces of globalisation are said to be contracting space, time and identity (Edwards and Usher, 2000), we might wonder how it is possible for our world to continue to be rent with individual, social and political divisions. Yet it is so – perhaps inevitably, and perhaps not surprisingly, given the continuing differences in priority and perspectives which shape both global and local affairs. As Jean McNiff has pointed out in an earlier volume in this series (McNiff, 2004) it can be argued that our inability to resolve differences might lie in the assumption that, in order to reach a resolution, it is necessary to achieve some form of compromise whereby either one party or both loses ground. McNiff proposes an approach to peace education – and to peace-making, which recognises and works with difference – specifically, the differences which determine the *agonistic* nature of human relations. I would like to take up the concept of working with difference, but from a different perspective. My intention in this chapter is to explore some of the ways in which, in the contemporary political and social context, divisions between 'I' and 'not-I' are created and perpetuated. Taking postmodern thinking as a starting point, I go on to draw on a range of interpretive perspectives, focusing in particular on postcolonial thinking and critical social theory.

Postmodernism and the Other

Critics of postmodern thinking have questioned its potential for challenging social and political divisions and inequalities (see, for example, Hill *et al*, eds, 1999; Cole 2001, 2004). However, I have argued elsewhere (see, for example, Atkinson, 2001a, b) that the postmodern disruption of unitary identity provides a powerful means of breaking down 'I/not-I' boundaries; and it is these boundaries, and their construction and maintenance, which I will explore in this chapter. (I am not alone in claiming the value of postmodern thinking in this field: St Pierre (2001), for example, explores the ethical dimensions of deconstruction, while Schutz (2000) argues that postmodernists – or rather, postmodern thinking – can 'do good'.)

My starting point is the notion of 'constitutive otherness': a notion which, as Cahoone (1996) asserts, is a key feature of postmodern thinking. Constitutive otherness is the creation of what is present through what is absent; the dependence of the centre on the margins; the dependence of the spoken on the unspoken. This dependence creates what Derrida (1974) calls 'violent hierarchies', of which 'I'/'not-I' is one. Into the text of 'I', postmodern and poststructural thinking reads the textual silences which keep 'I' safely separate from the Other (see Butler, 1993; Fine, 1994; MacLure, 1996; Stronach,

1996). This privileging of the centre over the margins operates both in the personal and the social arenas. The personal definition of self in contrast to that which is 'not-I' both excludes the Other from the normative categories by which the self is defined, and prevents the individual from recognising her/his own multiple selves. In the social arena, group identity negates 'that which it is not,' creating false unities among group members which deny the complex multiplicities of which 'the group' is composed.

In the spirit of the postmodern *bricoleur*, who takes conceptual tools up as and when they are perceived to be useful, I intend, in this chapter, to read these textual silences, this play of constitutive otherness, through a number of different interpretive lenses. It is my hope that this might provide a way of gaining a clearer insight into what in the world we are doing when, for example, 'We' in the West take massive retaliatory action against an invisible and ubiquitous enemy, in the aftermath of the attacks on September 11th 2001 on the two greatest symbols of American money and might – the World Trade Center and the Pentagon. As a starting point, I suggest that the whole rationale on which the recent and current actions of George W Bush and his allies are based, in the context both of the War on Terror and of the invasion of Iraq[1], depends on the operation of the notion of constitutive otherness. It would be foolish to imply, of course, that 9/11 and its aftermath have not already been the subject of extensive analysis across the social and political sciences, but comparatively little attention has been given to these events by writers in the field of education – an absence which several of the writers in this volume aim to address.

Culture, history and the colonisation of identity

The operation of constitutive otherness is closely linked to what post-colonial theorists describe as the colonisation of identity. Edwards and Usher (2000), drawing on Massey (1993) and Blunt and Rose (1994), identify the Enlightenment separation of space and time as a key factor in the advance of capitalism and colonialism, where 'history (time) is asserted over and played out on the inert body of geography (space)' (p 23). An implication of this separation is the impossibility, for the coloniser, of considering space, place, or time in any other than a Western sense; an impossibility evidenced by the coloniser's repeated inability to understand non-Western ways of knowing. Edwards and Usher link the colonisation of space-time to the historical power of the process of map-making (see also Sleeter, 2000) 'whereby particular spaces were made into 'places' (p 136) and suggest, again drawing on Massey (1994), that the contemporary Western preoccupation with the loss of a sense of place through globalising processes signifies in itself a colonialist perspective as the Western world robbed the colonised world of its sense of place long ago. (2000:34. In this sense, the very concepts of globalisation and postmodern existence may continue to reflect a colonising tendency.)

The creation of a 'place' called Iraq, through the decision-making of a collection of Western powers in the 1920s, represents a relatively modern example of this sort of colonial map-making, albeit without the banner of Empire. Not only did this process bring together, under the unlikely umbrella of a single nation-state, two deeply divided groups whose enmity stretched back for centuries – the *Sunni* and *Shi'a* Muslims, but it also provided a means whereby the sites from which much of Western civilisation sprang – ancient Mesopotamia, the cities of Ur, Babylon and Nineveh, the trade routes and fertile lands between the Tigris and the Euphrates – were wiped from collective memory by the erasure of the 'places' which were previously recognised – and, ironically, claimed by the West – as part of Our cultural heritage. This gives a deeply ironic flavour to George W Bush's remark, immediately following the September 11th attacks, that a blow had been struck at the heart of civilization itself – even if (as seems likely) Mr Bush failed to recognise the irony himself, alongside his failure to make a distinction, in planning his retaliation, between the actions of an extremist religious group (*Al-Quaida*[2]) and the intentions of a secular dictator (Saddam Hussein).

Hartsock (1990:160-161), drawing on the work of Memmi, 1967, and Said, 1978) shows how construction of the Other constructs the dominant Self. She summarises three characteristics by which Memmi identifies the construction of the Other:

1) as 'Not,' as a lack, a void;
2) as somehow not quite human
3) as an anonymous collective:
'In more colloquial terms, they all look alike.'

This is a process which can be seen at play in the homogenisation of identity which occurs in the Western construction of, for example, Muslims or Arabs (and the conflation of the two), and in the attendant Islamophobia which renders all who might fit this homogenous category (for which, for males at least, the qualifying criteria seem to be a certain skin-tone combined with a beard) subject to intense suspicion in the post-9/11 world.

Other postcolonial theorists take up the theme of the inescapability of colonialist thinking, reminding us (if a reminder were needed) that colonialism is not merely a lamentable mistake of the past, but an enduring feature of the present. Goldie (1995:232-3), analysing the semiotic construction of indigenous peoples, suggests that 'the indigene is a semiotic pawn on a chess board under the control of the white sign-maker' (the people of Afghanistan and Iraq providing rich examples, with their countries laid out ready for us to play). Goldie draws on Gilman (1985:18) to remind us of the way in which colonialist thinking continually redefines the boundary between self and Other in order to maintain their differences:

> Because there is no real line between self and the Other, an imaginary line must be drawn; and so that the illusion of an absolute difference between self and Other is never troubled, this line is as dynamic in its ability to alter itself as is the self. (Goldie, 1995:233)

This sort of flexibility has been demonstrated, in the UK, in the struggle within media and policy rhetoric to make sense of the apparently ambiguous notion of a British Muslim – a struggle which has led some commentators to return to the tactics of Norman Tebbit – the former Chairman of the Conservative Party and now member of the House of Lords, always outspoken in his public marginalisation of the Other – by claiming that the way to determine someone's true allegiance (and thereby their identity) is to see which side they cheer for in an international cricket match:

> It's an interesting test. Are you still harking back to where you came from or [sic] where you are? (Tebbit, *The Guardian*, 20 April 1990, in Smith, 1994: 106)

Othering and the Politics of Resentment: identity as a form of hatred

Cullingford, reporting on the development of prejudice and nationalism among young British children, describes 'identity as a form of
hatred':

> The perception of self is a matter of definition against others. The
> desire and the need to be independent, to be *unlike* others is
> closely embroiled in the counter-need to belong, to be *like*
> others. The question is always the extent to which personal
> identity is dependent on others. This is a cultural matter, as well
> as an emotional one. (Cullingford, 2000:219, original emphasis)

Similarly, McCarthy and Dimitriades (following Nietzsche) identify a
'politics of resentment' by which the Other is excluded and denied.
They describe the concept of resentment as:

> the specific practice of identity displacement, in which the social
> actor consolidates his identity by a complete disavowal of the
> merits and existence of his social other. Here, one becomes
> 'good' by constructing the other as 'evil' ... A sense of self, thus,
> is only possible through an annihilation or emptying out of the
> other. (McCarthy and Dimitriades, 2000:173-174)

This annihilation or emptying out of the other is, as we have seen over
the course of events following the 9/11 attacks, taken at times to
horrifyingly literal extremes. The necessity to annihilate the other –
either symbolically or literally – has resulted in an exponential rise in
Islamophobia across the Western world; the introduction of Western-
controlled governments in Afghanistan and Iraq; and the accidental
killing, as a necessary corollary to the War on Terror, of literally thousands of Afghan and Iraqi civilians.

Thompson's Modes of Operation of Ideology

Another interpretive perspective which can usefully be brought to
bear on this situation is Thompson's (1990:59-67) model of the
modes of operation of ideology, which provides a powerful tool for
the analysis of the discursive construction of the Other. He proposes
five modes of operation of ideology: legitimation, dissimulation, unification, fragmentation and reification, each characterised by specific
strategies of symbolic construction (see Figure 1). McCarthy and
Dimitriades' concept of a politics of resentment finds echoes, in parti-

Elizabeth Atkinson

Figure 1: Thompson's Modes of Operation of Ideology

Adapted from Thompson, 1990:59-67

Modes of operation of ideology	Strategies of symbolic construction
Legitimation: *The representation of relations of domination as legitimate*	**Rationalisation:** 'the producer of a symbolic form constructs a chain of reasoning which seeks to defend or justify a set of social relations or institutions, and thereby to persuade an audience that it is worthy of support' (p 61)
	Universalisation: 'By means of this strategy, institutional arrangements which serve the interests of some individuals are represented as serving the interests of all' (p 61)
	Narrativisation: 'claims are embedded in stories which recount the past and treat the present as part of a timeless and cherished tradition' (p 61)
Dissimulation: *Denying, concealing or obscuring relations of domination*	**Displacement:** 'a term customarily used to refer to one object or individual is used to refer to another, and thereby the positive or negative connotations of the term are transferred to the other object or individual' (p 62)
	Euphemisation: 'actions, institutions or social relations are described or redescribed in terms which elicit a positive valuation' (p 62)
	Trope: 'the figurative use of language or, more generally, of symbolic forms' (p 63)
Unification: *Emphasising the sameness between groups or individuals in spite of their differences*	**Standardisation:** 'symbolic forms are adapted to a standard framework which is promoted as the shared and acceptable basis of symbolic exchange' (p 64: Thompson identifies the establishment of a national language in a multilingual society as an example)

85

Modes of operation of ideology	Strategies of symbolic construction
	Symbolisation of unity: 'the construction of symbols of unity, of collective identity and identification, which are diffused throughout a group or plurality of groups' (p 64: Thompson identifies flags, national anthems, emblems and inscriptions as examples)
Fragmentation: *Dividing groups or individuals in order to sustain relations of domination*	**Differentiation**: 'emphasising the distinctions, differences and divisions between individuals and groups, the characteristics which disunite them and prevent them from constituting an effective challenge to existing relations or an effective participant in the exercise of power' (p 65)
	Expurgation of the other: 'the construction of an enemy, either within or without, which is portrayed as evil, harmful or threatening and which individuals are called upon collectively to resist or expurgate' (p 65)
Reification: *The presentation of transitory phenomena or states of being as though they were timeless, natural and permanent.*	**Naturalisation**: 'a state of affairs which is a social and historical creation may be treated as a natural event or as the inevitable outcome event or as the inevitable outcome of natural characteristics' (p 66)
	Eternalisation: 'social-historical phenomena are deprived of their historical character by being portrayed as permanent, unchanging and ever-recurring' (p 66)
	Nominalisation and Passivisation (turning actions into nouns and using verbs in the passive form): 'representing processes as things, deleting actors and agency, constituting time as an eternal extension of the present tense: these are so many ways of re-establishing the dimension of society without history' at the heart of historical society' (p 66)

cular, in Thompson's notion of the 'expurgation of the other': one of the strategies of symbolic construction by which the process of fragmentation operates within modern culture. This process serves to divide groups or individuals in order to sustain relations of domination; a process which can clearly be seen at work in contemporary US foreign and domestic policy.

Thompson's (1990:56) interest is in 'the ways in which meaning serves to establish and sustain relations of domination or, as Knowles and Malmkjaer (1996:44) put it 'the notion of ideology as meaning in the service of power'. (Ironically, Knowles and Malmkjaer are discussing children's literature; but perhaps the parallels between children's literature and policy rhetoric are not, after all, so surprising.) In particular, Thompson (1990:58) emphasises the concept of mobilising meaning through symbolic forms:

> Symbolic forms are not merely representations which serve to articulate or obscure social relations or interests which are constituted fundamentally and essentially at a pre-symbolic level: rather, symbolic forms are continuously and creatively implicated in the constitution of social relations as such. Hence I propose to conceptualize ideology in terms of the ways in which the meaning mobilized by symbolic forms serves to *establish and sustain* relations of domination: to establish, in the sense that meaning may actively create and institute relations of domination; to sustain, in the sense that meaning may serve to maintain and reproduce relations of domination through the ongoing process of producing and receiving symbolic forms. (Original emphasis)

Thompson is careful, too, to emphasise that symbolic forms go beyond the linguistic (in a sense which echoes Foucauldian notions of discourse). By 'symbolic forms' I understand a broad range of actions and utterance, images and texts, which are produced by subjects and recognized by them and others as meaningful constructs' (p 59). This is a point I shall take up later, but it is the notion of the mobilisation of meaning through these forms that is, I believe, of particular significance to our understanding of current events.

Rhetoric and representation

When George W Bush proclaimed, shortly after the attacks of September 11th 2001, that a blow had been struck at the heart of civilization itself, he set each of Thompson's modes of operation of ideology in motion simultaneously, neatly positioning non-Western culture and its representatives as unquestionably Other while at the same time asserting the symbolic dominance of the two targets of the attacks – the World Trade Centre and the Pentagon – as icons of Western civilization. This implicit acknowledgement of the overriding precedence of money and military power over other symbols of civilization – such as art and music, for example, or even democracy – allowed for another rhetorical turn: the legitimation of the subsequent military attacks on those who possessed neither money nor might, first in Afghanistan, then in Iraq. This was both accompanied and followed by a process of rationalisation (one of the strategies of symbolic construction through which legitimation is performed) whereby the maintenance of US power, for example, through both the political and the physical reconstruction of Iraq, was justified. Universalisation – another strategy of symbolic construction associated with the process of legitimation – is also at play here, in the assumption of universal benefits (for those who deserve them) arising from the US and UK military intervention in Iraq and its subsequent restructuring.

Thompson's second mode of operation of ideology – the process of dissimulation – is at work, too, in the presentation of current and recent events in Iraq, from the use of displacement to present the wholesale destruction of Fallujah[3] as entirely beneficial to its residents, to the ubiquitous euphemisation of military action through descriptions of 'shock and awe' tactics in Iraq and quaintly-named daisy-cutter bombs in Afghanistan. Thompson's fifth mode of operation of ideology – the process of reification – also operates here, in particular through eternalisation, whereby the particular stance of Bush and his supporters is presented as the representation of eternal truths; and passivisation, through which the continuing onslaught on the homes, streets and services of Iraqi towns such as Fallujah is presented as targets 'having been met', or specific areas 'having been secured'.

It is the combined processes of unification and fragmentation, however, which seem to play the most significant part in creating and maintaining the sense of Self and Other both within and beyond the boundaries of the Western world. Unification is achieved in particular through the standardisation of representation in terms such as 'the

American people' (and the concomitant statements and assumptions about what the American people want) and the American Way of Life. Those who do not conform to these notions of identity and unity become automatically Other, and this applies both to the enemy outside and the enemy within.

The enemy outside; the enemy within

The use of fragmentation, especially through the expurgation of the other, is particularly apparent in the relentless pursuit of the enemy, both outside and within Western society. Sometimes all it takes is a few carefully chosen words: the description of those fighting back against the Americans in Iraq as insurgents or rebels, for example, accompanied by the (American) soldier's-eye view of the fighting in Fallujah. Sometimes more subtle rhetorical moves are called into play, such as the introduction of legislation in the UK and the US to protect citizens from terrorism by allowing for detention without trial of those (such as the prisoners at Guantanamo Bay, as well as a number of prisoners held internally without trial in both countries) suspected of involvement in terrorist activities. But the play becomes even more subtle when it is possible to identify an enemy – such as *Al-Quaida* – which is potentially ever-present. *Al-Quaida* is invisible and unlocatable, therefore it can be considered to be everywhere – both outside and inside the boundaries of Western civilization. And this in turn legitimates the close surveillance of all (Muslims? Arabs? Non-Westerners?) who might be *Al-Quaida* sympathizers. This process has been taken to the extent, in the US, of monitoring the library loans of university staff known to have an interest in the affairs of the gulf states, and ostracising – and in some cases, removing from their posts – those who speak out against the US interventions in Afghanistan and Iraq (or, although this is not the issue under consideration here, against the US role in the ongoing conflict between Israel and Palestine). Surveillance at this level, where the minute movements of citizens are monitored and judged, might be seen as an example of Foucault's panopticon, by means of which all activities are observed from a single centralised vantage point (see Rabinow, ed, 1984:206) as well as summoning a chilling echo of the days of the McCarthy inquisitions.

The Power of the Visual

While Thompson's modes of operation of ideology can clearly be seen at work within linguistic discourses, there are other, equally powerful, discourses which underpin the process of Othering. Foremost among these, perhaps, is the discourse of visual images. The language of 'shock and awe' was reinforced by the firework displays of unprecedented military power (more firepower was expended in the attack on Bhagdad in March 2003, which constituted the first move in the 'liberation' of Iraq, than in the whole of the intervention in Kosovo of 1999). In an appalling visual/symbolic somersault, the proof that those suspected of involvement with *Al-Quaida* in Afghanistan were less than human was provided by the photographs of them being treated as less than human at Guantanamo Bay (where most of those originally taken prisoner in 2002 are still detained). And if we have any doubt as to the degraded and degrading behaviour of soldiers on the Other side (in whichever conflict we choose) we only have to look to the front-page images in our tabloid newspapers; or, where our press maintain an understandable sensitivity towards images of atrocities, consider the effects on the images in our minds of the *knowledge* that, for example, executions of hostages have been recorded on video. Where our own soldiers' behaviour seems to equal that of their enemies in degradation, however (as when US soldiers forced Iraqi prisoners to pose naked and wired for execution at Baghdad's Abu Ghraib prison in the Spring of 2004) we are careful either to expurgate these individuals as the enemy within, or to claim that they are not in any way representative of the civilised notions which we espouse.

Implications for Education: Policies and Practices of the Self

Whether in private practice, then, or in public policy, Othering acts as a powerful controlling force which produces prejudice and discrimination as regimes of truth. The discursive construction of the Other permeates our social practices at all levels, offering a far more persuasive map of the world than any of the liberal rhetoric of equality and diversity legislation or its related teaching. Without an attempt at a deconstruction of these processes, the normal everyday practices of education may only perpetuate and reinforce these binaries. It is for this reason that my own focus, in my work with university students (some of whom are training to be teachers; some

90

Elizabeth Atkinson

undertaking degrees in early childhood studies; some studying children's literature at Master's level) is on the ways in which we are implicated in this discursive construction. My approach to this involves the public confession and examination (within taught sessions) of my own prejudices, and a thorough exploration both of how they have come to be so firmly fixed through the effects of a range of social, cultural and political discourses, and of what alternative discourses can be brought into play in order to counteract their pervasive effects. We explore the metaphor (widely used in poststructuralist writing) of the *palimpsest*, the parchment from which the original writing has been erased in order for a new text to be written, but from which the old text stubbornly refuses to disappear altogether, and consider the ways in which this metaphor applies to the disjunction between my tacit and explicit beliefs. Having thus exposed myself as, under the surface, a racist, sexist, elitist middle-class snob, in spite of all my liberal philosophy, I use this as an example of the discursive construction of Self in opposition to the Other, and invite the students, privately, and without threat of exposure, to perform the same analysis upon their own public and private selves. This done, we relate the discursive construction of individual identities with the notion of Othering in the wider social, political and educational arenas, looking, as I have done in this chapter, at the mobilisation of meaning in the service of power. Without wishing to sound over-optimistic, I would like to suggest that such practices of the self might provide local solutions to the perpetuation of relations of domination (in classrooms, in families and in wider social and political spheres) which might just possibly, alongside the analysis of Othering in wider policy and practice, have global effects.

References

Atkinson, E (2001a) The responsible anarchist: postmodernism and social change, British Journal of Sociology of Education, 23 (1): 73 – 87
Atkinson, E (2001b) A response to Mike Cole's 'Educational postmodernism, social justice and societal change: an incompatible *ménage-à-trois*', *The School Field: International Journal of Theory and Research in Education*, 12(1 and 2): 87 – 94
Blunt, A. and Rose, G. (1994) Introduction: Women's colonial and postcolonial geographies, in. Blunt, A and Rose, G (eds) *Writing Women and Space: Colonial and postcolonial geographies*. New York: Guilford Press
Butler, J. (1993) *Bodies That Matter*. New York: Routledge

Cahoone, E (1996) Introduction to Cahoone, E (ed) *From Modernism to Post-modernism: An anthology*. Oxford: Blackwell

Cole, M (2001) Educational postmodernism, social justice and societal change: an incompatible *ménage-à-trois*, *The School Field: International Journal of Theory and Research in Education*, 12(1 & 2): 69 – 85

Cole, M (2004) Fun, amusing, full of insights, but ultimately a reflection of anxious times: a critique of postmodernism as a force for resistance, social change and social justice, in: Satterthwaite, J, Atkinson, A and Martin, W (eds) *Educational Counter-Cultures: Confrontations, Images, Vision*. (Discourse, Power, Resistance Series Volume 3.) Stoke on Trent: Trentham: 19 – 34

Cullingford, C (2000) *Prejudice: From individual identity to nationalism in young people*. London: Kogan Page

Derrida, J (1974) *Of Grammatology* (Trans G C Spivak). Baltimore: Johns Hopkins University Press

Edwards, R and Usher, R (2000) *Globalisation and Pedagogy: Space, place and identity*. London: Routledge

Fine, M (1994) Working the hyphens: reinventing self and other in qualitative research, in: Denzin, N K and Lincoln, Y S (eds) *Handbook of Qualitative Research*. Thousand Oaks, CA: Sage

Hill, D, McLaren, P, Cole, M and Rikowski, G (eds) (1999) *Postmodernism in Educational Theory: Education and the politics of human resistance*. London: Tufnell Press

Goldie, T (1995) The representation of the indigene, in: Ashcroft, B, Griffiths, G and Tiffin, H (eds) *The Postcolonial Studies Reader*. London: Routledge

Gilman, S (1985) *Difference and Pathology*

Hartsock, N (1990) Foucault on power: a theory for women? in: Nicholson, L J (ed) *Feminism/Postmodernism*. London: Routledge

Knowles, M and Malmkjaer, K (1996) *Literature as a carrier of ideology: children's literature and control. Chapter 2 of Language and Control in Children's Literature*. London: Routledge: 41 – 80

MacLure, M (1996) Telling transitions: boundary work in narratives of becoming an action researcher, *British Educational Research Journal*, 22(3): 273 – 286, also in: Stronach, I and MacLure, M (1997) *Educational Research Undone*. Buckingham: Open University Press: 116 – 131

Massey, D (1993) Politics and space/time, in: Keith, M and Pille, S (eds) *Place and the Politics of Identity*. London: Routledge

Massey, D (1994) *Space, Place and Gender*. Cambridge: Polity Press

McCarthy, C and Dimitriades, G (2000) Governmentality and the sociology of education: media, education policy and the politics of resentment, *British Journal of Sociology of Education*, 21(2): 169 – 185

McNiff, J (2004) The tragedy of peace education and its transformation, in: Satterthwaite, J, Atkinson, A and Martin, W (eds) *Educational Counter-Cultures: Confrontations, Images, Vision*. (Discourse, Power, Resistance Series Volume 3.) Stoke on Trent: Trentham: 117 – 131

Memmi, A (1967) *The Colonizer and the Colonized.* Boston, MA: Beacon Press
Rabinow, P (ed) (1984) *The Foucault Reader. An introduction to Foucault's thought.* London: Penguin
Said, E(1978) *Orientalism.* New York: Vintage Press
Schutz, A (2000) Teaching freedom? *Postmodern perspectives, Review of Educational Research,* 70(2): 215 – 251
Simpson, J (2004) *The Wars Against Saddam. Taking the hard road to Baghdad.* London: Pan Books. (First published 2003 by Macmillan)
Sleeter, C E (2000) Keeping the lid on: multicultural curriculum and the organization of consciousness. Paper presented at the annual conference of the American Educational Research Association, New Orleans, April
Smith, A M (1994) *New Right Discourse on Race and Sexuality. Britain, 1968 – 1990.* Cambridge: Cambridge University Press
St Pierre, E A (2001) Ethics under deconstruction. Paper presented at the annual meeting of the American Educational Research Association, Seattle, April
Stronach, I (1996) Fashioning post-modernism, finishing modernism: tales from the fitting room, *British Educational Research Journal* 22(3): 359 -375, also in: Stronach, I and MacLure, M (1997) *Educational Research Undone.* Buckingham: Open University Press: 14 – 33
Thompson, J B (1990) *Ideology and Modern Culture: Critical social theory in the era of mass communication.* Stanford: Stanford University Press

Notes

1   President Bush took the 9/11 attacks as a cue for an immediate operationalisation of the first steps in mounting an invasion of Iraq, in spite of the lack of any evidence that Saddam Hussein was connected with the events of September 11th. At the same time, the US and its allies mounted a wholesale attack on Afghanistan, designed to root out and destroy Bin Laden and his followers, which failed signally in this aspect of its mission, although it did succeed in removing the Taliban from power and replacing it with a US-supported government. While political commentators' views differ as to the extent to which the invasion of Iraq was a retaliation for 9/11, there is a general consensus that it gave Bush the opportunity he had been waiting for. As John Simpson comments (2004: 403):

> The invasion of Iraq was carried out for a variety of stated reasons, and one or two unstated ones, which were probably more important. It was done, we were told, in order to overthrow a particularly unpleasant tyrant, to protect the world from his dangerous weapons, to undercut the threat from international terrorism, to make the Middle East more democratic. It was also done, though no one put it into such words, to give Americans the sense that they had struck back at the dark forces which had reached out and attacked the heart of the American system on 11 September 2001. In addition, there must have been several people at the top of the Bush administration who thought that destroying Saddam Hussein would help to safeguard the position of Israel. As for the president himself, he may well have felt, privately, that going one step further than his father had gone would ensure his re-election in 2004.

As Simpson goes on to remark dryly, 'It didn't quite work out as expected'.

2   *Al-Quaida*, under the leadership of Osama Bin Laden, proudly proclaimed responsibility for the 9/11 attacks. Bin Laden went on to provide open taunts to the US administration in the form of a series of videos – the latest of which, at the time of writing, was released just before the November 2004 US election, in which he appeared, alive and well, demonstrating the inability of all the US military might to destroy him.

3   Fallujah is the Iraqi town which was identified by US forces as a key stronghold of anti-US insurgents during the continuing conflict in Iraq which followed the supposed end of the war. In spite of public warnings from Kofi Annan, the UN leader, that an attack on Fallujah would only serve to intensify the problems in Iraq, the US forces mounted a sustained attack on the city in November 2004 which was broadcast on international television entirely from the perspective of US soldiers and their allies.

PART TWO
PRAXIS: THINKING AND DOING

6

Linking the global and the local: some insights from dynamic systems theory

TAMSIN HAGGIS

In this chapter, Tamsin Haggis proposes an alternative to the endless oppositions of the paradigm wars, offering a conceptual framework for the understanding of inter-actions in educational contexts which incorporates both the global and the local, as well offering a rationale for accepting the unpredictable and the unexpected. Her analysis provides an important starting-point for this second section of the book, taking account of events at both the macro and the micro levels of education. Haggis offers an 'epistemology of the close-up', drawn from dynamic systems theory, which sheds new light on the emergence of patterns and behaviours which can be under-stood as the effects of multiple interactions, both between individuals and within and between groups and systems. Her analysis sets the scene for the explorations of inter-actions between professionals, and between professionals and policy-makers, offered by Boag-Munroe and Ollin in the following two chapters.

Furlong's (2004) recent discussion of 'the re-emergence of the para-digm wars' draws attention to the remarkable resilience of what Martin Hammersley (2002) has called 'two worlds theories' in educa-tional research (e.g. theory/practice; quantitative/qualitative; global/local). Although the last thirty years have witnessed a wide range of analyses and deconstructions of binary thinking from a variety of critical and postmodern perspectives (see, for example, Derrida, 1976; Kaufmann, 2001; Parker, 1997, Stronach and MacLure, 1997), such thinking appears to be particularly recalcitrant within educational discourses.

One reaction to this critique appears to be a tendency for contemporary discourses, for example, in relation to quantitative and qualitative approaches, to attempt various types of theoretical compromise. An example of this is the promotion of mixed methods (e.g. Gorrard *et al*, 2001), which appears to suggest that the different approaches are *complimentary* perspectives, which together provide a fuller, more rounded, perspective. In this view, a case study is seen as providing the detail that fills in a larger scale, more quantitatively-derived pattern. Such moves, however, side-step some fairly fundamental questions; for example, if a case study is simply the detail of a larger-scale pattern, why does a large-scale generalisation tend to have little or 'no applicability in the individual case' (Guba and Lincoln, 1998:198)? In reverse, why is there such trouble in using the insights derived from local, context-specific investigations in situations which lie beyond the original context of investigation? Whilst researchers working with postmodern perspectives may be confident that their analysis and interpretations can only engage with 'local narratives' and 'situated truths' (Sumara *et al*, 2001), the perceived pressure to relate the results of small-scale, local types of study to other, different, situations within a wider context still creates theoretical tensions for many researchers.

This paper will examine these tensions by attempting to create a 'departure' from the usual 'disciplinary orbits' associated with educational research (Derrida, 1976, in Stronach and McLure, 1997:3). Whilst postmodern and feminist perspectives attempt to challenge the assumptions of traditional sociology and psychology by using literary theory, or the visual and performing arts, the discussion here will use complexity theory, a perspective from the theoretical sciences, as its interpretative frame. Postmodernist and feminist approaches focus on discourse, text and power, and embody an intention to destabilize and complicate. Complexity and dynamic systems theories, on the other hand, have nothing particular to say about text, language, or power, and might be seen by postmodernists as an attempt at a new kind of metanarrative. It will be argued here, however, that this perspective offers a new way of examining educational research slightly differently from within, rather than from without, some of its traditional assumptions. Rather than trying to ignore, resolve or transcend the binary of qualitative and quantitative, this analysis will deliberately use a binary summary of these different positions in order to complicate and draw attention to the relationships which such polarities involve

A Binary to Explore Binaries

The suspicion with which many researchers now treat any kind of binary conceptualisation is arguably in danger of reducing the possibilities for thought, rather than, as originally intended, expanding such possibilities. Moran (2000) suggests that the current tendency to reject all oppositions is a misunderstanding of Derrida's (1976) intention, which was to force a questioning of the way that oppositions are valorised, rather than an attempt to overturn them. It could be argued that, at least in Anglophone cultures, binary concepts perform a crucial function in defining and delimiting an area to be discussed, with the extremes of opposed polar positions provide a starting point for dialogue. It is on this basis that the analysis here will begin by creating a working, binary definition of tendencies within different types of educational research.

For the purposes of this discussion, ('grand') theory and quantitative research will be taken to be connected in the sense that both try to produce general principles that will apply beyond specific contexts. Similarly, practice and qualitative research will be taken as connected in the sense that both attempt to deal with the complexities which arise in more localised, specific contexts. These general distinctions will be referred to as large and small scale approaches to research. It must be stressed that this is a temporary conceptual creation, which collapses a great deal of subtlety and potential argument. Furthermore, even within these parameters, it has to be recognised that researchers concerned with more localised, small (or medium) scale types of research are often also interested in creating theory, and, of course, that 'research is itself also a form of practice' (Hammersley, 2002:65). These are some of the problematic issues that this chapter sets out to explore.

The relationship between large and small-scale types of research is rarely examined in detail. Hammersley's discussion of macro and micro-level theories (Hammersley, 1984; Hammersley and Atkinson, 1995), for example, refers to 'a dimension along which the scale of the phenomena under study varies'. This suggests a continuum but does not say anything about the nature of each in relation to the other. Hammersley and Atkinson's discussion of attempts to integrate these two levels 'to show that there is only one level, not two' (*ibid.*) suggests that they are seen as separate; a position which Hammersley states more clearly in his more recent discussion of these issues. (Hammersley (2002) does also discuss problems with this idea of separated worlds, but he approaches the idea of what the worlds might have in common from a different perspective from that being discussed here.) In the earlier paper (1984), however, the suggestion that micro-level investigations can test macro-level theory implies that both are, in the end, operating within the same ontological and epistemological world. From this perspective, whatever it is that is being researched, identified and tested, at the two different levels, appears to be seen as ontologically consistent.

This assumption of ontological consistency also underpins the way that data are most commonly analysed, despite the sometimes very different philosophical positions which large and small-scale approaches may be aligned to. Unless the study is longitudinal, or biographical (and often even then), both quantitative and qualitative data tends to be analysed cross-sectionally. This way of creating categories of 'things held in common' (such as correlations, concepts, typologies, hierarchies) is so fundamental to research in the social sciences (Llewelyn, 2003) that it is rarely commented upon in conventional educational research discourses (despite the fact that postmodern and feminist analyses continue to question this approach from a variety of perspectives). The conventional approach could be seen as a *distancing* form of abstraction, in the sense that it assumes that the pattern that can be seen as the researcher becomes 'disentangled' from examples of the particular will be more useful for creating knowledge than any patterns that may exist at the level of the individual. The assumptions which underpin much cross-sectional analysis could be summarised as follows:

- Firstly, research can only be done by *abstracting* from specific examples

- Secondly, processes of abstraction self-evidently require the creation of *distance* from the particular

- Thirdly, distancing is required because this is the only way to perceive *meaningful connections*. Meaningful connections here are patterns of *similarity*

- Finally, connections, when assumed to exist, are seen to be *consistent* across all levels, from macro to micro (in other words, a case study will provide detail within a larger study)

Feminist and postmodern researchers have attempted to confound these assumptions by coming at them from unexpected angles, attempting to disturb and topple them through the use of perspectives from radically different disciplines. The analysis I am offering here, however, is far less ambitious, asking questions, at least initially, from within the same frame of reference. Even from within, however, potential inconsistencies and confusions soon appear. Though highly productive, this approach does not, for example, provide any account of what happens to the information which such commonality-seeking approaches have to discard; nor does it allow for the idea that what is discarded by the research may nonetheless be exerting an effect on whatever it is that is being investigated (Fogel *et al*, 1997:19). In addition, there are questions about issues such as the nature of the 'structural pattern' which a large-scale research study might be seen to articulate. A social science researcher might see such patterns as being representative of a dynamic aspect of social structure, such as gender relations, for example. The 'findings' of some large-scale educational research projects, however, can appear to suggest that a large-scale pattern which has been identified by the research refers not to dynamic social patterns, but to more fundamental, 'deep' structural mechanisms which are understood to underlie the apparent variety of different cases.

Such problems are arguably connected to a lack of clarity about how the patterns created at different levels of scale (small and large) relate to each other. Both 'social' and 'deep' structure understandings of the meaning of an aggregate pattern can appear to suggest that smaller-scale, individual or local patterns are able to provide more in-depth or detailed information about the pattern created at a larger scale, implying, as has been discussed above, an ontological coherence and consistency which transcends matters of scale. It could be argued, however, that the kinds of patterns which are visible from a distance are in fact quite *distinct* from the kinds of patterns that exist at the local level (Guba and Lincoln, 1998), in a way that is not simply the difference between what can be measured empirically, and what such a measurement may mean to an individual actor (Smeyers, 2001). This appears to be what underlies the commonly expressed idea that generalisations 'have no applicability in the individual case' (Guba and Lincoln, 1998:198). What exactly is a global pattern, if it fragments when it comes into contact with specific situations?

Even when attempts are made to address the relationship between the large and the small, analysis as distancing often appears to be seen as the only option. Hammersley and Atkinson (1995), for example, discuss 'four types of theory' in relation to both macro and micro levels. The most specific of the four types, referred to as 'micro-substantive research on particular types of organisation or situation' (238) gives 'doctor patient interaction' and 'police encounters with juveniles' as examples. Even in this most local level of theory, it is still a general principle that is sought. It appears to be simply taken for granted that all theory must, by definition, involve distancing from the particular (Flyvberg, 2001).

This situation seems somewhat incongruous when it is considered in relation to many current ideas in educational theorising. Though generalisable, statistically-based models of individual behaviour and cognitive traits remain popular in psychology, for example, these have been joined by newer perspectives which stress the importance of interaction, context, and the need to understand issues of particularity and difference in local situations. Generalised categories such as self, style, type and stage are increasingly being challenged by new interactional and social perspectives such as those of dynamic systems theory (Bosma and Kunnen, 2001), or critical and community psychology (e.g. Burman, 1994). Discussions of learning in areas such as adult education, reflecting the influence of feminist and postmodern critiques, have also broadened out from a reliance on atomistic, bounded categories such as 'adult learner', 'developmental stage', 'learning style' or 'special need', towards a recognition of the complexities of difference, and the context-specific nature of such difference (Edwards *et al*, 1996).

These moves could be seen as implying the need for an 'epistemology of the close-up'; a way of accounting for, and of speaking about, the difference and specificity which become apparent at a smaller scale. In terms of the gathering of research data, however, the dominant epistemology is still largely based upon a deliberate *retreat* from particularity, and upon the production of categories based on similarities; both processes which are likely to obscure and silence the ways in which things might be different. Current habits of categorising at both levels also have a tendency to produce static types of concept, rather than concepts which represent the fluidity and change involved in process and interaction (Stehr and Grundmann, 2001).

An Epistemology of the Close-up?

Johnson (2001) suggests (following Weaver, 1948) that there are three types of scientific enquiry. The first deals with problems involving very limited numbers of variables, and concerns issues such as the movement of the planets around the sun (the approach underpinning Newtonian mechanics). The second approach deals with problems which are characterised by 'millions or billions of variables that can only be approached by the use of statistical mechanics and probability theory' (2001:46), which he calls 'disorganised complexity'. This perhaps could be seen as a fair description of the approach taken in much Social Science research. He suggests, however, that there is a field between these two approaches which deals with a still substantial number of variables, but with one crucial difference:

> much more important than the mere number of variables is the fact that these variables are all interrelated... these problems, as contrasted with the disorganised situations with which statisticians can cope, *show the essential feature of organisation*. We will therefore refer to this group of problems as those of *organised complexity*. (Weaver, 1948, in Johnson, 2001:47. Original italics.)

Much large-scale educational research can perhaps be conceptualised as attempting to deal with 'disorganised complexity'. The standing back involved in attempts to uncover general principles entails deliberately discounting relationships *within* individual systems (people, cultures, classes, schools), as the interconnectedness of the elements within these types of units are seen to be too specific to be useful for the purpose of extracting a general principle. By contrast, dynamic systems theories (Fogel *et al*, 1997; Richardson, 2000; Valsiner, 1998), whether conceived of as versions of complexity theory (Cilliers, 1998; Byrne, 1998) or as theories of emergence (Johnson, 2001), concern themselves precisely with the interactions and relationships that occur within specific (open) systems.

A dynamic system is seen to consist of a large number of components which are interacting dynamically, with the interactions being confined to the local level (Cilliers, 1998). These multiple interactions are non-linear, and involve complex feedback loops which continually adjust and modify the both the 'parts' of the system and the system itself. As the system is an open one, the interactions can also affect the boundaries of the system itself, and indeed have effects beyond the system.

If there is a sufficient number of these interactions, and if they take place over a sufficiently long period of time, specific forms of order, or organisation, will periodically emerge from within the system:

> (Dynamic systems) solve problems by drawing on masses of relatively stupid elements, rather than a single, intelligent' 'executive branch'.... In these systems agents residing on one scale start producing behaviour that lies one scale above them: ants create colonies; urbanites create neighbourhoods; simple pattern-recognition software learns how to recommend new books. (Johnson, 2001:18)

Two examples discussed by Johnson describe this in more detail. The behaviour of ants, for example, is believed to come about not as a result of the directions of a queen, but as a result of simple forms of chemical communication between individual ants, which relay information about local conditions. The sheer size of the number of interactions, and the fact that these take place over time, result in emergent behaviour at the level of the colony (moving away from danger, for example, or towards food). Similarly, neighbourhoods within cities organise themselves along lines of social class, and cities themselves continually change and adapt in ways that have not been planned.

Discussion of the unpredictability of emergence in this kind of description of dynamic processes is often misunderstood to imply randomness, chaos or indeterminism. Non-linear systems, however, are in fact seen to be operating causally, though this causality is not of the deterministic, linear kind. What distinguishes it from more linear types of deterministic process is the fact that it is impossible, due to the speed and number of interacting variables, for many of the deterministic processes which are going on to be tracked or observed (Goldstein, 2000). For this reason, the results of the interactions cannot always be predicted, because it is not possible to know in advance what will interact with what, or indeed, what has interacted with what up to that point, and what has resulted from previous unknown interactions. In this sense the history of the interactions both within and beyond the system is crucial in determining the form of future emergences. Furthermore, this is seen to be a completely decentralised process, in that the order which is produced is seen to emerge solely from the multiple interactions. There is no key variable, no centrally-guiding programme or brain, and no one principle factor which makes everything happen. This does not, however, imply that anything at all can emerge, as emergence is ultimately constrained by certain features of the system itself, and by its interaction with factors and systems beyond its own boundaries (Fogel *et al*, 1997).

The implications of this conceptual framework have not yet been investigated very much in relation to approaches to educational research, or to the study of learning (see, however, Fenwick, 2003; Osberg and Biesta, 2003). In terms of attempting to find alternative epistemologies of difference, specificity and context, however, these ideas are interesting in that they privilege the importance of local interactions, and the interconnectedness of multiple, different elements in a local situation. The stress on dynamic interactions, for example, provides the potential for talking about 'learners' and 'context' as different kinds of interwoven process which are continually creating and being created by each other, rather than as static objects, manifesting characteristics, surrounded by an environment and affected by teachers. This perspective, however, does more than simply highlight processes of change and flow; it suggests that in fact there *is* only change and flow, in the sense that *it is the interactions themselves which are the system* (a person, from this perspective, is entirely 'composed' of interactions). The fact that the interactions produce changing forms of order does not necessarily imply something static, or even bounded. A sense of 'self' may emerge from the interactions of brain and environment, and function to order consciousness, but this does not have to imply that such a sense of self is either static or essential.

Theories of Emergence and Educational Research

A dynamic systems approach could not be used to talk about many kinds of population research, when a 'population' refers to an abstract category which has deliberately been created in order to track statistical patterns in relation to a large number of *different* systems (e.g. different schools, different students). This kind of population, does, of course, exist within a number of larger connected systems: 'British society', for example, 'working class culture' or 'the English university system'. This conceptualisation of the larger system, however, is not necessarily part of the framing of population-based research, which may be more likely to focus on a population as a category which contains a range of examples of the variation presented by many different, smaller units within the larger system. For example, 'Scottish dyslexic students' are likely to be investigated in relation to their individual psychologies, rather than the way in which such psychologies might exist in relation to certain cultural/systemic interactions within a particular social group. Similarly, a dynamic systems approach could not be used to talk about themes across data from different interviews, as a theme is an abstract category which has been extracted from the different systems (and systems of meaning) which the individual interview texts represent.

A dynamic systems perspective draws attention to the importance of the interactions *within* open systems. Research mechanisms which deliberately cut across systems cannot, by definition, track the ways in which different elements within a system react together to create certain types of outcome. Views from outside selected systems can track what can be seen to emerge from the different systems, but not the processes which led to these types of emergence. This reverses Silverman's (2001) notion that qualitative research can only describe the 'what' and 'how', with quantitative research providing the answer to 'why'; here it is the study of a particular set of systemic interactions which would provide clues as to the 'why' of specific forms of emergence.

These ideas could offer a new perspective on the problems outlined above in relation to the connection between macro and micro-levels of research activity. Research results and/or theory are usually aggregated abstractions, which it is nonetheless expected will be 'applied' to specific situations in a way that is meaningful to that specific situation. Though researchers are often blamed for the difficulties or failures involved in these attempts at connection, such failures could be because the logic/pattern which exists at the abstract level is simply not echoed further down the line. Patterns which exist at the level of the situated, particular example are arguably quite different from larger, aggregate patterns, because they are produced in a different way. From a dynamic systems perspective, patterns at the local level are the emergent properties of the multiply interacting variables which make up the open system which is the focus of attention. These emergent properties are *specific to the system being investigated* (although this does not preclude the possibility that similar properties might emerge from the interactions of a different, but similar open system). By contrast, an abstraction (e.g. a research model, or a policy innovation) is created by aggregating the similarities that can be seen when a number of unconnected open systems are viewed from a distance. What can be seen from a distance, however, is not an 'underlying' principle which unites the different cases, but simply a particular kind of shape. Selective qualitative investigations carried out within large-scale studies cannot, from this perspective, 'illuminate' 'or 'flesh out' the pattern of connections that exist between different systems, because such patterns only *exist* at a distance. Individual cases, on the other hand, are operating in relation to their own sets of variable interactions, which the distance pattern, by definition, has had to filter out of view.

Interacting Multiple Worlds: Distinct, but Interwoven

For some early attempts to use this approach in the analysis of data, see Haggis, 2004a and b. These papers report on two different analyses of the same set of interviews with a small group of mature students talking about learning in higher education. In both cases the results of a normal, distancing type of analysis are compared to a second, more 'indeterminate' type of analysis, which explores the patterns which begin to emerge when multiple factors in an individual case are considered in detail, without looking for causalities or even correlations. What emerges from this, particularly when contrasted with the dominant models of learning in higher education, is an argument that an understanding of *difference* could be as important in understanding learning as an understanding of commonalities. The analysis also explores how patterns of meaning begin to emerge within individual accounts, when using this approach, in ways that are quite different from the type of pattern which might emerge from a cross-sectional analysis. What these papers argue for is not necessarily different from what many qualitative researchers are already doing in biographical and life-history types of analysis. Dynamic systems/complexity theory, however, might be able to provide a different kind of language for talking about what it is that non-generalising studies attempt to do.

A dynamic systems perspective appears to reverse most of the assumptions outlined in the first part of this chapter. Abstraction which operates through creating distance from the particular could be seen, far from potentially enabling the isolation of 'key principles', instead to be actively destroying the very interactions and connections which constitute a particular system. The only way to try to understand the functioning of such a system seems to be to study it 'close-up'; in relation to its own multiple interactions. Distancing approaches, by contrast, compare emergences from these interactions with the emergences from other, different systems. In some situations it would only require a conceptual shift to move from one type of analysis to the other; distancing abstractions carried out in relation to separate, unconnected systems could become 'close-up' abstractions if the systems being investigated were instead conceptualised as being interrelated features of the larger systems that contain them.

The perspective outlined here begins to provide an articulation of why generalisations cannot be applied to particular cases, or why a case study cannot simply provide the detail of a larger scale pattern. The interactions within a system are constrained both from within the system itself (in relation to its initial conditions and circumstances) and by its interaction with other, different systems which simultaneously exist both within and beyond its own boundaries (such as culturally enacted discourses of gender, class, etc.). The history of the interactions within any given system, however, and what this interaction history produces in terms of emergence, is always particular to the individual case. A cross-system pattern which has been created through comparing the external features (or emergences from) a number of different systems is thus ontologically distinct from the patterns of interaction which could be described at the level of a particular system. Because some of the interactions within smaller systems are also interactions within larger systems, however, an abstraction created in relation to different systems within a population (for example, 'characteristics of dyslexic students') might also represent some of the interactions of the larger system pattern as well ('effects of British societal attitudes to expressions of dyslexia').

The interrelatedness of distinct systems creates the paradoxical situation of an ontological distinction between the 'two worlds' which (perhaps bizarrely, for the western mind) is at the same time non-dualistic. The worlds are separate, whilst being at the same time completely enmeshed. What connects them, however, is not the common underpinning of a deep structural unity, which becomes ever more secure as the scale at which the pattern can be shown to persist becomes larger. From a dynamic systems perspective the worlds instead make up a multidimensional 'space of flows' (Castells, 1996); an interconnected system of interwoven larger and smaller systems, which are interacting dynamically in relation to boundaries and constraints which are themselves constantly undergoing modification. Although each set of systemic patterns is determined by the individual make-up and history of that particular system, systems are themselves partly constituted by 'elements' of other systems (though these consist of interactions, rather than entities), and are thus constantly interacting with aspects of themselves which are, at the same time, beyond them.

Conclusion

Dynamic systems theories appear to offer a new way of looking at things which previously could not easily be seen. The focus on phenomena as open systems composed of interactions, rather than objects; the impossibility of tracking multiple causalities which nonetheless produce patterns of order and meaning; and the importance of time, history and specificity, all appear to offer something new in relation to the ancient divisions implied by dualities such as theory and practice, large and small, and quantitative and qualitative forms of research.

Dynamic systems thinking could hold out theoretical promise for researchers who may be trying to find ways of illuminating complex, human aspects of learning which tend to be reduced or left out of many current research frameworks. It does this in a number of ways. Firstly, it provides an acknowledgement of the complexity of phenomena, rather than attempting to reduce complexity to simplified abstractions. Secondly, it provides a rationale for a focus on the ways that things are interconnected, rather than demanding various forms of separating out from context. In this sense, it offers a way of engaging with the often rather general idea of 'context' in quite specific ways. Thirdly, it offers a way of thinking about process and change, rather than modelling state, 'type' and condition. A possible application of this in education could be to change the distancing, abstracted question of 'what works?' into a specific, process question such as 'what is happening when something is working'?

Finally, this type of thinking articulates a different vision of causality and determinism. Processes of interaction and emergence, although largely untrackable, are seen to be generated in a way that is logical and consistent with the interactions between different parts of (and beyond) the (open) system. It may be impossible to track the pathways that lead to the emergence of schizophrenia, a meaningful sense of the world, or motivation to learn, but the appearance of these conditions and orientations, from a dynamic systems perspective, is an outcome which is likely to be consistent with the interacting factors involved. This idea offers the potential of a different way of thinking about why emergences can be difficult to understand when they are viewed from a perspective beyond the system that generated them, and when they are compared with emergences from other, different systems. It is only when a system is observed from a vantage point which is *outside* of that system that things appear to be 'messy', contradictory or unexplainable; in relation to the internal dynamics of the system, what emerges is seen to be a direct result of the various interactions involved, even though these cannot be precisely measured or anticipated.

This suggests, perhaps surprisingly, a position that appears to be congruent with a more 'natural science' view of phenomena as being based on principles of ordering and consistency. Naturally occurring systems do produce changing forms of order, in the sense that, if they did not, there would be no system (selves, groups, cultures). Such order, however, may not exist in the form of 'underlying principles' which can be identified and then applied to multiple occurrences of different phenomena. Unexpected patterns of natural order may, in fact, exist more obviously in the very places where one might least expect to find them; in the local, the situated, rather than being visible from the perspective of a 'god's eye view'.

References

Bosma, H and Kunnen, E S (eds) (2001) *Identity and Emotion*. Cambridge: Cambridge University Press

Burman, E (1994) *Deconstructing Developmental Psychology*. London: Routledge

Byrne, D (1998) *Complexity Theory and the Social Sciences*. London: Routledge

Castells, M (1996) *The Rise of the Network Society*. Oxford: Blackwell

Cilliers, P (1998) *Complexity and Postmodernism*. London: Routledge

Derrida, J (1976) *Of Grammatology* (trans G C Spivak). London: Johns Hopkins University Press

Edwards, R, Hanson, A and Raggat, P (eds) (1996) *Boundaries of Adult Learning*. London: Routledge

Fenwick, T (2003) Rethinking processes of adult learning www.ualberta.ca/~tfenwick/ext/pubs/print/adultlearning.htm

Furlong, J (2004) BERA at 30. Have we come of age? *British Educational Research Journal*, 30(3): 343 – 358

Fogel, A, Lyra, M and Valsiner, J (1997) *Dynamics and Indeterminism in Developmental and Social Processes*. New Jersey: Lawrence Erlbaum

Flyvbjerg, B (2001) *Making Social Science Matter*. Cambridge: Cambridge University Press

Gorrard, S, Rees, G, Fevre, R and Welland, T (2001) Lifelong learning trajectories: some voices of those 'in transit', *International Journal of Lifelong Education*, 20(3): 169 – 187

Goldstein, J (2000) Emergence: a construct amid a thicket of conceptual snares, *Emergence* 2(1): 5 – 22

Guba, E and Lincoln, Y (1998) Competing paradigms in qualitative research, in: Denzin, N and Lincoln, Y (eds) *The Landscape of Qualitative Research*. London: Sage

Haggis, T. (2004a) Meaning, identity and 'motivation': expanding what matters in understanding learning in Higher Education? *Studies in Higher Education*, 29(3): 335 – 352

Haggis, T. (2004b) Constructions of learning in Higher Education: metaphor, epistemology and complexity, in: Satterthwaite, J, Atkinson, E and Martin, W (eds) *The Disciplining of Education: new languages of power and resistance*. (Discourse, Power, Resistance Series Volume 2.) Stoke on Trent: Trentham Books: 181 – 197

Hammersley, M (1984) Some Reflections Upon the Macro-Micro Problem in the Sociology of Education, *The Sociological Review, 32(2): 316-324*

Hammersley, M (2002) *Educational Research: Policymaking and Practice.* London, Paul Chapman

Hammersley, M and Atkinson, P (1995) (2nd Edition) *Ethnography.* London: Routledge

Johnson, S (2001) *Emergence.* London: Penguin

Kaufmann, J (2001) Oppositional feminist ethnography: what does it have to offer adult education? American Educational Research Conference Proceedings www.edst.educ.ubc.ca/aerc/2001/2001kaufmann.htm

Llewelyn, S (2003) What counts as 'theory' in qualitative management and accounting research? *Accounting, Auditing and Accountability Journal,* 16(4): 662 – 708

Moran, D (2000) *Introduction to Phenomenology.* London: Routledge

Osberg, D and Biesta, G (2003) Complexity, Representation and the Epistemology of Schooling. Proceedings of the 2003 Complexity Science and Educational Research Conference, Edmonton, Canada, October: 83 – 99 Available at www.complexityandeducation.ca

Parker, S (1997) *Reflective Teaching in the Postmodern World.* Buckingham: Open University Press

Richardson, K (2000) *Developmental Psychology: How nature and nurture interact.* London: Macmillan

Silverman, D (2001) *Interpreting Qualitative Data.* London: Sage

Smeyers, P (2001) Qualitative versus quantitative research design: a plea for para-digmatic tolerance in educational research, *Journal of Philosophy of Education,* 35(3): 477 – 495

Stehr, N and Grundmann, R (2001) The authority of complexity, *British Journal of Sociology,* 52(2): 313-329

Stronach, I and MacLure, M (1997) *Educational Research Undone.* Buckingham: Open University Press

Sumara, D, Davis, B and Laidlaw, L (2001) Canadian identity and curriculum theory: an ecological, postmodern perspective, *Canadian Journal of Education,* 26(2): 144 – 163

Valsiner, J (1998) *The Guided Mind.* Massachusetts: Harvard University Press

7

Critique and practice: closing the pedagogic gap

SUE CLEGG

Sue Clegg takes up the issues raised by Tamsin Haggis, interrogating the relationship between critical theoretical work on education and the development of policy and practice, and challenging the assumption that thinking, at the level of theoretical abstraction, will by itself show us what needs to be done: that all we need to do is to get our theory right and then put it into practice. Looking at the gaps between educational theory and practice, Clegg puts forward a way of connecting abstract theory and day-to-day practice that moves beyond the weary rehearsal of conventional discussions of this old divide, reconciling research 'for' and research 'about' higher education. She is thinking carefully about thinking – and arguing for a strenuous and sensitive engagement with practice. This chapter prepares us for the deeply theorised resistance-in-action celebrated in Lambert's performance poem.

Introduction

The impetus for this chapter came out of attempts to intervene in a series of debates that are taking place in higher education both nationally and internationally, and also out of a set of local concerns about how the sorts of research I am engaged in relate to practice. I was struck that theory to practice gaps appeared to be more amenable of resolution at the level of research into learning and teaching – what Macfarlane (2004) following Malcolm and Zukas (2001) describes as

113

'for' higher education, rather than work 'about' higher education. Yet the critical voice as exemplified by *Discourse, Power, Resistance* must include broader 'about' higher education questions involving the social, political and economic location of contemporary discourses of higher education. Yet, arguably, it is this voice that is most disconnected, most obscurely theoretical, furthest from practice. In part this is reflected in my own work. The work I do in collaboration with colleagues is closest to the practical artistry of teaching, and has the most immediate impact (Clegg, 2004a). However, it could also be argued that it is susceptible to deconstruction as contributing to erosion of teacher autonomy insofar as it becomes complicit in (well-meaning) attempts at influencing policy on the ground. Moreover, I still feel compelled to write critically 'about' higher education; I think rightly so. It is only through a broader awareness of the relations of higher education that we can come to any understanding of the contradictions and dilemmas we face. This understanding at the most fundamental level impinges on the practice of higher education in terms of what is possible. It provides the basis of critical social science thinking. However, the 'pedagogic gap' Malcolm and Zukas (2001) locate does not seem capable of any easy closure. There are two strands to this argument; one epistemological, about the relationship of theoretical knowledge to practice-based knowledge, the other political, which concerns the relationship of critique to practice as social action, both within and outside the academy. Both strands imply collective realisation: practice is irreducibly social. I therefore conclude the chapter with some comments about the effects on me personally of FAAB (Hey *et al*, 2003), and also some reflections based on my attempts to initiate action around one of the most basic of bourgeois feminist demands: gender equity in higher education.

The chapter will, therefore, interrogate the relationship between critical theoretical work on higher education and the development of policy and practice in higher education. In particular it will take up the themes of evidence-based practice and the idea of Institutional Research (IR) which are prevalent in thinking about higher educational research and represent the ideologically dominant account of theory to practice links. The rhetoric of these models risks producing knowledge for domestication rather than critique (Land, 2001). However, the relationship between critical work and practice is by no means straightforward. The importance of Schön's (1983, 1987) problematic of developing an epistemology of practice still confronts us in theorising the relationship between research and practice. There is no simple relationship between abstract theoretical and empirical work, and the practical wisdom of professional practice. Moreover, in my own case, I am working at one remove in an academic development unit, so my relationship to pedagogic practice is primarily through dialogue with staff and in the formulation of policy. Collaborative research with colleagues creates the conditions for this dialogue around the purposes of research and its translation into practice contexts. However, even under these conditions there are issues of different voice, both between researchers, practitioners and policy makers, but also in the sorts of speech and writing that emerge from projects. The critical voice appears the most abstract and removed from practice; closer to practice the degree of control over the conditions of practice tends to restrict the possibilities for radical change. While small changes take place on the ground, critical rhetoric fails to connect, and dialogues in spaces like the conferences on Discourse, Power, Resistance remain at a distance from the messy and increasingly more difficult realities of mass higher education. At the DPR conference FAAB (Hey *et al*, 2003) reasserted (as they did at BERA, 2003) the political purpose of critique in a joyous, funny, collective dramatisation of the conditions of work in higher education, reminding us that change is a collective political project, not just the work of theory. This chapter will attempt to reconsider the relationship between critique and practice in the light of that experience.

The structure of the chapter follows from these concerns. The first section begins by examining the current debates about Institutional Research (see LTSN, 2004, The Association for Institutional Research 2004) and evidence-based practice (see Evans and Benefield, 2001) as a way of locating the epistemological problems of theory and practice. This part of the chapter reprises some of the problems of simplistic theory/evidence/practice linkages which have often been characterised as falling into that broadest of all epistemological catch-alls – positivism. While this might seem epistemological old-hat, it remains work constantly in progress because the underlying impetus to provide objective criteria and measures for audit and policy remains an ever-present social reality. This section concludes with some thoughts, based in a critical realist epistemology, that attempt not a resolution but at least a more satisfactory statement of the problem. The second section considers the burgeoning area of research 'for' higher education or, as it is sometimes described, pedagogical research. In this section I look at some of the limitations of these traditions and consider how such work might be located in relation to the idea of critical pedagogy which connects work both 'for' and 'about' higher education. Section three looks more closely at the critical work about higher education and considers the linkages to higher education practice. The final section, rhetorically titled 'beyond pessimism', considers practice as social and collective action involving the struggle for a public voice, space and pleasure[1] in transforming relations within higher education and beyond.

Institutional Research and Evidence-based Practice

Debates about the relationship between research/evidence and practice have recently re-surfaced in two dominant guises in higher education: institutional research and evidence-based practice. Both are research 'for' higher education in the broader sense of being in the service of improvement, and neither is new. Institutional research has a longer, largely US (The Association for Institutional Research, 2004) and European (EAIR, 2004) pedigree, but has been recently taken up in the UK context through the Generic LTSN led by Norman Jackson and seems likely to continue under the auspices of the Higher Education Academy (2004). At the same time the migration of evidence-based practice from its origins in medicine, through health and social policy into education, has continued (Evans and Benefield, 2001), and is manifest in higher education in the debate about the systematic review of Progress Files (Gough *et al*, 2003), which was the first of its kind in the sector. While neither of these traditions lay any claim to critique, both claim a relationship to practice and policy making. The debates about the utility of these approaches have, therefore, yet again brought to the fore the issues of the relationship of theory to practice. The gap between research and scholarship, between evidence and practice, has attracted much attention since Schön's (1983) attempt at developing an epistemology of practice. He pointed out that data produced in the research domain, usually under positivist assumptions, cannot simply be translated into practice. Following

Schön (1983) we can argue that, in principle, the relationship between theory and action is not a simple linear one. However, both the dominant model of IR, and the sorts of systematic review procedures preferred in the evidence-based movement appear to be premised on pre-Schönian notions of research and dissemination (McCormack *et al*, 2001).

The dominant US style of IR privileges objective data, often quantitative, as the basis for policy and action. It also separates the act of producing and presenting data, usually carried out by professional institutional researchers, from the act of policy formation or practical pedagogy in response to these data, enacted by manager academics or teachers. Yet this sort of separation, and the linkages presumed, are precisely the ones that Schön critiqued. The existence of this gap has been commented on by contributors to the public e-mail discussions that have been initiated though the Generic LTSN. Contributors have emphasised the situated, context-specific nature of practice and the desire of practitioners to know why something works rather than simply that it does under certain conditions. Indeed, this concern with the explanatory power of research is fundamental as the conditions of practice, whether they be policy-orientated or pedagogical, are always specific. If practitioners are to make sense of what the research means for them, then this must involve an understanding of the underlying processes so that adjustments can be made that suit the particular circumstances of practice. Equally, in order to develop and implement institutional policy, policy makers need an understanding of their local institutional and disciplinary cultures (Henkel, 2000), which are highly variable. The ability to translate a knowledge of general principles into practice forms the essence of practical artistry, and is the basis of professionalism of any sort.

The context within which IR is currently being debated, moreover, is shaped by the broader picture and the debate that has been raging about evidence-based practice within the wider educational community and beyond (eg Evans and Benefield, 2001). The terms of this debate are in many respects also reverting to pre-Schönian epistemological assumptions with the development of centres dedicated to synthesizing findings, which are then disseminated to policy makers and practitioners as the evidence-base for action (McCormack *et al*, 2001). These centres include the Evidence for Policy and Practice

Information and Co-ordinating Centre (2003), which was established in 1993 'to address the need for a systematic approach to the organisation and review of evidence-based work on social interventions' (The Evidence for Policy and Practice Information and Co-ordinating Centre, 2003). This aim mirrors similar developments in health care; the Cochrane Collaboration (2003) was set up in 1993 as an international organisation involved with the preparation of systematic reviews. These initiatives have at their core the idea of informing policy and practice based on using evidence sifted through systematic review. Practitioners, policy makers, and users are then expected to take evidence neutrally conceived, and apply it to practice. The attractions of this model are obvious and derive from the evident advances in medicine, where the pace of change means that practitioners need good summaries as aids to clinical decision-making. The extension of the evidence-based movement outside the biomedical field into health care and social policy more generally, however, is hugely controversial (Elliot, 2001, French, 2002, Oakley, 2000, 2001, Stronach and Hustler, 2001). Moreover, the evidence-based movement is implicated with a more general distrust of professional judgement in delivering quality, and acts as a mechanism for rationing services.

These developments have inevitably found their way into higher education. The first systematic review looked at Progress Files (the UK misnomer for Personal Development Planning), although it is worth noting that this occurred after national policy had been decided (QAA, 2001) and acted as a confirmatory rationale rather than informing the policy-making process (see Lather, 2003). Such reviews, however, fall far short of knowledge practitioners need for understanding. Systematic reviews aggregate findings from chapters located by means of standardized search terms and sifted for quality based on the utilization of procedures which approximate to the randomized control trials and which, therefore, report clear outcome measures from the research. However, practitioners need to understand the underlying mechanisms in order to make professional judgments about the relevance of findings in their own practice context. These will inevitably be different from the context of gold-standard randomised control trials designed as isolated programme evaluations (Pawson, 2002a, 2002b). In the example of the systematic review of Progress Files, the authors were able to conclude that personal development planning worked, but they explicitly declined to offer an analysis of how or why this might be so, as their chosen methodology explicitly precluded this objective. Proponents might wish to argue that this is merely a first stage. However, this is somewhat disingenuous because, if the assumptions underlying systematic review are faulty, then its conclusions must be of questionable value. Systematic review is premised on a procedural understanding of objectivity and rigour, rather than the search for understanding; a different approach is required rather than simply building on flawed foundations (Pawson, 2002a, 2002b). Indeed, basing further work on Personal Development Planning on the existing systematic review is likely to compound the problem, since it will direct attention to disparate studies unified only by the form of investigator intervention and the reporting of outcomes, rather than debating what the mechanisms might be. More of the same will, therefore, not rectify its flaws; rather a different approach is required, which begins with thinking about the hows and whys of successful interventions. The confirmatory evidence from the systematic review of Progress Files might help bolster compliance, but by its very nature cannot provide insight into the development of practical pedagogies (Clegg, 2004b).

This is not the first time such arguments have been made. The development of action research was one response to attempting to resolve the problem of the gaps between the contexts of research and those of practice. But this approach has been attacked for not producing the sorts of generalisable empirical data which the evidence-based movement presumes can be derived from large-scale studies or Random Control Trials (RCTs). The core issue is about what sorts of knowledge can impact on practice. This is not a question of method as such: large-scale surveys and well-designed RCTs have a place alongside qualitative inquiry, and rational theoretical argument. My argument is that we still need a fundamentally Schönian approach to theory/practice gaps, and that the challenge of developing an epistemology of practice is as pressing now as it was three decades ago. The evidence-based policy movement and IR movement aspire to address the gap through the provision of better data, but data as such are not the core of the problem.

'For' Higher Education

Research 'for' higher education is burgeoning and in many instances is conducted in close collaboration with practitioners, if not by practitioners themselves. We now have numerous reports of practice, often in the form of qualitative case studies, which describe various innovative approaches to practice and student responses to them (for example in the ILTHE Journal *Active Learning*). Because these reports describe the practitioners' underlying philosophies or approaches to learning and teaching, these case studies appear to offer greater insight into the hows and whys of practice. Certainly many can claim to be close to practice and have an impact on the teams of practitioners who are involved in innovation. Moreover, because of the ways these are taken up by academic developers, curriculum designers, and through the formal and informal institutional and national networks, they can influence thinking in particular discipline areas or indeed predispose practitioners to adopt new technologies, as in the case of e-learning (for examples see *ALT-J*). Interestingly, in the debates about IR there has been an expressed desire on the part of some participants to share practitioner accounts, or 'vignettes'of practice, as a more practical source of inspiration. However, much of this sort of research and evaluation is susceptible to the critique outlined above. It can fairly claim to narrow the theory-practice gap socially and organisationally, but remains rooted in the local and descriptive, and is often lacking any convincing theorisation about why things appear to be working rather than that they do. Moreover, there is an ever-present danger that successes are reported in a self-justificatory parade which is increasingly encouraged by the cultures of audit and compliance. In other words, this research could be characterised as involving domestication rather than critique (Land, 2001), taking the status quo as given in trying to find out how we might do things technically better, rather than questioning the purposes behind what we are doing.

Work which apparently has greater claims for sophistication both in terms of its methodology and its attempts at theorisation, and can justifiably be argued to have had a huge impact on thinking in higher education, can be identified from within the phenomenographic tradition (Marton, Hounsell and Entwistle, 1997). This work has given higher education a number of influential concepts including, notoriously, deep, surface and strategic learning. However, as Haggis (2003) has argued, this work on student conceptions of learning is limited in its theoretical scope, and has ignored the more critical questions of purpose and social location. With no disrespect to the originators of the phenomenographic approach or to contemporaries working within that tradition, one could argue that the belief in the benefits of deep learning has become one of the truisms of practice, sitting alongside reflective practice as one of the mantras of higher education (Ecclestone, 1996). In this context it is interesting to note that work that is emerging from the ESRC TLRP 2 funded project led by Entwistle (ESRC, 2004), is beginning to complicate our understanding of ways of thinking and practising and has led him to unpack concepts such as 'constructive alignment' (Entwistle, 2003). This work is having to grapple with tutors' conceptions of subject-influenced ways of knowing, which bring the local and the global into a closer relationship, as disciplinary epistemologies are simultaneously both local and intimately connected to international currents in disciplinary thinking. The advantage of this work, and hopefully more large-scale funded projects, is that it can connect theoretical development with comparative data sets and systematically explore the contextual factors which characterise small-scale case study work.

My own work with colleagues might be characterised as falling between these two forms. It is based on small-scale local case studies, but aspires to a degree of theoretical sophistication and to elements of critique. In much of my ongoing work, however, my relationship is at one remove, since I am helping colleagues explore their own practice. The process involves the research team of which I am part collecting and analysing data in close collaboration with colleagues, but essentially on their behalf (Clegg, 2004a). This distinguishes it from both the traditions of critical pedagogy and action research where the stuff of the practice is the teachers' own direct engagement in the classroom. Some people would advocate these as the ideal stances for knowledge production in higher education, based on the traditions in other sectors of education. However, leaving aside for one moment the difficulties in any setting, there seem to be particular reasons why action research is likely to have limited application in higher education. Action research depends on socialisation into a particular set of values associated with teaching, whereas higher education teaching has barely begun to reach the status of a profession in this respect (Macfarlane, 2004). The dominant form of enculturation in higher education, despite recent changes, is still into a discipline and disciplinary ways of thinking. Given the rewards and status associated with disciplines it seems likely that only a minority of academics are going to make pedagogy their major research focus.[2] In practice, therefore, collaboration and interdisciplinarity are the rule. This can be immensely creative, but begs the question of the extent to which it is possible to sustain critical practice in what are increasingly unfavourable conditions. Given the enormous changes in higher education systems and the external socio-economic pressures it might be argued that the conditions for critical pedagogy are being eroded and that what critique accomplishes is merely sitting on the sideline crying foul. The possibilities of radical praxis are, thereby, considerably undermined.

'About' Higher Education

The preceding sections have traced two different approaches to research 'for' higher education. Both rest, to a large extent, on a bracketing out of the larger questions of the purposes and conditions of higher educational practice. Yet there is now a large critical literature that analyses the relations of higher education itself and takes higher education as such as its object of study. Barnett's (2003) recent work identifying pernicious ideologies is one example, but there is also a large feminist literature that has spoken about the relations inside higher education. Mahony and Zmroczek (1997, also Hey, 2003) have edited work looking at the complex ways in which classed, gendered, racialised and sexualised forms of domination continually intersect the ways in which higher education is lived, while both Reay (2004) and Hey (2001) have analysed the subaltern position of contract researchers and women's marginalised role within the academy. This literature is interesting because it speaks to ways of being inside the academy in a way that both illuminates and connects to the broader social formation, and also acts as a critique of some of the dominant accounts in the sociological literature which take class to be a 'zombie category' (Hey, 2003; see also Clegg, 2004b). This literature which is too large to review here, and includes multiple-theoretical stances, stands as a powerful testament to the power of critique. However, with some exceptions, the tone of much of this work is highly theoretical. It seems (as in this chapter) that, when we seek to criticise in order to give our voice legitimacy in the academy, we use its clothes. This is, of course, both understandable and legitimate. The processes we are analysing are complex; theory is not window-dressing. Indeed, without theoretical work we are likely to be left with naïve ideas of evidence, of 'what-works', and the sort of reductive analysis which reduces problems to plain speech and a quick political fix. However, the relationship of critique to practice remains problematic in part because much critical work points to resilience of forms of domination. What then of the spaces for critical practice?

One of the ways of trying to link questions of theory to practice in higher education has been through the idea of critical pedagogy, whereby theoretical critique is linked to the experiences of students in ways that could connect to broader social action. To quote from Elizabeth Ellsworth, who, writing as long ago as 1989, began in turn to shed doubt on critical pedagogy as a way out of the impasse:

> Students often asked what was meant by critical .....and I referred them to the answers provided in the literature. For example, critical pedagogy supported classroom analysis and rejection of oppression, injustice, inequality, silencing of marginalised voices, and authoritarian social structures. Its critique was launched from the position of the 'radical' educator who recognises and helps students to recognise and name injustice, who empowers students to act against their own and others' oppression (including oppressive school structures), who criticises and transforms her or his own understanding in response to the understandings of students. (Ellsworth, 1989: 299-300)

Ellsworth noted that these descriptions exist at a very high level of abstraction and, moreover, do not engage with the specifics of real interventions in the classroom. Her chapter analysed her own attempts, and what she described as the politics of partial narrative, whereby different groups of students related in different ways to their experience of participating in her course 'Media and Anti-racist Pedagogies' which became 'Coalition 607' out of a recognition of multiple voices. Her analysis problematised the idea of empowerment and the failure of critical pedagogy to situate the nature of teacher knowledge. As she rightly observed: 'Critical pedagogies are always implicated in the very structures they are trying to change'(Ellsworth, 1989:310).

Rather than critical pedagogy, Ellsworth advocated the value of 'defiant speech' (Ellsworth, 1989:310). Drawing on the work of both Lather (1998) and Ellsworth (1989), Perriton and Reynolds (2004) have more recently argued that refusal may actually be a more liberating stance. They, like the contributors to the special edition *Gender and Education* edited by Tanton (1999), have drawn attention to the gaps between theory and practice in the discourse of empowerment itself.

These arguments are, of course, tied up with a much larger set of debates about traditions within Marxism and post-structuralism. However, I want to make a rather more modest and prosaic set of connections. Firstly, writing which crosses the boundaries of 'for' and 'about' higher education and has the confidence to use understandings of the micro-dynamics of higher education to pry open the larger political issues (and by virtue of this dialectic the reverse), seems to me immensely fruitful; Ellsworth's paper remains important because she does this. A more recent example from an avowed Marxist perspective is by Mike Gonzales (2003), and the work I cited by Reay (2004) and Hey (2003) would also fall into that category, taking the minutiae of the lived experience of higher education (in their case contract research) to cast light on its real relations. All three examples in different ways involve politics of refusal: a refusal of indifference (Gonzales, 2003), a refusal of the normalisation of inferiority (Reay, 2004; Hey, 2003) and a refusal of abstract accounts that in their turn become oppressive (Ellsworth, 1989). The second connection that I want to make is about the importance of time and history in our analyses; critical pedagogy itself comes out of particular socio-economic circumstances and possibilities. Reflecting on critical pedagogy, Giroux (2001), one of its leading theorists, recognises the ways in which the recent past has been more hostile. The analysis of the conditions of higher education, therefore, connects to the possibilities of action on it and in it. This is evident for example in the renewed energy that writers such as Gonzales (2003) take from the growth of new forms of activism outside it, and of course is a major theme in much of Segal's (1987, 1999) writing in chronicling the changing relationships between feminist theorising in relation to the fortunes of the women's activism. The conditions are certainly not of our own choosing; but, nonetheless, people continue to remake history. The question of practice inside the academy, and the relationship of theory to practice are, therefore, not solely individual and theoretical, they are public, collective, embodied and actual.

Beyond Pessimism

While there are more than adequate grounds for the pessimism of the intellect in relation to the scope for practice in higher education, I also want to suggest that the relationship of critique and practice must, most importantly, involve actions. Collective activity is informed by theory, and in turn informs theory, but is not reducible to it. In Collier's (1997) example the concrete sciences, such as singing, cannot be reproduced from abstract science, such as the physiology of voice production; the performance as such matters. The same is true for teaching or any other practical art. This is why I have argued for the importance of work that offers accounts of the lived realities of peda-gogy and practice in higher education. Our understanding of theory and practice gaps can be illuminated by a more sophisticated episte-mology; but praxis, irreducibly, requires action.

In my conclusions I want to consider some small-scale interventions in higher education, rather than the broader politics of movements outside it. The first involves an event which took place at the last British Educational Research Conference (BERA, 2003) in many ways the official voice for educational research in the UK (with its counterparts in Europe EERA and in America AERA). Billed as a normal symposium: *The state we're in – education, education/ research and education/researchers – a feminist review* by Hey *et al*, the abstract promised:

> This will be an interactive session comprising a series of critical feminist commentaries that offer alternative and alternately creative – de- and re-constructions. The organisation of the symposium will be innovative. We intend to run this symposium thematically, dia-logically and multi-vocally, linking in and out of a number of themes and it will therefore comprise contributions of varying lengths and modes of delivery rather than a series of distinct, indivi-dual chapters, though for communicative and administrative clarity's sake we have pragmatically represented the narrative of the ideas of the symposium in a linear format and attached designated 'author(s)'. Our themes centre on exploring the complex relation-ship between theory and practice as these are presently being en-gineered. (Hey *et al*, 2003:1)

What followed was funny, engaging, moving; involving pastiche and parody, rewrites of classic comedy sketches and favourite musical anthems (*River Deep, Mountain High*), and also quiet statements in lyrical language of the pain that working in higher education can cause. As a bitterly funny commentary on the élitism of higher education, and the collusive ways in which we as academics are complicit in the competitive practices of research selectivity and as a defiant enactment of the politics of refusal – it was simply glorious! As individuals these are women academics who have made major contributions to the theoretical literature dealing with post-compulsory education; but in breaking out of its theoretical conventions they used (and parodied) theory in ways that gave hope, certainly to me, and judging by the riotous applause, to most of the audience. This was certainly not the usual reaction of a group of academics at a BERA symposium. Why it was so important, I would argue, is that it connected theory and practice, and showed that we can act, and can defy the seemingly endless ways in which the practices of higher education seek to compartmentalise us and our students.

It was also a challenge for us all to act. Many different forms of small refusals of indifference, and of positive engagement by students and staff still occur in higher education. The pleasures of academia remain in those spaces and places in which real communicative action takes place. What is often lacking are ways of making these into public collective acts. There are numerous ways of making connections, but making the time and spaces in which to realise collective intent seems of central importance (Clegg *et al*, 2003). This may involve action around the most basic and straightforward issues. Everyone acknowledges that gender equity (even in its crudest sense of equal pay) has not been achieved in higher education, despite the fact that everyone is signed-up to espousing equity as a fundamental value. Yet, as anyone who has ever done this (in my case for three decades!) will know, when one speaks about the issue in committee meetings and the like, a weary embarrassment or slight irritation not infrequently follows as people are forced to listen *again* to 'that woman'. The refusal to be silenced seems to me one of the most simple of political acts. However, many of the women's networks that had sustained activisms of even this puny sort have been eroded. Bird (2001), for example, documents the ways in which interdisciplinary experiments that sustained programmes such as women's studies have been eroded. What I have found is that even the small act of organising a meeting, bringing people together to discuss gender equity, can be enormously rewarding. About 80 people recently attended such a meeting addressed by Miriam David, leading to discussions about what we could do. What was astonishing was not what we concluded in terms of desired improvement, or even our understanding of the situation, which at one level was very basic and could have been said at any point in the last three decades. David (2003) is quite correct in her analysis of the ways in which things have also changed, but it seems that the real pleasure was in collectively reasserting some very basic demands. This is not an isolated example. Sheila Scranton at Leeds Metropolitan University has recently revived their women's network, of which I was a member for many years, and reports that the response has been the same. People are delighted and revitalised by being part of a collective voicing.

I recognise that this chapter has only touched on the issues; but I have attempted to reassert the importance of continually trying to connect critique and practice. The chapter started with IR and evidence-based practice, and I think it is important to recognise that there is an official narrative of the connection of academic work and research to practice that does indeed drive the policy agenda, even if, as Lather (2003) so pithily reminded us, as an *ex post facto* rationalisation. So critique has to work to continually re-demonstrate the epistemological and political flaws of the theory to practice connections posited by these traditions. However, if we only do that we will have failed, as the realities of higher education will continue to change from under us. We also need to engage with the positive politics of refusal, and the joyous engagement with collective projects that the concept of practice must involve. The examples in this chapter involve feminist forms of action, but argument is not confined to these. Higher education itself produces gender divisions, and hence solidarities, in particularly powerful ways. However, if one looks beyond higher education to the anti-war movement and to the truly global scale of the challenges, then solidarities based on particularity will not be enough; but the global and local do connect, and above all, to borrow from Gonzales (2003), we must act 'against indifference'.

References

Barnett, R (2003) *Beyond all Reason: Living with ideology in the university.* Buckingham: Open University Press

Bird, E (2001) Disciplining the Interdisciplinary: radicalism and the academic curriculum, *British Journal of Sociology of Education* 22(4) : 463-478

Clegg, S (2005) Evidence-based practice in educational research: a critical realist critique of systematic review, in: *Sociology of Education*, 26(3) (Forthcoming)

Clegg, S (2004a) Using Research to Inform Policy and Practice LTSN Generic Centre and SEDA, *Institutional Research Conference*, Sheffield Hallam University: 18th February

Clegg, S (2004b) Critical Reading: Progress Files and the production of the autonomous learner, *Teaching in Higher Education*, 9(3): 287-298

Clegg, S, Rowland, S, Mann, S, Davidson, M and Clifford, V (2003) Reconceptualising Academic Development : Reconciling pleasure and critique in safe spaces *Exploring Academic Development in Higher Education.: Issues of Engagement* at Clare College: University of Cambridge, September

Cochrane Collaboration (2003) http://www.cochrane.org/docs/descrip.htm Accessed 1.11.03

Collier, A (1997) Unhewn Demonstrations, *Radical Philosophy*, 81: 22-26

David, M (2003) *Personal and Political: Feminisms, Sociology and Family Lives.* Stoke-on-Trent: Trentham Books

EAIR (2004) http://www.eair.nl/ Accessed 29.03.04

Ecclestone, K (1996) The reflective practitioner: mantra or a model for emancipation, *Studies in the Education of Adults*, 28(2): 146-161

Elliott, J (2001) Making Evidence-Based Practice Educational, *British Educational Research Journal*, 27(5): 555-576

Ellsworth, E (1989) Why doesn't this feel empowering? Working through the repressive myths of critical pedagogy, *Harvard Educational Review*, 59(3): 297-324

Entwistle, N (2003) Concepts and Conceptual Frameworks Underlying the ETL project Occasional Report 3 http://www.ed.ac.uk/etl/publications.html Accessed 29.03.04

ESRC (2004) Teaching and Learning Research Programme http://www.tlrp.org/ Accessed 29.03.04

Evans, J and Benefield, P (2001) Systematic Reviews of Educational Research: does the medical model fit?, *British Educational Research Journal*, 27(5): 527-542

French, P (2002) What is the evidence on evidence-based nursing? An epistemological concern, *Journal of Advanced Nursing*, 37: 250-257

Giroux, H A (2001) *Theory and Resistance in Education.* Westport: Bergin and Garvey

Gonzales, M (2003) Against Indifference, *Teaching in Higher Education*, 8(4): 493-503

Gough, D A, Kiwan, D, Sutcliffe, S, Simpson, D, and Houghton, N A (2003) Systematic map and synthesis review of the effectiveness of personal development planning for improving student learning, http://eppi.ioe.ac.uk/ EPPIWebContent/reel/review_groups/EPPI/LTSN/LTSN_June03.pdf Accessed 26.1.04

Haggis, T (2003) Constructing Images of Ourselves? A critical investigation into 'approaches to learning' research in Higher Education, *British Educational Research Journal*, 29(1): 89-104

Henkel, M (2000) *Academic Identities and Policy Change in Higher Education*. London: Jessica Kingsley

Hey, V (2001) The construction of academic time: sub/contracting academic labouring research, *Journal of Education Policy*, 16(1): 67-84

Hey, V (2003) Joining the Club? Academia and Working-class Femininities, *Gender and Education*, 15(3): 319-335

Hey, V, Brine, J, Hey, V, Lambert, C, Leathwood, C, Meo, A and Reay, D (2003) The state we're in – education, education/research and education/researchers – a feminist review, BERA Conference, Hariot-Watt, Edinburgh, 11-13 September

Land, R(2001) Agency, context and change in academic development, *International Journal for Academic Development*, 6(1): 4-20

Lather, P (1998) Critical pedagogy and its complicities: A praxis of stuck places, *Educational Theory*, 48(4): 487-497

Lather, P (2003) This Is Your Father's Paradigm: Government Intrusion and the Case of Educational Research, *Discourse, Power, Resistance; New Directions, New Moves*, University of Plymouth, April 2003

LTSN Generic Centre What does 'evidence based' mean in higher education? http://www.ltsn.ac.uk/genericcentre/index.asp?docid=20033 Accessed 29.03.04

Macfarlane, B (2004) *Teaching with integrity: the ethics of higher education practice*. London: RoutledgeFalmer

Mahony, P and Zmroczek, C (eds) (1997) *Class Matters: 'working class' women's perspectives on social class*. London: Taylor and Francis

Malcolm, J and Zukas, M (2001) Bridging pedagogic gaps: conceptual discontinuities in higher education, *Teaching in Higher Education*, 6(1): 33-42

Marton, F, Hounsell, D and Entwistle, N (eds) (1997) *The Experience of Learning*. Edinburgh: Scottish Academic Press

McCormack, B, Kitson, A, Harvey, G, Rycroft-malone, J, Titchen, A and Seers, K (2001) Getting evidence into practice: the meaning of 'context', *Journal of Advanced Nursing*, 38: 94-104

Oakley, A (2000) *Experiments in Knowing: Gender and Method in the Social Sciences*. Cambridge: Polity Press

Oakley, A (2001) Making Evidence-based Practice Educational: a rejoinder to John Elliott, *British Educational Research Journal*, 27(5): 575-576

Pawson, R (2002a) Evidence-based Policy: In Search of a Method, *Evaluation*, 8: 157-181

Pawson, R (2002b) Evidence-based Policy: The Promise of 'Realist Synthesis', *Evaluation*, 8: 340-358

Perriton, L and Reynolds, M (2004) Critical Management Education: From pedagogy of possibility to pedagogy of refusal?, *Management Learning*, 35(1): 61-
77

QAA, Guidelines for Progress Files (2001) http://www.qaa.ac.uk/crntwork/
progfileHE/guidelines/progfile2001.pdf Accessed 13.1.03

Reay, D (2004) Cultural capitalists and academic habitus: Classed and gendered
labour in UK higher education, *Women's Studies International Forum*, 27:
31-39

Schön, D (1983) *The Reflective Practitioner.* New York: Basic Books

Schön, D A (1987) *Educating the Reflective Practitioner: how professionals think
in action.* New York: Jossey-Bass

Segal, L (1987) *Is the future female?: troubled thoughts on contemporary
feminism.* London: Virago

Segal, L (1999) *Why feminism?: gender, psychology, politics.* Cambridge: Polity

Stronach, I and Hustler, D (2001) Old Whine in New Battles, *British Educational
Research Journal*, 27(5): 523-525

Tanton, M (1999) Special Issue Gender and (management) Education, *Gender and
Education*, 11(3): 245-356

The Association for Institutional Research (2004) http://www.fsu.edu/~air/home.
htm Accessed 29.03.04

The evidence for policy and practice information and co-ordinating centre (2003)
EPPI-Centre: *Introduction*, http://eppi.ioe.ac.uk/EPPIWeb/home.aspx
Accessed 1.11.03

The Higher Education Academy (2004) http://www.heacademy.ac.uk/ Accessed
29.03.04

Notes

1   I would like to thank Val Clifford, Mike Davidson, Sara Mann, and Stephen Rowland
who were co-participates at an invited event *Exploring Academic Development in
Higher Education.: Issues of Engagement* at the University of Cambridge. We collectively authored a chapter *Reconceptualising Academic Development: Reconciling pleasure and critique in safe spaces* during the course of this remarkable conference, which
directly influenced my thinking for this chapter. Although it is difficult to pin down the
exact influences of this experience I would also like to thank the organisers for creating
a wonderfully stimulating environment in which to write and think. I would also like
to thank the members of FAAB for their BERA performance, which also had huge impact on my thinking. Both these events stand out as exemplars of the ability of collective
work to energise and motivate the individual.

2   I would like to thank Dai Hounsell for this insight which followed when I was a dis-
cussant for the TLRP 2 at BERA (2003). Dai argued that the tie to discipline was such
that only a small minority of academics would wish to engage in pedagogic research,
and that collaboration with higher educational researchers was a better characterisation
of the process in practice than action research.

8

'The naming of cats is a difficult matter': how far are government and teachers using the same words to talk about educational concepts?

GILL BOAG-MUNROE

In this chapter, Gill Boag-Munroe explores the dissonances and disjunctions between the language of UK education policy (and of its policing through Ofsted, the Office for Standards in Education) and the language of individual members of the teaching profession, taking as her starting-point the principle that language, thought and action are deeply interwoven, and that an analysis of one will therefore shed light on the others. Boag-Munroe identifies the spaces between these policy and professional discourses as actual and potential sites of teacher resistance, and examines, through a synthesis of post-Vygotskian activity theory and Critical Discourse Analysis, the ways in which teachers construct themselves and their professional activities in opposition to, or resistance against, the imperatives of government requirements and reforms. This chapter offers an example of the complex interactions described by Haggis in the previous chapter, and foreshadows the forms of resistance identified in the following chapter by Ollin.

The naming of cats is a difficult matter,
It isn't just one of your holiday games;
You may think at first I'm as mad as a hatter
When I tell you, a cat must have THREE DIFFERENT
NAMES. (Eliot, 1974:9)

Introduction

This chapter developed from a wider study into how teachers work simultaneously in two activities: the first of which I am for the moment calling schooling, and the second, Initial Teacher Education (ITE). The research arose from my own work as subject and senior mentor in an 11 – 18 secondary school in the English Midlands. Using post-Vygotskyian Activity Theory (see 'Methodology and design of the research' below) I have been investigating the rules; conceptual and linguistic tools, and power relationships within the two activities, and looking at the kinds of tensions and contradictions that arise for the person trying to work simultaneously in both activities. I decided, following Vygotsky's idea that language precedes thought (Vygotsky, 2000, [1934]:218) that an investigation of the conceptual tools should begin with an investigation into the language tools in use in the activities. From analysis of the language and conceptual tools, I could go on to refine my understandings of the other elements of the activities. I offer here some early interpretations of how teachers understand the language tools and power relationships within the activities of schooling and Initial Teacher Education and how they may be resisting them.

Background

Fullan (1991) argues that 'Educational change depends on what teachers do and think – it's as simple as that.' (p 117). Actions are informed by thought, and Stubbs (1996) and Fairclough (1995) argue that if the language of an activity is investigated, it will reveal the underlying assumptions which inform the actors' thinking. If thinking is shaped by language (Vygotsky, 2000 [1934]), and actions are shaped by thought, then if educational change is to happen, the language in which education policy and practice is shaped must also change. There is evidence (see, for example, Fairclough, 2002) that the current Labour government shapes education policy through discourses previously alien to teachers, in order to trigger new ways of thinking about the aims and functions of education. These new discourses are linked to ways in which the government is conducting its foreign and domestic policies – including educational policy – to secure its economic future in a globalised world (Olssen *et al*, 2004). Change, then, is being forced with the aim of securing and expanding the present power base.

If change is happening in education, and if that change is being driven by government policy and language use, then an investigation of the language which teachers use to talk about their work should offer an indication of how far the new language of education as used by government has been adopted by teachers to form their pedagogical concepts, and perhaps how far teacher thinking about education has come into line with government thinking. However, as Argyris and Schön (1992) argue, there is a difference between what teachers may say (espoused theories) and what they do (theories in use). At this stage of my research, I am focusing more on what teachers say – 'espoused theories' – than on what they do.

The literature on ITE policies (e.g. Apple, 2004; Ball, 1994; Bowe *et al*, 1992; Chitty and Dunford, eds, 1999; Cochran-Smith and Fries, 2001; Hodgson and Spours, 1999; Wilkin, 1996) suggests that there are possibly five main strands of thinking currently running through education policy and practice. From the Conservative era 1988 – 1997, the key concepts underlying policy-making generally were neo-conservative and neo-liberal. From the neo-conservative strand emerged language to do with tradition, national culture, moral values, all used to maintain and foster elitism. Such ideas gave rise to a National Curriculum in which were embedded the elitist notions of what is appropriate for children to learn if they are to become good (white, middle-class, entrepreneurial, male) citizens of their nation state. Interwoven with these ideas were those of neo-liberalism, which promoted market forces and introduced competition, targets and marketisation to the education sector. Instead of co-operation between schools, a culture of public-relations glossy self-promotion developed, alongside league tables of results in national tests and Ofsted inspections. (Ofsted is a government department whose self-proclaimed role is to 'improve the quality and standards of education ... through independent inspection and regulation' (Ofsted, 2004).) This ensured that teachers were discouraged from co-operating across schools so that their position in spuriously constructed performance leagues could be maintained.

Developing from this, under New Labour, a discourse of managerialism emerged, using the language of performance, accountability, standards and effectiveness (Fairclough, 2002). Concepts of lifelong learning and knowledge economy were prominent as pillars of the government's policy on education, alongside policies of partnership between government departments and business. These policies were implemented through increased concern with 'delivery of programmes rather than courses which followed specifications instead of syllabi. Education managers were concerned with measuring output, quantifying results. Instead of checking, teachers were to audit or carry out skills audits; instead of keeping records, they monitored, assessed, recorded, reported and were accountable for their pupils' performance. The people or groups acted upon, delivered to, measured or counted were lost under a numerical juggernaut. Targets were to be met, regardless of the ability of those who were being acted on in the classroom to meet the target. As Rowland (2003) says, a regime was established in which '...the teacher should force compliance upon the student, whose response should be one of servility and conformity to expectations.' Under such a regime, '[R]esponsibility for learning (or lack of it) lies with the teacher, not the learner' (p 19). The mechanism of inspection was retained in this strand of thinking, so that command and control of those chosen to implement the policies could be ensured and even increased, whilst the power of the teacher in the classroom was further eroded (Buckingham and Jones, 2001). Rowland (2003) points out that there was a 'political assumption taken to be common sense...that the market will and should be in control' (p 18).

Teachers, on the other hand, were increasingly concerned with issues of professionalism (e.g. Goodson and Hargreaves, eds, 1996; Locke, 2001; Gore and Gitlin, 2004), as they perceived that their autonomy in their workplace had diminished. While teachers' understanding of professionalism was based on a comparison of their work and status with that of lawyers and doctors, government appeared to be conceptualising professionalism for teachers as similar to that for the Armed Forces or Civil Servants, where the employee is regarded as apolitical, and required, as a professional, to carry out the political will of the government of the day. Teachers have traditionally neither defined nor positioned themselves as Civil Servants (although, in effect, it is arguable that they have always been so). Successive governments from the 1980s onwards, though, have manoeuvred teachers, by erosion of power and status, into a position where they can no longer offer the kinds of resistance to education policy rhetoric that they traditionally did (Buckingham and Jones, 2001).

More recent erosions of status have been achieved through government use of the word 'profession' and its lemmas (the root 'profession' with its various suffixes: professional, professionalism, professionally) in ways which exclude the notions of autonomy that teachers are so keen to associate with professionalism, thus kidnapping the concept so that teachers no longer have control of the concept and how it is used. The word as a negotiating tool has been silenced, made to bend to government ways of meaning, so that it no longer has the potency the teacher seeks.

Alongside teacher assertions of their professional status, and to some extent growing out of them, was academic concern to develop teachers as reflective practitioners, (following Schön, 1987) with the ability to interweave theory and practice, evaluate their own performance in order to improve on it, and develop their own action research projects to further improve performance. Reflective practice is about self-awareness and change, about 'respect for the right of individuals to exercise self-direction' (Osterman and Kottkamp, 1993: 185). Concepts of personal power and action, and of behavioural and organisational change, characterise this discourse.

Across these discourses was an increased use of the modifier 'effective' to describe teaching. Harris (1998) reviews the literature relating to 'effective teaching' and sees it as 'highly dependent upon the nature of the educational outcomes and goals that the teaching is aiming to foster' (p179). When used in the specialist way that Harris clearly intends, the concept of 'effective teaching' is meaningful and specific. However, I would argue that in many documents, and specifically those generated by government, the use of the word 'effective' seems simply to suggest that anyone disagreeing with government strategies could not be considered 'effective'. Throughout the Hay McBer Report on Teacher Effectiveness, for example, the word is used so excessively that it is ultimately rendered meaningless, except (and this is a significant exception) to suggest that 'effective' teachers are not only those who are working in prescribed ways, but are somehow a separate, elite group (Hay McBer, 2000).

In this chapter, I aim to present data drawn from three classroom teacher mentors in one school to show how they are participating in or resisting the discourses outlined here.

Methodology and Design of the Research

The conceptual frame of the study is post-Vygotskyan Activity Theory, an analytical heuristic which allows the elements of an activity, defined by its object, to be explored. Following Engeström's model (Engeström *et al*, eds, 1999) there are six elements to an activity: a subject, working on an object to transform it, using tools, and operating within a context of rules, community and division of labour. Analysis of an activity using this heuristic draws out how the focus subject can work and is working on an object, and highlights any tensions or contradictions in the activity. A tension is understood as something which destabilises the activity (Daniels, 2004) but does not cause a change in the activity system to be highlighted. A contradiction is understood as paradox, or concepts which mutually exclude each other: the resolution of the contradiction involves the construction or adaptation of tools to resolve the paradox, and leads to expansive learning through a redefinition of the object (Engeström, 1987). There are four sites in which contradictions can arise (Chaiklin, 2001):

- Primary contradictions arise *within* the constituent components of the activity, for example between one rule and another

- Secondary contradictions arise *between* the components of the activity, for example between object and tool

- Tertiary contradictions arise between the object of one activity and that of an emergent activity

- Quaternary contradictions arise between a newly emergent activity and neighbouring activities with which it overlaps

In my study, I argue that there are two activities being worked in simultaneously: the activity of schooling, which is about the teacher's work with pupils in the classroom; and ITE, which is about the teacher's work with student teachers in the whole school context. (see Figure 1). If a teacher is working in two activities at the same time, the possibilities for secondary, tertiary and quaternary contradictions between the different elements of the activity are increased from the fifteen possibilities in a single activity, to forty-six possibilities within and between two activities. That calculation takes no account of any contradictions which may arise between the subject's work in the two focus activities, and the work in any additional activities they may be acting in or inhabiting. Nor does it take account of the possibilities for primary contradictions: there may be tensions or contradictions between and within the conceptual and linguistic tools in use within a single activity, for example, which constrain the ways in which the subject is able to work on the object. Figure 1 (below) illustrates how the two activities of schooling (1) and ITE (2) overlap. (QCA is the Qualifications and Curriculum Authority, which is responsible for the production of national end-of-key-stage tests, taken by pupils in England at the ages of 7, 11 and 14. TTA is the Teacher Training Agency, which controls Initial Teacher Training through the production of a set of published standards which trainees must meet in order to qualify.)

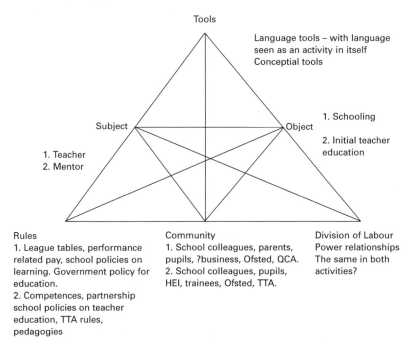

Tools

Language tools – with language seen as an activity in itself
Conceptial tools

Subject

Object

1. Schooling

2. Initial teacher education

1. Teacher
2. Mentor

Rules
1. League tables, performance related pay, school policies on learning. Government policy for education.
2. Competences, partnership school policies on teacher education, TTA rules, pedagogies

Community
1. School colleagues, parents, pupils, ?business, Ofsted, QCA.
2. School colleagues, pupils, HEI, trainees, Ofsted, TTA.

Division of Labour
Power relationships
The same in both activities?

Figure 1: How the Two Activities Overlap

With Vygotsky, (2000 [1934]:212) I believe that there is 'such a close amalgam of thought and language that it is hard to tell whether [a word] is a phenomenon of speech or a phenomenon of thought'. I therefore decided that the best way to understand how the subject teacher was working within the activities was through a study of the language in use in the activities, which would lead me to an understanding of the conceptual tools in use. However, Activity Theory offers no frame for analysing language and I needed to find an additional, compatible frame for this. I resolved this issue by incorporating into each activity an integral activity of language, through which the language tools, rules, community, power relationships and object can be explored to amplify understandings of the elements of the activity under study. The elements of activities are developed in relation to language: for example, language tools are letters, signs, words, paralinguistic features; tones and so on; the rules of language are drawn from grammar and local usages; power is signified by the registers and dominant discourses in use in the language activity (see Figure 2). (For a further discussion of this, see Boag-Munroe, 2004.) The language activity could then be investigated using Critical Discourse Analysis (Fairclough, 1995): analysis of the data using the two frames combined would allow me to develop a more delicate understanding of how teachers were currently working in the two activities. CDA views language as a form of social practice, and analyses discourses to uncover the power relationships which form and are formed by them. Fairclough's version of CDA has been adopted because his concept of 'orders of discourse' – 'the ordered set of discursive practices associated with a particular social domain or institution [...] and boundaries and relationships between them' (Fairclough, 1995:12) chimes with the concepts of 'community' and 'division of labour' in Activity Theory. This interplay of analyses leads to a finer understanding of what is happening within the activity under study.

For the full study, I have studied two cases, one in each of two schools. Each case consists of two mentors (teachers in schools who work with student teachers on their practicum) one of whom works within science, a core subject area (that is, one compulsorily studied by all secondary-age pupils and tested nationally at ages 14 and 16); and the other in a non-core (optional) subject area: Business Studies in one school, Religious Studies in the other. Each school works within a different Initial Teacher Education partnership,: a contractual arrangement between a school and a University or College (referred to hereafter as 'Higher Education Institution' or 'HEI') to provide school-based teaching experience for student teachers.

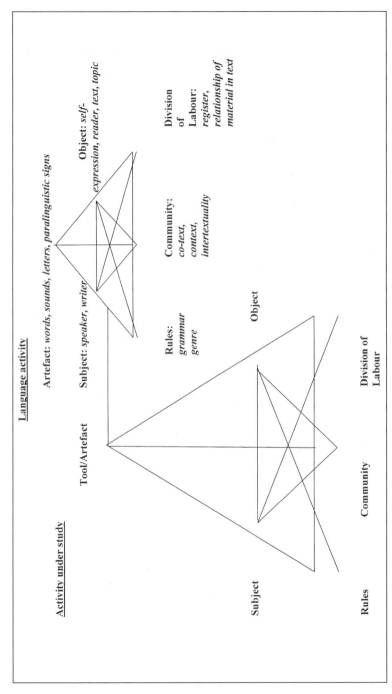

Figure 2: The interrelationship of language and activity (from Boag-Munroe, 2004)

Evidence has been collected in the form of semi-structured interviews with the subject mentors and senior mentors (those teacher mentors with oversight of all initial teacher education in the school) to elicit teacher views about their work in both the classroom and mentoring roles. I have also collected data via the internet, from government documents relating to ITE and classroom teaching and, for the purpose of the present phase of the study, I have used the most recent Ofsted (Office for Standards in Education) report for the school in the study.

The findings presented here emerge from the analysis of some of the data collected from one of the schools in the study, anonymised as Middlemarch School, a 13 to 18 comprehensive school situated on the border of a rural county and a heavily urbanised county in the English Midlands. The subjective and informal voices of the senior mentor ('Will') and two subject mentors ('James' and 'Celia') are heard alongside the objective and formal voice of the school's Ofsted report. Interviews with the three mentors were transcribed and processed through the WordSmith computer programme, which analyses word frequency; concordances specified words; and highlights key words within a corpus. The aim of this was to highlight words which suggest particular discourses in use, or their absence. The Ofsted report was similarly 'WordSmithed', and the two sets of data compared to show whether the two groups – Ofsted and mentors – were using similar lexis. The transcripts and the reports were also analysed using Critical Discourse Analysis (CDA) methods drawn from Fairclough (2003) and Jäger, (2000), to tease out some of the conceptual tools in use by the teachers in the two activities of schooling and ITE, together with their perceptions of rules and power relationships.

Findings
Tools
To find out which discourses teachers were cohabiting with government, I took a cluster of key words from Fairclough's (2002) analysis of government language. I added words which the Word-Smith programme (which provides a computer-generated word frequency list) identified as frequently used by Ofsted which belonged within the discourses inhabited by policymakers; and added the two key words from teacher discourses: 'professional' and 'reflect*'. (An asterisk by the word indicates that the base form of the word and its lemmas –

achieve, achieved, achieves, achievement, for example – were counted.) In addition I investigated the use of words central to the work of teachers: 'teach*' and 'learn*' to see how policy imple- menters actually used the words.

A comparison of the use of these words suggests that teachers are not currently using the key words in the Ofsted discourses, and therefore are not yet entering the policy discourses which are intended to shape their professional activity. Only Will, the senior mentor, inhabits the 'professional' discourse, and only James, the most recently qualified teacher, enters the 'reflective' discourse more than once.

Figure 3: Table to Show Comparative Frequency of Key Word Use by Middlemarch School Mentors and Ofsted

Discourse indicator (total number of lexical items in text)	Will (10,592) Senior Mentor	James (11,117) Bus. Studs. Mentor	Celia (6,382) Biology Mentor	Ofsted (27,226)
Teacher Discourses				
Professional	14	2	1	4
Reflect*	1	4	0	1
Managerialist Discourses				
Accountable	0	0	0	3
Achieve*	2	12	0	35
Assess*	1	0	0	52
Deliver*	0	1	1	0
Effective	0	0	0	32
Manage*	13	18	1	54
Measure*	3	0	0	9
Performance	6	2	0	21
Progress*	4	1	1	148
Quality	0	0	0	55
Target*	2	6	0	26
Neo-conservative discourse				
Standards	0	2	0	109
Common to all				
Learn*	9	7	5	81
Teach*	95	68	49	229

Only James talks about 'standards', though the other two refer dismissively to 'tick* boxes' when they want to indicate the competences or standards to be met by students[1]. Nor is 'effective' a word which teachers use to talk about their work, possibly because they see it as otiose. Together these two absences suggest an emerging resistance to the discourses used by the more powerful member of the education community.

Resistance arguably also emerges from the persistence of the focus of teachers on teaching rather than learning. If, as current debates on education suggest, the focus of work in the activity of schooling is on learning outcomes, then 'learn*' should be the dominant concept. However, 'teach*' is used almost three times as frequently as learn* by Ofsted, but almost ten times more frequently by teachers, showing that, in the interview context at least, they are focusing on what *they* do in the classroom more than on what their pupils or student teachers do. This tends to play into the 'delivery' metaphor beloved of the managerialist approaches to education, although this may be an effect of the way that the interview was developed.

Ofsted's views of pupil learning was discussed in the interviews in metaphors of conveyor belt 'progress', quantities of examination results 'achieved' and positive-negative vertical scales of 'performance'. James is the only teacher to talk about 'achieving' in both activities: his business background and curriculum subject may influence this. Similarly, he uses the concept 'manage' slightly more than Will, who, as Deputy Head is himself a manager, and considerably more than Celia. His understanding of the word, however, is quite narrow: rather than managing in the sense of manipulating their behaviour or desire to learn, he sorts his pupils according to what they are willing to do. He also reported that he found the language of teacher training 'bizarre' and 'stupid', making him feel invisible. When asked what he thought about the TTA competences James answered:

> I think the competences should be rewritten. [...] it's almost like an educational language which I'm still juggling with...I feel like I am not even present because I am struggling just to understand the language that we're talking about here.

His use of 'juggling' and 'struggling' metaphors suggest that he finds it difficult to hold ('I'm still juggling...') or assimilate ('I am struggling...') He suggests that he wants to comply, to enter government discourses, but is unable to because the concepts are not yet part of his thinking about education.

Concepts of what it means to be a teacher are explored in a wide range of literature. Edwards *et al* (2004:34) argue that most of them can be clustered in metaphors of nurturing (as planting seeds, fostering growth or development) or architecture (scaffolding, building). The concepts found within the study vary between the government and the teacher mentors. Where the government offers a mechanistic and managerial approach expressed through competences, James feels that competences cannot capture what it is to be a teacher, though he does focus on teacher tasks with little sense of interaction with pupils except as 'having fun':

> Now what evidence... what basically am I looking for? I'm looking for this person who can stand up in this class and that they can teach them, that they can set their work, that they can plan their work, that they can set homework, that they can mark it, that they can talk to a mum or dad if they need to, and that they can have a bit of fun and laugh with the kids when they want to as well. And I have got this wonderful document here that I have got to inwardly digest.

At the time of the interview, James was considering leaving the profession: his reasons reveal how he feels oppressed by the work:

> I have only been teaching seven years. It's the *confrontational* element that I object to... I hate to say it but my whole life is *driven* by this group of youngsters going for that exam, that group for this exam and that group for that exam. And I think it's awful that we are *dominated* by this... (my italics)

For the other two mentors though, 'teaching' involves enjoyment of the subject (Will and Celia); enjoyment of working with young people (Will and Celia); personal development of the pupil (Will and Celia); making a contribution to society (Will) and desire to help young people (Celia). For all of them, there is frustration because while they may be willing to comply with government as their employer, they feel that what government asks of them is in conflict with their own guiding concepts: they feel they want autonomy in deciding how to do the job they have prepared for.

The competences of teacher training were not viewed positively by any of the mentors. Will dismisses them as 'tick boxes' which say very little about the essential intangible qualities which he believes make a teacher. James, ironically, when talking about GNVQ (General National Vocational Qualification) syllabi, which require the collection of evidence to demonstrate work done, spoke approvingly of the structure and organisation of them:

> ... the old GNVQs I was taught where you had performance criteria and the range of statement and all this. And it was very, very organised... I thought it was a very good structure.

The subject of exams was a difficult one for all three teachers who, while they generally felt that exams were important, did not see them as the object of schooling. For Will it was more important that 'that's your job and that's your contribution to society, and that's your contribution to those kids' lives. That you make them a bit better when they leave than when they came'. Again, Will: 'I love seeing people make sense of the world around them and feeling a bit more in control.' Celia felt that 'results are important' because 'it reflects directly on to you and people will grade you accordingly', but the pressure to achieve was 'from outside'. Exams, though, were not everything. For her, success was 'kids who choose to do A-level science... even if they are going to be like D or E kids and couldn't do it...' The ordering of educational priorities in ways different from those of government again hints at the will to resist some of the effects of policy.

James, though, did appear to be more exam focused than the other two in his classroom work. Discussion of dealing with pupils was focused clearly on using the exams as a motivator for them to do the work. He preferred to separate the pupils who wanted to work from those who were not interested, and to put his energy into working with those who wanted to do the exams.

> So within a certain group I know that I can expect to get very, very little work out of them. So I take the best five out and put them in another group and put five other Charlies into that group and say okay when this class comes along I am going to achieve this.

Ofsted's concepts of schooling, as represented in the report on Middlemarch school, appear to be expressed in terms of quantifiable aspects. Pupils move through the key stages rather than developing, learning, or growing. They are presented as objects on which the education system works, with no voice or volition. The quality of teaching and management of pupils are considered and graded; pupils make progress, acquire information and even respond, but seem to learn very little. For Ofsted, there is little consideration of empathic concepts such as caring, reassuring, and supporting in their account of schooling. Quality and effectiveness are judged instead.

Interestingly, given its place in the discourse of teacher education, the concept of 'reflect*' is not an important part of any of the participants' discourse, with only James using the idea more than once. However, as anticipated, for Ofsted, concepts of performance, standards and quality, which belong to the discourse of performativity, feature very strongly, whilst for the teacher mentors these are comparatively insignificant.

Rules

Government sets rules which are framed at the top and commanded downward, with policing mechanisms and the bribe of additional money for the school to ensure they are followed. Formally written rules in the form of statutes, handbooks, National Curricula and frameworks are issued to teachers, and Ofsted inspects to ensure compliance. Rules are to do with counting, keeping evidence, accountability, with teachers being accountable for pupil performance – or lack of it. Ofsted reports, it is made clear on the front, have legal authority derived from statute ('Inspection carried out under Section 10 of the School Inspections Act 1996'). They are numbered: each school has a unique reference number; the reporting inspector has a reference number; the Ofsted contract has a reference number; the paragraphs in the report are numbered; pupils are counted and their results quantified. Stages of their education are numbered, from the year they are in to the key stage they are at. They are 'high' or 'low' 'attainers' who have 'standards of attainment' which is 'above' or 'below' national average. 'Progress' is viewed as an elevating conveyor belt on which pupils are placed at Reception age and on which they are expected to remain until the end of Year 13, regardless of their own wishes, abilities or interests.

There was frustration from the teachers that they could not always access or understand the rules within which they were required to work. Will in particular, as deputy head and senior mentor in the school, was exasperated at trying to understand the rules relating to the new pay spine for teachers. 'It's a nightmare, it's a joke almost...So what's the news today and how do you know.' There's a sense of being 'pawns in the game, really' (Will). 'I think there is that feeling of, I suppose it is, being disempowered from what you are doing... they are alienated from what they are doing, to be honest.' (Will). The confusion of metaphors of bad dreams, pranksterism and chess games reflects the confusion that Will is feeling as he tries to express his exasperation.

> Teachers no longer have any autonomy in their classroom, and they feel isolated, alienated and disempowered as a result.

> But as a classroom teacher you can't help but feel more and more alienated from what you're doing. There is quite a long history to it, it's not new, but with the National Curriculum saying this is what you must teach and this is how you must teach it...

Division of Labour

When asked about school policies on ITE in the school, Will said that the majority of staff were enthusiastic about being involved in ITE and often asked to have students. He talked about it being a whole school policy to be involved in ITE, though he was a little hazy about whether everyone was aware of it and whether they were happy about it.

> Gill: So you've got a school policy that the school will be involved?

> Will: Yes

> Gill: And is everybody happy with that?

> Will: I think so on the staff. I haven't asked people because it might be negative but the only... well, let sleeping dogs lie almost.

His aim to present a strong picture of rules which are collegially developed are undermined by his reluctance to involve his colleagues in discussion about the policy to have student teachers in the school, and in this he mirrors government in making assumptions and imposing his decisions. Yet he valued mutual support and reassurance, seeing it as a stronger motivator than external pressure to do the work.

that's only mirroring what the government is doing with performance management themselves. No wonder staff are leaving. They're getting reviewed, they're getting their boxes ticked. They're being told, okay, you can do this and do that but it's not what you want. It's not the way. You want reward; you want recognition that you're doing well and like to be rewarded as well as have it acknowledged...

and again

You need to be able to talk to people about the frustrations they're feeling, anger they're feeling, how they feel about themselves when kids have told them to fuck off two or three times a day. It's those kind of saying well, I'm okay are you okay approach we need to take a bit more. Touchy-feely a bit more.

From the data collected from this school, a rather negative picture develops. Where teachers want to be treated and to treat each other as colleagues, they were finding that they no longer had time to work collegially as other pressures intervened and separated them from each other. Celia talks about working through her lunch times with pupils and student teachers; Will talks about the staff common room being deserted during breaks and James comments on how isolated he feels as a lone Business Studies teacher. Will in particular talks about the 'alienation' and 'disempowerment' that he feels in teaching at the moment. He feels that tick boxes are 'depersonalising'; that there is 'insecurity in the profession' because teachers no longer know what is coming next; and above all, there is the frustration of trying to understand the rules. All these feelings suggest that he perceives the Division of Labour in both schooling and ITE to be hierarchical, which is in tension with his own desire for collegiality.

Celia's views of the Division of Labour emerge from her comments on the relationship she has with her partner HEI. She has very little contact with the HEI, largely because both she and her partner Subject Tutor work part time. So there is a sense of being separate from the HEI rather than working in the partnership intended by the current organisation of ITE.

Conclusions
While this study was not complete at the time of writing, there is emergent evidence that teachers' responses to policy initiatives are as

complex as their work. Resistance, on the current analysis, emerges in the space created by the growing language and conceptual distance between government and teachers, which teachers are filling with their own ways of acting.

The present findings suggest that rather than changing teachers' practices by changing the language of education, policy makers are alienating teachers and making it more difficult for them to do what they came into the profession to do: work with and pass on their enthusiasm for knowledge to children. I have tried to privilege the voices of the teachers in the dataset in this chapter, because all of them felt that they no longer had a voice, and I wanted to remedy that. From what they say, it is apparent that for them there are tensions between the rules that government imposes on them in their work in both activities, and the rules that they develop for themselves from their own understandings of what teaching is about. They are increasingly isolated and disempowered in their work by a hierarchical and alien division of labour, and are unhappy at losing their autonomy in the classroom. There is a strong feeling from all the mentors in this dataset that they want to share their own knowledge, skills, passions and understandings about the work of teaching in empathic ways, but they resent being forced into mechanical box ticking which they perceive as meaningless. The language of policy makers is alien to these teachers, who do not use the language of managerialism, do not appear to be using the government's concepts of managerialism to inform their work, and have not yet found 'other tongues for speaking' (Atkinson, 2003:6).

Resistance to prevailing policy discourses, therefore, emerges from the very fact that the mentors are not entering the discourses of performativity and managerialism. They appear to resist by ignoring the linguistic resources (such as TTA and QCA documents) which form the rules and conceptual tools they do not want to use, though sometimes they argue that they are trying to understand but failing to do so. They are deciding, consciously or unconsciously, to continue inhabiting existing discourses to reflect their view of teaching and mentoring as essentially nurturing, rather than delivery, processes. Government discourses are perceived as inaccessible, and so ignored, and any gap which that ignoring leaves is filled by the teachers' own discourse. This, ironically, plays into their desire for autonomy, which is therefore achieved by default.

References

Apple, M (2004) Doing things the 'Right' way: legitimating educational in-equalities in conservative times, in: Satterthwaite, J, Atkinson, E and Martin, W (eds) *Educational Counter-Cultures: Confrontations, Images, Vision.* (Discourse, Power, Resistance Series Volume 3.) Stoke on Trent: Trentham: 3 – 18

Argyris, C and Schön, D A (1992) *Theory in Practice: Increasing Professional Effectiveness.* London: Jossey Bass

Atkinson, E (2003) Education, postmodernism and the organisation of consent, in: Satterthwaite, J, Gale, K and Atkinson, E (eds) *Discourse, Power, Resistance: Challenging the Rhetoric of Contemporary Education.* (Discourse, Power, Resistance Series Volume 1) Stoke-on-Trent: Trentham: 3 – 12

Ball, S J (1994) *Education Reform: a Critical and Post Structuralist Approach.* Buckingham: Open University Press

Boag-Munroe, G (2004) Wrestling with words and meanings: finding tools for analysing language in Activity Theory, *Educational Review*, 56(2)

Bowe, R and Ball, S J with Gold, A (1992) *Reforming Education and Changing Schools: Case studies in political sociology.* London: Routledge

Buckingham, D and Jones, K (2001) New Labour's cultural turn: some tensions in contemporary educational and cultural policy, *Journal of Educational Policy*, 16(1): 1-14

Chaiklin, S (ed) (2001) *The Theory and Practice of Cultural-Historical Psychology.* Aarhus: Aarhus University Press

Chitty, C and Dunford, J (eds) (1999) *State Schools: New Labour and the Conservative Legacy.* London: Woburn Press

Cochran-Smith, M and Fries, M K (2001) Sticks, stones and ideology: the discourse of reform in teacher education, *Educational Researcher*, 30(8) 3-15

Daniels, H R J (2004) Activity, discourse and pedagogic change. Paper presented at the Third International Bernstein Conference, Clare College, Cambridge, July

Edwards, R, Nicoll, K, Solomon, N and Usher, R (2004) *Rhetoric and Educational Discourse: Persuasive Texts?* London: RoutledgeFalmer

Eliot, T S (1974) *Old Possum's Book of Practical Cats.* London: Faber and Faber

Engeström, Y (1987) *Learning by Expanding.* Helsinki: Orienta Konsultit

Engeström, Y, Miettinen, R and Punamaki, R-L (eds) (1999) *Perspectives on Activity Theory.* Cambridge: Cambridge University Press

Fairclough, N (1995) *Critical Discourse Analysis.* Harlow: Longman

Fairclough, N (2002) *New Labour, New Language?* London: Routledge

Fairclough, N (2003) *Analysing Discourse: Textual Analysis for Social Research.* London: Routledge

Fullan, M (1991) (2nd edition) *The New Meaning of Educational Change.* London: Continuum

Goodson, I F and Hargreaves, A (eds) (1996) *Teachers' Professional Lives.* London: Falmer Press

Gore, J A and Gitlin, A (2004) [Re]Visioning the academic-teacher divide: power and knowledge in the educational community, *Teachers and Teaching: Theory and Practice*, 10(1): 35 – 58

Harris, A (1998) Effective teaching: a review of the literature, *School Leadership and Management*, 18(2):169 – 183

Hay McBer (2000) *Research into Teacher Effectiveness: A Model of Teacher Effectiveness.* London: Department for Education and Employment (DfEE)

Hodgson, A and Spours, K (1999) *New Labour's Educational Agenda.* London: Kogan Page

Jäger, S (2000) Discourse and knowledge: theoretical and methodological aspects of a critical discourse and dispositive analysis, in: Wodak, R and Meyer, M (eds) *Methods of Critical Discourse Analysis.* London: Sage Publications

Locke, T (2001) Questions of professionalism: erosion and reclamation, *CHANGE: Transformations in Education*, 4(2)

Ofsted (2004) www.ofsted.gov.uk

Olssen, M, Codd, J and O'Neill, A-M (2004) *Education Policy: Globalization, citizenship and democracy.* London: Sage

Osterman, K F and Kottkamp, R B (1993) *Reflective Practice for Educators.* Newbury Park, CA: Corwen Press, Inc

Rowland, S (2003) Learning to comply: learning to contest, in: Satterthwaite, J, Gale, K and Atkinson, E (eds) *Discourse, Power, Resistance: Challenging the Rhetoric of Contemporary Education.* (Discourse, Power, Resistance Series Volume 1.) Stoke on Trent: Trentham: 13 – 26

Schön, D A (1987) *Educating the Reflective Practitioner.* San Francisco: Jossey-Bass Publishers

Stubbs, M (1996) *Text and Corpus Analysis.* Oxford: Blackwell

Vygotsky, L (2000) *Thought and Language.* (ed. Kozulin). Cambridge, MA: The MIT Press (Originally published in Russian, 1934)

Wilkin, M (1996) *Initial Teacher Education: The dialogue of ideology and culture.* London: The Falmer Press

Details of the WordSmith Tools programme can be found on www.oup.co.uk

Note

1   Ofsted opts for the term 'standards' – the word favoured in government policy documents from 1997, when new Labour came to power – rather than the earlier term 'competences' which had been introduced in the 1980s and concretised in government policy on education in 1992 (Wilkin, 1996:156). Both terms refer to the list of minimum knowledge, skills and attitudes which the Teacher Training Agency considers students must have in order to become qualified teachers.

9

Professionals, poachers or street-level bureaucrats: government policy, teaching identities and constructive subversions

ROS OLLIN

In this chapter, Ros Ollin challenges dominant notions of the teacher as victim, and explores the ways in which teachers employ subtle methods of resistance under the disguise of what De Certeau (1984) calls 'la perruque': the wig. Ollin explores the ways in which these constructive subversions operate within Gramscian and Foucauldian concepts of power: a conceptual framework which sees power as two-way and relational, rather than simply as the domination of one group (in this case, policy makers) by another (in this case, teachers). This chapter offers a further exploration of the forms of teacher resistance explored by Boag-Munroe in the previous chapter, and adds another dimension to the interlocking spheres of interactions explored by Haggis at the beginning of this section, placing a firm emphasis on the significance of the individual as a locus of both power and resistance.

This chapter considers how a positive and energising discourse could be employed in discussions of teachers and their responses to bureaucratic, centralised control. I envisage this as an initial attempt to counteract a prevailing 'culture of victimhood' whereby teachers are portrayed as powerless victims trapped in a web of hegemonic power (Smyth and Shacklock, 1998). Ironically, this disempowering portrayal is often carried out by writers and educationalists in broad sympathy with the teaching profession who, by drawing attention to the problems engendered by managerialism and targeted accountability, may seek to spur the profession into large-scale action. I do not deny the validity of much of the research into the low morale and pressures experienced by teachers in all educational sectors. Nor do I deny the validity of any aspirations which support the rights of teachers as a body to change those initiatives which contradict their own knowledge and experience. However, I would suggest that there is a parallel perspective to be considered, concerned with the subtle and complex interplay between external factors and individual agency which operates on a daily basis throughout the education system. The ways in which writers represent teachers and the ways in which research is interpreted may demonstrate a tendency to dismiss as insignificant, if not irrelevant, the small acts of resistance and what I will term 'constructive subversions' demonstrated within teachers' working practices. By drawing on theories from a number of different epistemological and philosophical areas, I hope to suggest that the space for individual action, and its effect on policy implementation, may be far greater than is often acknowledged.

The policy context within which teachers operate has been extensively considered by writers on education. Much has been written about the increasing convergence in global government policy trends characterised by a centralisation of control, an emphasis on performativity, accountability and marketisation, communicated through a discourse of managerialism. The effect of these restrictive frameworks and government policy initiatives on the work of teachers and academics has been extensively documented (Lea *et al*, 2003; Ollin, 2002; Ball, 2001; Easthope and Easthope, 2000; Avis, 1999; Dale, 1997; Halsey *et al*, 1997; Hargreaves, 1994; Torres, 1989). This has engendered a lively and wide-ranging debate on the professional identities of those involved in teaching and, more broadly, on the nature of teacher professionalism itself (Bathmaker, 2001; Sachs, 2003; Day, 2000; Whitty, 1997). A significant feature of much of this work is the representation of teachers as being under a state of siege, as powerless victims of forces beyond their control. Ball uses comments from demoralised teachers to support his analysis of the intrusion of the 'technical intelligentsia' which 'drives performativity into the day-to-day practices of teachers' and forces them to 'play the game' in school inspections

Ros Ollin

(Ball, 2001:147). In the post-sixteen context, the lack of active mass resistance is presented as having a damaging effect on education:

> In further or higher education, the passivity of lecturers and academics undermines the possibilities of revitalising what is left of the academic community. (Hayes, 2003:88)

Exhortations for action tend to concentrate on large-scale collaborative resistance undertaken by the teaching community as a whole. For example, the recent call from Sachs (2003) for symbolically 'disruptive work' and the need to challenge the dominant discourse of education is aimed at generating collective action rather than individual resistance. This would support a concept of professionalism which includes the obligation to speak out in public as a cohesive body (Carr, 2000). However, I would suggest that there can be many different kinds and levels of resistance which writers on education need to take into account. These can include resisting practical changes affecting working practices; resisting the *processes* by which change is implemented; resisting inroads on personal or professional identity; resistance to a general state of things by opposition to a political or ideological stance. For each type of resistance, action can take place at the micro-level (the individual and particular), as well as the macro-level (the large-scale and public), with continuous interplay between the two (Giddens, 1984). I will argue in this chapter that many theoretical perspectives on power and change acknowledge the significance of this micro-level activity in undermining large-scale structures of control.

It may be useful here to explore briefly different notions of power and their relationship to resistance, as inherent in the notion of resistance is the notion of power – power that is resisted against or power that is exercised to overcome resistance. However, the concept of power is in itself problematic, characterised in different ways depending on which ontological stance prevails. I would suggest that, broadly speaking, power can be conceived as either hegemonic or organic. In Marxist philosophy, power is hegemonic, characterised by centralised political and economic control and the presence of a dominant discourse which 'normalises' potentially contestable sites (Gramsci, 1971). The relationship of the 'resistor' to the source of power is conceived here as a duality consisting of the monolithic dominant and the rebelling subordinate.

An alternative notion characterises power as an organic entity, located not in one space but endlessly formulated and reformulated within socio-cultural networks and social relations (Foucault, 1997). Power here may not be overtly represented, but becomes covertly internalised and normalised within the practice of individuals and groups. Of significance to this chapter is that the Gramscian hegemonic and the Foucauldian relational concepts both acknowledge the potential of individuals to exercise resistance. Far from characterising people as victims, Gramsci has a liberating notion of the power of individuals to think and to question social and political norms – the development of a social consciousness which he argues is not something that can be imposed upon people, but arises from their own working lives. He further suggests that any contradictions between the results of political ideology and the lived experience of the individual should be seen in terms of an ideological struggle. Interestingly, Gramsci suggests that although resistance may occur as an overt ideological struggle, it also may be construed as an ideological *struggle even if those involved are unaware of this.* I would suggest that this viewpoint could indicate a caveat to those writers on education who dismiss individual acts of principled assertion as 'mere' resistance (Moore *et al*, 2002) as it places those acts inevitably in the public and ideological domain, even though the individual intentionality derives from the private domain of personal principle.

Although the hegemonic concept postulates a binary relationship of power and resistance, Foucault's notion of resistance is of a far more fluid and elusive nature, weaving through different social fabrics and taking coloration from the surrounding context or circumstance. It functions through a knowledge of the rules of a particular environment, its regulatory systems and how its discourse is employed. This knowledge can then be used by individuals as a basis for developing the tactics which will enable them to survive in complex and sometimes hostile environments. This idea of tactics is given a more active and empowering slant by De Certeau (1984) discussed later in this chapter.

So far, I have considered briefly two different philosophical and political conceptualisations of power and have argued that both notions allow for the significance of individual agency. I will now consider a different theoretical field altogether, that of strategic management and change. I will suggest that, within the conceptual framework of management theory, government policy developments and implementations can be represented as large-scale change strategies, exemplifying, according to the theoretical base, either hegemonic or Foucauldian notions of power. Classical planned models of change, linked to Taylorist models of control (Taylor, 1911) are underpinned by what could be termed a hegemonic ontology where power is located in one place – the top – and with that power being used to force, coerce or persuade groups or individuals into compliance with the change required. This compliance model is consistent with the normative motions of an authoritative policy hierarchy (Brodkin, 2000) and can be found in the coercive discourse of some government members, such as Charles Clarke, the current UK Secretary of State for Education and Skills. It can also be found in the policing-oriented inspectorial system exemplified by the ruthless and punitive approach adopted by Chris Woodhead, the former UK Chief Inspector for Schools, who resigned in November, 2000.

More recent theorists on strategic management reject the rather static and simplistic notions of power inherent in classical management theory, and acknowledge the complexity and instability of the change process (see, for example, Fullan, 1999). This thinking is reflected in contemporary management theories related to processual, cultural models of change. In these models, power is no longer seen as located in one particular space, but functions as a set of fluid and evolving relationships which form as a result of different sets of alliances or circumstances (Dawson, 1994; Fullan, 1999). This is far closer to Foucault's notion of power as organic, residing not in one place or person, but within networks of relations of power (Foucault, 1997). Important to the theme of this chapter is that strategic management theory using a processual approach recognises the *micro-* as well as the macro-political and cultural dimensions of strategic policy change and also, the importance of acknowledging different loci of power in the implementation of policy initiatives (Dawson, 1994).

While both classical and processual theories include the possibility of resistance to change, however, conceptualisations of resistance differ among different strategic management models. In the classical planning model, resistance is seen as entirely negative, to be pre-empted, beaten down, appeased or managed. Resistance in this model means that the power at the top is directly challenged by those on whom the power is enacted. The confrontational nature of this power-resistance binary lends itself to large-scale public challenges to those in control of policy by groups of people such as professional bodies or trades unions, or to large-scale inertia such as that demonstrated by many teachers in response to policy changes (see Boag-Munroe in this volume). However, resistance is characterised differently in the more contemporary processual, cultural change models. Here resistance, in the form of disagreement or conflict, is seen by some writers as a means of ensuring that the change takes into account the multiple perspectives of those involved, with the possibility of reaching a level of compromise about the nature of the changes to policy or practice to be enacted (Fullan, 1999). In the latter model, power is recognised as being located at *all* levels within an institution, at practitioner level as well as at management level. Of significance to the theme of resistance is that processual models of strategic management acknowledge a very real possibility of individual practitioners changing the content or process of a policy enactment. As Fullan suggests:

> The individual educator is a critical starting point because the leverage for change can be greater through the efforts of individuals (1993:12)

So far in this chapter, I have tried to indicate that different theoretical fields all recognise that there is space for resistance at the level of the individual, as well as through the collective public voice. I have also suggested that it is possible for individual resistance to have an impact on policy. I will now look at this theme in more detail through the work of Michael Lipsky on street level bureaucracy and then move on to discuss an empowering version of individual agency through looking at Michel de Certeau's writing on poaching and *la perruque*.

The research of Michael Lipsky (1980) presents a useful challenge to the notion of passive acceptance and the portrayal of individuals as powerless in their enforced enactment of government policy. His concept of the 'street level bureaucrat' encompasses those public sector workers who interact directly with the public and can exercise considerable discretion in how they work. He includes teachers among the list of public sector workers to whom this analysis applies. Of relevance to this chapter is that Lipsky's research attributes a significant amount of discretionary power to street level bureaucrats, including the power to interpret policy according to their own capacities to carry out the work and control what and how they choose to implement. Lipsky identifies that common environmental features of public sector employees operating at street-level are the significant resource constraints and heavy workloads under which they must function. These affect the strategies they use to cope with their job, which display a number of features comparable to research on teachers' coping strategies (Moore and Edwards, 2003). Lipsky sees the street-level bureaucrat as essentially self-determining, with considerable power to interpret and enact the job in the way that they choose. He suggests that the demands of accountability, which seeks to increase congruence between worker behaviour and management policy through administrative controls, have little effect on the street-level bureaucrat who will find ways of producing the minimum required. Although Lipsky's representation of the street level bureaucrat devising individual coping mechanisms under stress is, in one sense, a depressing view, in terms of the notion of resistance to a managerialist environment, there is some cause for optimism. Although he recognises that the idealism and commitment of many practitioners is affected by the pressurised context of work, he does see them as exerting very substantial power over their own work practices. This autonomy can also have the far more wide-reaching effect of changing government policy at street level. Hence by individual interpretations of policy, that policy is transformed. The effects of policy transformation from the 'top to the bottom' have been researched elsewhere and represented, for example, in what Reynolds and Saunders term *'the implementation staircase'* (Reynolds and Saunders, 1987).

However, although Lipsky writes about the power of the employee, he does present their resistance to policy initiatives in terms of the coping strategies of a beleaguered workforce. Hence, to a certain extent he still contributes to a representation of 'victimhood'. De Certeau (1984) has a far more empowering notion of resistance, captured in his work on the everyday practices by which ordinary people reclaim their own meanings from those presented to them through the processes and products of mass enculturation. He distinguishes between strategy and tactics, where strategy is determined by those with 'will and power', delineating a space from which influence can be exerted over external targets or threats, and tactics – 'the art of the weak' –

operating within a space that is not their own. In other words, tactics comprise a 'set of practices that strategy has not been able to domesticate' (Buchanan, 2000:89).

De Certeau's (1984:18) idea of resistance is in the form of 'subtle, resistant activity' and includes 'innumerable ways of playing and foiling the other's game... that is, the space instituted by others'. However, although he seems to almost suggest a kind of guerilla tactics here, in which the resistance is a negative, if playful act, elsewhere he indicates ways in which people take positive action to transform existing spaces and, through making their own space within them, affirm their sense of self. They do this through their discourse – stories which affirm an alternative way of viewing the world, which refuse to legitimate a dominant ideology. They also do this through their own practice, in particular what De Certeau (1984:24) refers to as la perruque (the wig) which is 'the worker's own work disguised as work for his employer'. De Certeau (1984:25) suggests that this practice is prevalent in most places and that by doing this, the worker actually 'diverts time... for work that is free, creative and precisely not directed for profit'.

I would suggest that the power of De Certeau's analysis is in the representation of the capabilities of individuals and small groups caught in larger systems to retain those things that are important to them and co-exist with, whilst refusing to legitimate, systems of dominance and control. The discourse he uses is of play, joy and creativity – an essentially liberating discourse about the practices of ordinary people. I would suggest also that much research on teachers marginalises the capabilities of individuals and small groups caught in larger systems to retain those things that are important to them and to co-exist with, *whilst refusing to legitimate*, systems of dominance and control. This corresponds to various research findings about teachers' resistance to relinquishing what they consider to be important to good practice (Smyth, 2001). I would further suggest that De Certeau's concept of la perruque might be adapted to include the possibility that an individual's notion of their own professional identity might cause a particular type of 'poaching' from the employer's time. This poaching would involve the worker taking time to engage in the types of practices which satisfy them that they are behaving in accordance with their own notions of personal and professional identity. The worker's

Ros Ollin

own work here is the professional practice they define as good and appropriate, and 'disguised as work for the employer' represents a 'strategic compliance' (Shain and Gleeson, 1999, in Bathmaker *et al*, 2003) with external managerialist demands.

My point here is that there are many ways in which resistance to government ideologies, represented through policy, can take place, and that many of what I will term constructive subversions can take place. These are acts which may take place at an individual or small group level, but can have the effect of subverting policy intentions and even transforming policy itself. They are constructive for this reason, but constructive also because they serve to reinforce a positive and empowered notion of teacher identity rather than the besieged victim too often portrayed.

It has been suggested that a culture of pragmatism has effectively de-politicised teachers (Moore *et al*, 2002). It has further been suggested that active subversion of policy only exists at senior management level (Moore and Edwards, 2003) through what has been termed strategic pragmatism. However I would suggest that there are many examples of these tactics being used by teachers at the 'street level'. A significant number of research findings which present teachers as compliant and powerless are currently predicated on large-scale challenge as being the only means of countermanding government policy. However, a closer look at how the teachers are actually undermining policy by their small-scale acts of principle might support a different reading of some of the research evidence. A recent book researching teacher's lives warns against underestimating individual teachers:

> Beware of making judgements about teacher technicisation which underestimate or do not take into account the power of local, institutional and personal professional contexts. (Day, 2000:126)

Day further states:

> The teachers in this study had clearly adapted and during the transition from initiation to internalisation of change had reasserted their autonomy. (*ibid*:126)

Let me state clearly that I am not suggesting that writers on education should adopt any simplistic, propagandist view of teachers happily implementing government policy as portrayed in much of the government-inspired literature. I am proposing that, in its desire to take a

159

critical viewpoint on centralised policy, educational research does not neglect or minimise the capability of individuals to retain what they consider is important, and by so doing resist, to some measure at least, the external pressures for them to act otherwise. I would suggest that the constructive subversions that many teachers engage in on a regular basis represent a principled version of *la perruque* where the tactics of the 'weak' have the potential to form a powerful alternative framing of what is important in education. A number of commentators on education have called for large-scale public actions to produce an assertion of teachers' identities and professional practices. I would argue that there is room for both this overt activism and for less public, but nevertheless, constructive subversions. Both have an important part to play in the development of an alternative discourse which removes teachers from a position of victimhood. I would suggest that it is important for both teachers and those who write about teachers to be aware of the frames (Schön, 1993) within which their discourse is created, and to become aware of the possibilities of reframing towards a more positive and empowering vision of teachers' potential to bring about change.

References

Avis, J (1999) Shifting Identity. New conditions and the transformation of practice – teaching within post-compulsory education, *Journal of Vocational Education and Training*, 51(2): 245 – 264

Ball, S (2001) Performatives and fabrications in the education economy: towards the performative society, in: Gleeson, D and Husbands, C (eds) *The Performing School: Managing teaching and learning in a performance culture*. London: RoutledgeFalmer

Bathmaker, A (2001) Neither dupes nor devils: teachers' constructions of their changing role in Further Education. Paper presented at the fifth annual conference of the Learning and Skills Research Network, Research-Making and Impact on Policy and Practice, Robinson College, Cambridge, December 2001

Bathmaker, A, Avis, J and Kendall A. (2003) Biography, values and identity: becoming a lecturer in Further Education. Paper presented at the International Conference of the *Journal Of Vocational Education and Training*. July 2003

Brodkin, E Z (2000) *Investigating policy's practical meaning: street-level research on welfare policy*. Working paper: Project on the Public Economy of Work. Chicago: University Of Chicago

Buchanan, I (2000) *Michel de Certeau; Cultural Theorist*. London: Sage

Carr, D (2000) *Professionalism and Ethics in Teaching*. London: Routledge

Dale, R (1997) The state and the governance of education: an analysis of the re-structuring of the state-education relationship, in: Halsey, A, Lauder, H, Brown, P and Wells, *A Education: Culture, Economy, Society.* Oxford: Oxford University Press

Dawson, P (1994) *Organizational Change: A processual approach.* London: Paul Chapman

Day, C (2000) Stories of change and professional development: the costs of commitment, in: Day, C, Fernandez, A, Hauge, T and Moller, J (eds) *The Life and Work of Teachers: International perspectives in changing times.* London: Falmer

De Certeau, M (1984) *The Practice of Everyday Life.* (Trans S Rendall). Berkeley: University of California Press

Easthope, C and Easthope, G (2000) Intensification, extension and complexity of teachers' workload, *British Journal of Sociology of Education,* 21(1): 43 – 57

Foucault, M (1997) *Discipline and Punish: The Birth of the Prison* (Trans A M Sheridan- Smith). Harmondsworth: Penguin

Fullan, M (1993) *Change Forces.* London: Falmer

Fullan, M (1999) *Change Forces: The Sequel.* London: Falmer

Giddens, A (1984) *The Constitution of Society: Outline of the theory of structuration.* Berkeley: University of California Press

Gramsci, A (1971) *Selections from the Prison Notebooks.* London: Lawrence and Wishart

Halsey, A, Lauder, H, Brown, P and Wells, A (1997) *Education: Culture, Economy, Society.* Oxford: Oxford University Press

Hargreaves, A (1994) Restructuring restructuring: postmodernity and the prospects for educational change, *Journal of Education Policy.* 9(1): 47 – 65

Hayes, D (2003) Managerialism and professionalism in post-compulsory education, in: Lea, J, Hayes, D, Armitage, A, Lomas, L and Markless, S (eds) *Working in Post Compulsory Education.* Buckingham: Open University Press

Lea, J, Hayes, D, Armitage, A, Lomas, L and Markless, S (eds) (2003) *Working in Post Compulsory Education.* Buckingham: Open University Press

Lipsky, M (1980) *Street-Level Bureaucracy: Dilemmas of the individual in public services.* New York: Russell Sage Foundation

Moore, A, Edwards, G, Halpin, D and George, R (2002) Compliance, resistance and pragmatism: the (re)construction of schoolteacher identities in a period of intensive educational reform, *British Educational Research Journal.* 28(4): 551 -565

Moore, A and Edwards, G (2003) Teaching school management and the ideology of pragmatism. Paper presented at the International Conference, Knowledge and Discourse: Speculating on Disciplinary Futures. Hong Kong, June 2002.

Ollin, R (2002) Professionals or prisoners: the competency approach to professional development, in: Trorey, G and Cullingford, C (eds) *Professional Development and Institutional Needs.* Aldershot: Ashgate

Reynolds, J and Saunders, M (1987) Teacher responses to curriculum policy: beyond the 'delivery' metaphor, in: Calderhead, J (ed) *Exploring Teachers' Thinking.* London: Cassell

Sachs, J (2003) Teacher activism: mobilising the profession. Plenary Address presented at the annual meeting of the British Educational Research Association, Heriot Watt University, Edinburgh, September

Schön, D (1993) *The Reflective Practitioner*. London: Temple Smith

Shain and Gleeson (1999) Under new management: changing conceptions of teacher professionalism and policy in the Further Education sector, *Journal of Education Policy*, 14(4): 445-462

Smyth, J and Shacklock, G (1998) *Re-making Teaching*. London: Routledge

Smyth, J (2001) Undamaging 'damaged' teachers: reclaiming teachers' pedagogical work. Paper presented at the annual meeting of the Australian Association for Research in Education, Freemantle, December

Taylor, F W (1911) *The Principles of Scientific Management*. New York: Harper Bros

Torres, C (1989) The capitalist state and public policy formation: framework for a political sociology of educational policy making, *British Journal of Sociology of Education*. 10(1): 81-102

Whitty, G (1997) Marketisation, the state and the re-formation of the teaching profession, in: Halsey, A, Lauder, H, Brown, P and Wells, A *Education: Culture, Economy, Society*. Oxford: Oxford University Press

10

The Silkscreen Vickies: identity, images and icons (in the age of the Research Assessment Exercise)

VICTORIA PERSELLI

In this chapter, Victoria Perselli identifies her love of art and music as a vehicle for taking time out from the constraints and pressures of 'business as usual' in academia; roaming across the boundary spaces between relaxation and work. In doing so she offers an unusual critique of her situation as a female scholar operating within the highly competitive, regularised and policed environments of contemporary educational systems. Beginning with the work of Andy Warhol, and his Silkscreen series, she muses on the constantly changing significances of what she terms female sexual assertiveness. Taking us through a gallery of icons and personal interactions, Perselli explores glamour as a form of response and resistance to powerful de-sexualising, neutralising forces, of which she names the RAE as a prime example; at the same time delivering a vision of a post-medium approach to representation and research by drawing parallels with images of female idols of the silk and silver screens. Her discussion recalls Isherwood's plea, in the first section of this book, for a return to the recognition of the corporeal, the personal and the erotic as central to our identities. There are links here, too, to Pinar's analysis of the deep psychology of educational and political practices, and to the passion of Lambert's poetic plea in the final chapter of this book.

Introduction

In this chapter, my aim is to draw together several strands that have fascinated me and preoccupied my thoughts over the past couple of years, in order to devise some kind of research or teaching tool in relation to female sexuality. In particular I want to explore the notion of glamour and its connection with what I have here termed female sexual assertiveness. In flagrant disobedience of any utilitarian research remit, I begin with elements of things I like: Andy Warhol and the Pop Art movement, and the images of glamour icons from the 60s that have so powerfully influenced the development of rock music and the music video genre today. I shall refer specifically to the output of the band No Doubt, whose lead singer and 'front' is Gwen Stefani, by coincidence cover-featured in American Vogue in April this year (2004), the time of the Discourse Power Resistance (DPR) conference at which this paper was first presented.

I have chosen to work from visual images of women created largely by men in the fields of art and the mass media, towards images of women constructed largely by themselves in music and rock video, in order to suggest that at last it is becoming possible for women to express their sexuality in an assertive, overt and – to my mind – refreshingly humorous way. This, I hope, will open doors for discussion on the multifarious forms of female sexuality that can be discerned in the present day; in particular via the visual and performing arts. This thesis is tempered by the ironic observation that both the commercial art of Warhol and the rock video genre coexist in and through the advancement of late capitalism. It by no means assumes that women are now more liberated *per se* in their sexuality; rather, that these media offer opportunities for distinct forms of sexual self-expression, consciously developed from the era of the great divas as depicted by Warhol *et al*, to be discernible and therefore debatable within a more general discourse of female sexuality.

My title, 'The Silkscreen Vickies', represents a postmodern play on Warhol's Silkscreen series (Jackie, Marilyn, etc.) and a wry sideways glance at the (supposedly) self-defining female research scholar who is, nevertheless, a product of the inherently commercial and competitive medium of the Research Assessment Exercise (RAE)[1] in the UK. As always I am keen to put on display the inside-outside nature of my way of working, in terms of forging a method and methodology, as much as to arrive at something thought-provoking, tragic or funny about the paradox of being a woman and an educational researcher in the age of the RAE.

Defining the Research Object in relation to Female Sexual Assertiveness

I love the beginnings of a new piece of writing, especially if it involves experimentation with unfamiliar media and ideas so far randomly assembled and unformed. I love the sensation of risk stemming from not knowing what the research process will throw up, not least since it involves delving into one's own feelings and experiences as a source of reference, to see what (else) is there. I had a hunch that I could open up an area provisionally labelled 'female sexual assertiveness' via a parade of famous women under the iconic banner of the platinum blonde/vamp/bad girl: Marilyn Monroe, Shirley Temple, Maria Callas, Ursula Andress, Brigitte Bardot, Sophia Loren, Dusty Springfield, Deborah Harry, Chrissie Hynde, Gwen Stefani, as depicted in moving and still image, as well as via their own song lyrics, in the case of the singer-songwriters. I was also secure in my own mind that all this frivolity and fluff – in masculinist terms – would yield a very serious discussion of women and their roles within tightly bounded power structures.

An aspect of female sexual assertiveness that attracted me was that it would generally be perceived as predatory. This suggested a highly stylised version of woman as sex-symbol and femme fatale, together with her younger counterpart or former, more parochial self; the singular, competitive alpha female, unmistakably dominant within a group of girls 'out on the prowl'; looking for sexual experiences and being unabashed to ask for them, potentially exciting and threatening to men and to other women alike, driven by biology and psyche as much as by social or historical construction. But this line of thought also conjured the volatile and vulnerable, as though bad girls will (pretty much always) come to a bad end... Thence to another traditional take on the subject, whereby something depressive or needy must be lurking behind the rolled-gold signifiers of predatory sex (thick lipstick, tight skirt, spiked heels and glossed hair): the woman coveting a need for love, affection or protection – and seeking it in the wrong places.

However, the more I pursued this the more I recognised the complexity of trying to make any generalisable statements about female sexual assertiveness that would hold true for either my starting point, which was iconic figures as portrayed in the 60s, in film, music and in the mass media, crystallised by Warhol and Pop Art (McCarthy, 2000), or recent performance artists such as Gwen Stefani, Christina Aguilera, Pink, whose images are explicitly derived from the work of their predecessors, and at least implicitly suggestive of Warhol *et al.* The only thing I could claim assuredly is that, in common with certain other public figures 'famous for being famous' (Jacky Kennedy, for example), for me they all represent variations on the theme of *glamour.*

So why might this be important just now? Here are some other random ideas: that glamour (and by extension fantasy) are significant aspects of both the human condition and female sexuality which educational research doesn't often address, except perhaps condescendingly; that the work of Warhol provides an interesting critical lens with which to look (ironically and tongue-in-cheek?) at female sexuality within the academy, the marketisation of researchers and our commercial worth in the era of the Research Assessment Exercise (Warhol: 'I want to be a machine'; 'In the future, everyone will be famous for 15 minutes'); that there was a neat contradictory streak between this and my prior work, which approaches related ideas on identity and selfhood from the perspective of *Marxian* teaching (Perselli, 2004a). As I threw together (well, not exactly, but more of that later) my poster presentation for Discourse Power Resistance, these were the threads running through my head, together with a conviction that something significant on the changing feelings and attitudes around women's sexuality and self-expression in this area, in the here-and-now, would emerge from this montage of ideas (Denzin and Lincoln, 2000:3-5) – and with it a tool for teaching or research (Kincheloe and Steinberg, 1998) that could prove useful to women.

Glamour, Commerce and Culture

Before going any further I want to draw attention to what I appear to be omitting from the discourse. In this text so far I have named exclusively white, western artists who have become successful and achieved their celebrity status within a system of late capitalist economic reproduction. The reasons are relatively simple. Firstly, it's where I'm coming from. These are the images I remember as being influential in my childhood, and these are the specific artists and songwriters in the present day whose work I enjoy because it speaks to me with expressions of sexuality I find refreshing and, I think, illuminative of how women's views of their own sexuality have changed over time. What needs to be articulated immediately – and in no sense as a form of lip-service either – is the extent to which all these glamorous images and icons can be related (back) to Black and non-Western cultures and identities. Indeed, listening to Stefani lyrics or to recently emerging artists (Joss Stone, Erykah Badu, Amy Winehouse) gives me an entree *into* Black music (jazz, soul, funk); something I was never adequately exposed to as a child, or more recently as a classical musician. In combination they offer illustrations of a wide range of ways of being in the world as a woman that are more relevant than anything I have ever encountered – speaking now as a teacher and teacher educator – via the English National Curriculum or the UK Standards for Qualifying to Teach; where female, Black and non-western culture, history and society have been miserably neglected. The possibility of deconstructing the concept of glamour across racial, socio-economic and gender boundaries seems obvious enough. Glamour, whilst being a vital part of the human condition (perhaps the only steadfast claim one can make, it's such an irreducible, slippery object), is not a fundamental trait of Woman, and whilst it tends to be associated with women in western culture (via the supposedly objectivising male gaze), is neither female nor male in essence. Plenty of examples of male manifestations of glamour spring to mind – again not from white, western, heterosexual film, music or mass media exclusively. Although glamour in the mass media is inclined to be highly racialised, gendered and a product of late capitalism (in advertising, for example: his Rolex watch to her Louis Vuiton handbag) accessible to the ordinary citizen only in imitative forms, this division is tenuous and can be playfully/problematically exploited (the football megastar David Beckham wearing a sarong, for example). To go further, the specific signifiers of feminine glamour have in any case throughout history been appropriated by both heterosexual and homosexual men in deliberative ways: formerly in *commedia del arte*, carnival, pantomime, transvestism and drag; more recently in the rituals attached to stag nights, in clubbing and house parties, in gay iconography (for an illuminative analysis of gay sexuality in popular film see Seidman, 2002: 123-161, also Dilley, 2002) and Bollywood.

Secondly, I would actually argue that words like 'appropriation' or 'debt' are inadequate to describe the kinds of boundary-crossing that occurs with regard to non-verbal forms of artistic, ritualistic, religious or self-expression via music, visual art, drama, film and video, body language and body art. Debt (appropriation, derivation) suggests that we know for sure where the object (glamour and its signifiers or Zydeco or Garage, say) came from and to whom it belonged – some essence – when it might be more realistic just to make a polite acknowledgement of recent, and therefore easily ascribable, sources (bling bling (jewellery) to hip hop, for example). The student of social history already knows how interdependent past/present really are, and 'debt' (appropriation, derivation) cannot be the right word to use for the objects and forms of beauty one sees in film, the knowingness expressed in song writing, the uncontrollably transgressive habit of visual/musical/dramatic codes and conventions. Thus the claim of a white, western heritage through the persona of, say, Marilyn Monroe (or Elvis Presley if one requires a male counterpart), is ridiculous; behind these figures there will always be someone else (maybe Black, maybe gay, maybe from the schools of blues or jazz) who got there first, culturally speaking.

Thirdly, as with all research projects, there is the necessity to delineate boundaries and demarcate starting points; and in this instance and with DPR readers very much in mind, to have some fun and gain pleasure from exploring areas I already enjoy in a haphazard way as time out from the 'business as usual' of trying to interpret meaningfully a relentless deluge of hastily concocted educational reform. If my selection is personally predisposed, this does not cause me too much *angst* for one very good reason. From past experience as a researcher thinking about Difference, what I already know for sure is the ways in which the object of study one chooses automatically and productively throws attention onto its opposite number. This is totally born out at the DPR conferences, where it would be impossible to have a sustained conversation for very long regarding Women's Sexuality, or White Women, or Heterosexual Women Singer Songwriters, or Working-class Gay White Women in Film, before someone (thankfully) says: so why haven't you mentioned anything about Men's Sexuality,

Black Women, Gay Women Singer Songwriters...? Where is Billie Holiday? Where is KD Lang?! A vigorous research community thinks both locally and collectively; it strives to consider self always in relation with/to others; to make worthwhile connections from the personal to the political, the self to the social and vice versa. So although I feel trepidation at embarking on the topic of sexuality at all, especially when it randomly incorporates things that happen to fascinate me and with everything that this seemingly omits, I do trust in my research community's ability – at DPR conferences, at Trentham Books and in the wider world of readers and researchers – to turn this work from the proverbial sow's ear... into a beautiful silk purse.

Finally, as the conference discussion below demonstrates, not all women (or men) warm to the images that represent glamour, or are particularly interested, one way or another, in glamour as a characteristic of sexuality. Some women decisively object to being exoticised or fetishised in this way – and would argue, possibly, that this is an act of aggression against them. The sexualities of women and the outward forms of expression these take are as multifarious as those of men. However, this conveniently brings me to a social reality that might begin to be disentangled in these pages, which is that a) women can and do make choices of their own about their sexual preferences, appearance and behaviours, and that b) the notion of glamour in relation to sexual assertiveness, as defined here, runs contrary to the view that the female human body is intended for monogamous and/or reproductive relations – and that whilst this is a constant source of celebration and inspiration in the arts and creative media, in education it is inclined to be treated as a problem or even a threat (see Atkinson, 2004: 55-68; Reardon, 2004: 103-113). Here sex and sexuality cannot be considered in isolation; there are other axes of power and struggle. Who exactly has a purchase on glamour and, by extension, fantasy: the rich? the famous? the commercially successful? The distinguishable features of sexuality (of which glamour is just one) are visibly interrelated with aspects of race and ethnicity, age and social class; cutting across the male/female binary, whereby gay sexuality, the sexualised body of the pregnant (solo) teenager, the pose and dress of gangster rappers or, more recently, that of working class ladettes, all represent apparent contestations of the (exclusively) monogamous or reproductive purposes of sex. It's not that one particular set of values and views on sexuality is wrong, merely that school environments and teaching curricula which refuse to represent or at least acknowledge the multifarious takes on sex and sexuality, family and interpersonal relations and, in particular, the dreams and aspirations of young people that present within a pluralised society, are highly likely to fail (Bay-Cheng, 2003:61-74). For a teacher, self-awareness regarding where the boundaries lie between aggressive imposition of one's own sexual culture (i.e. hegemony) and assertion of individual/group freedom of expression or choice in these matters can and should usefully inform decisions about how sex, sexuality, morality and the ethics of interpersonal relations (the I/thou conversation) might be taught (if at all). This in turn has implications for a host of related issues such as citizenship, religion, gender or socio-economic segregation, the privacy of the individual and health education – however challenging that may be for us as educators.

So if glamour is the main object, what are the research tools?

Feminine/feminist nuances of female sexuality are beautifully illustrated in the songs of Gwen Stefani. Particularly appealing is the way in which apparently benign, passive sentiments – the submission of an ultra-feminine, ingenuous woman to the hypermasculine bad guy – is contradicted by her stage presence (an *androgynous* Marilyn; a fantasy send-up of BDSM (Bondage, Discipline and Sado/Masochism) culture) and through the contours, textures and colours of the music itself. Stefani frequently manages to appear to be saying one (submissive, accepting) thing whilst simultaneously representing another. The play on ultrafeminine versus hypermasculine, good girl/bad girl, innocent/knowing is so light in touch that the overall impression is of someone taking these historicised and gendered images and just playing; sending up the whole caboodle with breathtaking self-confidence; evoking glamour through banal detail (*It's My Life, Bathwater, Excuse Me Mr., Underneath It All*: No Doubt: 2000, 2003) as much as through stereotypical symbols of money, power or fame. Where I believe Stefani is rigorously faithful to her sex – via the songs and the various stage personae which encapsulate all and more of the glamour images I was conjuring earlier – is in her refusal to remain invisible to the (indifferent) male gaze; in short, whatever impression she aims to achieve, Stefani never sells out on female desire (Bay-Cheng, *ibid.*).

My poster presentation for DPR consisted of a series of overhead transparencies (OHTs) using quotations from Warhol, from the Research Assessment Exercise, references to song lyrics, principally Stefani and 'No Doubt'. I also referenced the Vogue website, where, by happy coincidence, pictures of Stefani formed the cover and feature article for the April version of American Vogue. Complications of printing, copyright and intellectual property make it impossible to reproduce exactly either song lyrics or visual images on these pages, so readers must go to the sources or visit the referenced websites for these. However, I hope that the extracts and discussion below, supplemented with material of my own, convey a flavour of the DPR event – which, in any case, side-tracked substantially from its original intentions. (See also Perselli, 2004b, for further discussion of visual imagery and imaginative conjecture in educational research.)

IMAGE 1: Female Sexuality and the DPR Abstract

In my first, draft abstract for DPR I made an unconscious assumption that research into female sexual assertiveness necessarily involved issues already topical in education:

> I anticipate that this will facilitate discussion around notions of sex and sexuality in relation to, for example, globalisation, marketisation, bureaucratisation, 'inclusion' and 'liberation' (for whom exactly? where? when? how?) in the age of HIV/AIDS and what the implications might be towards better understandings (in the academy, in schools and beyond), of this aspect of education

and that there must be an extant moral justification behind the work. I disliked this abstract, because when I started out I had no meaningful standpoint on any of the above, other than obliquely via very small-scale work I had done before, so why posture a moral imperative if there wasn't one? As a researcher and teacher I was actively striving to move away from an objectives-outcomes regime, and with it any preconceived morality/sexuality assumptions too. All I had wanted to do was to have some fun with female sexuality... just to see...? One of the attractions of researching glamour icons is precisely that they do not make explicit commentary on any of the issues which we are inclined to obsess over as teachers and educators – and that was partly the point: 'taking time out from business as usual'. In particular I felt a distaste in linking female sexual assertiveness with

STIs (sexually transmitted infections); not because they have no relevance, but again because this would effectively pre-empt participants' responses to the stimuli. But sex, I now realise, lends itself all too readily to regulation (Foucault, 1990): for social stability (in the idealised sense), for the acquisition of wealth and power (the church, the state), for economic productivity (Abramson and Pinkerton, 2002); and an unsubtle morality or health discourse forecloses too quickly on glamour, as would, I think, an unsubtle Marxism. More to the point, an unsubtle sex education programme forecloses on the experiences of real people:

> How might our programs change if the self were seen as constituted through the social rather than in opposition to it?' (Silin, 1995:99)

> Social scientists cannot conduct research that is empirically whole and socially useful if they are too elitist or too frightened, or if they are too preoccupied with structure (Dance, 2002:32)

> The circumstances under which people become educated about human sexuality stand in sharp contrast to the manner in which they typically learn about other important human characteristics and behaviours. (Abramson and Pinkerton, 2002: 75)

> The unaccounted problem becomes how to imagine which knowledge will allow for new practices of the self when the dominant knowledge of sexuality is so caught up in, and constituted by, discourses of moral panic, protection of innocent children, the eugenics of normalcy, and the dangers of explicit representations of sexuality. (Britzman, 1998:73)

A broader take on sex and sexuality might yield something far more dynamic and vital. Besides which, if we really were living *in the age of* HIV/AIDS there would be no contest and therefore no discussion. However it would have been naive to think that I could introduce sexual assertiveness as a focus without engaging regulatory discourses at some stage in the research. In my final submission I consequently reworded my abstract and eliminated this dimension altogether, but by now this had become a more informed, active rejection.

IMAGE 2: Warhol and the RAE

As far as I am aware the Research Assessment Exercise is a pheno-menon of the U.K. without parallel elsewhere in the world. As a method of government funding for educational research it is highly contentious (Stronach, 2004:3-20; HMSO, 2003; www.hero.ac.uk/rae). I exploited the criteria of the RAE to examine my position as a teacher and researcher whose work centres on aspects of identity and selfhood – often defined by assessment in one form or another in the English education system – and how this permeates the professional and private domains (Perselli, 2004c).

Here are the categories under which I am invited to contribute my research output for the RAE:

> international meetings
> sponsoring organisations
> international collaborations
> conferences
> distinctions
> fellowships
> prizes
> distinguished positions
> externally funded invitations
> community recognition

It seems to me that the ability of a remote central UK assessment board, ostensibly devoid of teacher researchers, to actually judge the worth of one's work and award research funding on such vague terms is tenuous indeed. Never mind! When Warhol was a teenager he won first prize in an art competition at school for his painting entitled *The Broad Gave Me My Face, But I Can Pick My Own Nose*, so perhaps there was hope still for me?

Throughout his early life Warhol hated his facial profile and later had corrective surgery on his nose. If I make myself more attractive, will I get invited to more of the above, I wonder? Or does no-one give a damn what you look like; how you feel about your appearance; your sexuality?

IMAGE 3: Jackie Kennedy on the Steps of a US Air Force Plane, Followed by JFK and Officials.

It hadn't escaped my notice that my female icons or idols were mostly American, or (apparently) conformed to American standards of glamour, and that to make it big in the research world you probably have to 'crack the American market'. I had also noticed that most of the academic publishing houses are US/UK owned, so the empiricist model had affected me deeply. In a story I wrote a while back for a book on teacher identities (O'Reilly Scanlon, Weber and Mitchell, 2004) I depicted myself 'descending from the plane, clutching this little bag of wares to sell, thinking, Who is out there? Who will buy this?' Wow! Coming across this picture of JK and JFK on a pirate Warhol website made me wonder if I had seen it before. I certainly don't remember much about JFK at all, but the figure of Jackie intrigued me throughout my childhood and adolescence, and parallel clips of The Beatles and various other celebs *returning* from the States at London airport, being mobbed by adoring fans, are very vivid.

Warhol: 'In the future, everyone will be famous for 15 minutes'. Hmm. In the future, will educational researchers achieve celebrity status on this level, I wonder? If so, I want a piece of it! Alternatively, notorious criminals also get deported back to/escape from the UK by plane; it could go either way... Who are the Bad Girls of the RAE? Are they seeking love/affection/recognition in all the wrong places? Glamour and sleeze, merit-marks and corruption; opposite sides of the same coin. Equally compelling, for sure.

IMAGE 4: Marilyn

The platinum blonde... blonde jokes... Blondie (Deborah Harry's band). Warhol depicted a world of 'inaccessible glamour and celebrity'; yet it was also a world anyone could buy a piece of, in imitation or for real (*Dreaming*; Blondie, 1979). He painted celebrities like Marilyn Monroe (whose real name was Norma Jean) and ordinary things one would come to think of as ubiquitously part of 20th century life, such as coca-cola and Campbell's soup. I was intrigued to discover that every day at noon Warhol actually went home to the flat he shared with his mum, where she heated up Campbell's soup for him. W H Auden performed the equivalent in poetry, incorporating features of the industrial and mechanical age into his writing; debunking certain myths about what poetry ought to be about – and how it should be written. Why doesn't education research include more about the ordinary materiality of things? Making the familiar strange (and vice versa), isn't that our business too?

Last time I was in America I bought a whole array of Campbell's soups, with fascinating flavours we don't have in the UK, but I couldn't bring them back because I only had carry-on, so I knew they would get confiscated in security. International travel, information technology and mass media can free up ideas, create openings and enable new kinds of relationships to be formed, but at the same time security, safety, commodification (for example, not being able to quote song lyrics or show pictures without complex fee-paying procedures) inhibit me from replicating these ordinary things, now that they have become artefacts of my research. Nevertheless, the very idea that educational researchers, rushing from DPR in Plymouth, UK (my home town) to AERA (the American Educational Research Association annual meeting) halfway across the globe at San Diego, might step outside the bubble of unreality that constitutes the conference circuit, to notice a Vogue cover on a news stand, skim the Stefani sleeves at a Virgin Megastore, or study some soup can labels in a hypermarket, makes me smile.

When I worked as a SENCO (Coordinator for Special Educational Needs) in an infant department of an urban primary school, I spent a long time pursuing professional development activities: first a postgraduate diploma, then a Master's degree and finally my PhD. I was very committed to improving my practice and being better at my job. But one day a fashion journalist friend of mine 'phoned to say that she had a spare place for a makeover and fashion shoot for her magazine: was I interested? Could I fill the slot? I did, and afterwards, because I knew people would get to see the pictures sooner or later anyway, I pinned them up, a bit tongue-in-cheek, on the SENCO pin-board at school. 'Oh yes!' said one parent, 'it's about time this place had a bit of glamour'. Wow, I thought; you could spend your whole life convincing people that you are adequately qualified to teach their child without ever attending to these other perspectives; unconsciously judging and being judged on points of dress or style or body-language, as though they don't exist. Glamour has this ambivalent power: on the one hand to set you apart from the crowd, on the other to make you more visible, to release fantasies. I think this is important in ordinary life, particularly for women workers in education, where both the domestic and professional demands can be extraordinarily harsh and frequently in conflict with each other.

IMAGE 5: I want to be a Machine

A major Warhol exhibition opened at Tate Modern, London, on February 7th, 2002. Donna De Salvo, Senior Curator, on Warhol:

> More than any other artist of his generation, Warhol showed that the ubiquitous imagery of mass culture had come to reflect and shape contemporary life [Coke etc.]. This powerful subject matter... has often obscured his radical explorations into different media. He painted and drew with silkscreen, made moving images appear still, stitched together identical photographs, and filled a room with silver balloons. His life's project was to explore the aesthetic and cultural associations of the term 'media', questioning structural boundaries in a way now heralded by some as 'post-medium'.

> Although he described his approach as 'machinelike', his work was far from uniform. He created an art of endless permutation, re-inventing the same images and themes again and again. His capacity to *discover difference within what appeared to be the same uncovered a world of nuance in the every day.* (De Salvo, 2002; italics added)

Discovering difference in the same, the every day – yes!! This is why we must talk about feminisms in the plural, and why the attitudes to the pictures and ideas stimulated in the DPR session are so multifarious: one woman says she is left cold by them, another advocates abstinence in sex, someone else quotes Adrienne Rich 'feeling like a porn star' when she is having sex (is this a bad thing, a good thing? we wondered), a fellow presenter relates back to her village in Africa and the way women and girls are schooled into their femininity in the dress they wear. Many accounts emerge that are illustrative of diverse sexual values and perspectives and I begin to wonder if we will ever get through the material for all the talking (and would that matter?).

IMAGE 6: No Doubt: Stefani preparing for a video shoot, with silk, furs, long black gloves, heavy black leather belt

Warhol: 'You live your dream America, that you've custom made from art and schmaltz and emotions, just as much as you live your real one.'

But he also said 'You can only live life in one place at one time'.

Both these quotations, combined with the fantasy-like dressing up for a video shoot, the expression of intent on the women's faces in the photograph, suggest to me that you must cherish your life and live your art; savour all its good things.

Warhol proceeded to paint his Disasters series, such as Electric Chairs, Race Riot and Tunafish Disaster. This use of art as social commentary is in keeping with the direction the Pop Art movement was heading generally. His car wrecks, mushroom cloud and the suicides (e.g. of Marilyn Monroe) 'suggested the rift between media promises of health and happiness and the very real desperation of lives that did not find a place in such one-dimensional narratives' (McCarthy, 2000: 68).

Warhol also made portraits of his mother, he attended mass nearly every day, he painted religious themes, many of which were not disclosed during his lifetime. This aspect of the private/public persona is compelling; that you could be apparently researching one thing whilst simultaneously preoccupied with another, which, for whatever reason, you don't want to reveal just now.

Observation-surveillance-transparency-criticism-acclaim: all aspects of the artistic process that are aspects of the life of the public intellectual too. There can be value and no little honesty in being coldly indifferent, and there is value in subjective emotional engagement (and dishonesty in feigning emotion); it depends what you are talking about and what you are trying to say. Foucault (2001) discusses this in terms of the Greek *Parrhesia*; the speech of someone, the *parrhesiastes*, who speaks the truth and says everything she has in mind, even if it differs from what the majority of people believe. I resent the assumption that I have to Care in order to be ethical; also that I may be assessed on my work in ways that are inappropriate to its intentions or effects.

We proceed with three further OHTs in a similar vein, incorporating real-life conversations and reflections that the songs and the art inspired:

Hey Joe
VP phone call to brother:
'Why are we so deviant, Joe?'

Joe:
'Because we were raised by circus folk.'

Happy Birthday
VP text message to Friend 1:
'Happy birthday, babe.
YOU CAN ONLY LIVE YOUR LIFE IN ONE PLACE AT ONE
TIME.
Andy Warhol said it, but I got it first off you...

And the druggie house off Broad Street,
the one that's all boarded up
[my home: New England style clapboard front on remodelled 1970s
semi],
looks good enough to me.'

Detox 1
Friend 2, text message to VP:
'What's up babey? You OK?
You want a chat?'

VP:
'Don't know. Don't think so.
Let's just say, the usual words don't seem to be working.
– shxx Z., I really need to get out of here.'

Detox 2
Daughter to VP:
'It sounds really interesting [this project].
I just think it could be difficult to bring off. I wouldn't know where
to start.'

VP:
'Well, I've fermented this in my head for a long time.
It's almost as though you have to detox first.'

'No Doubt' Sleeve Note for *Running* (No Doubt: The Singles, 2001):

Filtered through the band's sensibilities, the track was maturing
beyond those initial influences. But it was far from done. At first,
No Doubt attempted a 'spacier' version of 'Running' but everyone
involved agreed it buckled under its own weight. That's when
producer Nellee Hooper added his Midas touch. In a process of

studio alchemy, the track was boiled down to its essential elements and at long last it came together.

Conclusion

So what were the anxieties that made it so difficult to get started? What was the 'detox' you have to go through in order to begin to write? How does post-medium research mature beyond its initial influences? Stefani also talks of '... a pure moment of celebration and experimentation'; how does that come about?

I love the No Doubt sleeve notes and lyrics because they speak, as Warhol does, to a young (research young?) generation as much about the creative process as about the work, in simple language that is refreshingly accessible and thought-provoking. One anxiety was simply that the audience at DPR might not relate to either the objects and tools or the theme, so I was truly delighted that the many people who attended the session did know and love the Stefani songs, also her voice and appearance which is witty, unselfconsciously ironic, highly androgynous yet simultaneously playing with feminine gloss and glamour, and of course totally lacking in deference. This is the allure of the rock genre; that it can be all these things at once. But I was also delighted that participants could follow the method and feel free to disagree. Since I was leading the session I wasn't able to record individual views (was this teaching? was it research?), but in a way that was better because the naturalness and spontaneity was its high point: 'a pure moment of celebration and experimentation'. The fact that I was generously allocated 75 minutes in which to present, yet still our discussion spilled over well into the evening, ending with a large circle of women and men: young postgraduate students, art students, experienced academics, mothers, boyfriends, grandmothers, all talking about sexualities and very much in the plural, was enough.

A second anxiety ran deeper. I had to work very hard with background reading, listening and thinking before beginning to write ('I've fermented this for a long time'); partly through daily tensions and stresses – the discipline demanded to put these on hold should not be underestimated – partly through fear that I might make gratuitous self-disclosures of no consequence to anyone, partly through transgressing into areas of research I didn't know how to handle. I was also concerned not to overkill on Warhol or Stefani; it was just like the lady said, sometimes less is more, things can buckle under their own weight. I do hope, therefore, that in these pages I have left enough space for interpretation and maybe inspired some readers to consider post-medium methods in the context of their own work.

Returning to female sexual assertiveness and the ways in which many participants spoke of themselves, their daughters or granddaughters, it does seem as though women are becoming more knowing, or at least more articulate, about their sexuality; relating this to pleasure and desire as distinct from emotional intimacy or biological necessity. This chimes with recent research: Laina Bay-Cheng (2003, *ibid.*) in her discussion of teen sex refers to sexual self-efficacy and sexual agency, which 'involves the negotiation of sexual desires, contextual factors and the ability to assert the resulting decision' (p65). The impression is mirrored in the lyrics of the singer-songwriters, where negotiation and reasoning are taking place in a complex matrix of social relations and situations, with an implied and sometimes overt sexual entitlement for women. Similarly, the image of the glamour girl has shifted over time. Whereas at one time we might have assumed, with my parade of women icons, that the accoutrements of glamour were primarily capitalist (and capitalism is certainly seductive in this way; evidenced by aspirational (designer) clothing, luxury goods and venues; the craving for expendable income to the point of excess), this now seems simplistic because it belies the creative function of glamour as a manoeuvre out of the desexualisation that comes through drabness and monotony; be it slavery of body or mind. Economic and political independence – at least for some women, some of the time – combine with opportunities for self-determination which rely neither on material wealth nor material power. Punk rock, the movement that occurred in the interim period between the 60s icons and the present-day performers, could arguably be seen as the antidote to capitalistic glamour that has since allowed Stefani *et al* to redefine its parameters in performance art. There are unselfconscious, self-parodying and self-referential strategies being used in song, still image and video which resonate with audiences in terms of women's refusal to be invisible or to be victims, which, I think, carry over usefully into other identity formations too (Seidman, 2002, *ibid.*). By deliberately glamourising the RAE, for example, one might – now here's a thing – dignify the role...?

Whatever we might feel about mass markets and globalisation, the interpretations we make of oppression or repression, sexual morality or sexual health discourses (and for sure there are plenty of conversations to be held about all of these), there is evidence in the real world, when we are attentive to the ordinary things people do and say, of cultural knowledge evincing cultural change: there are far more versions of female sexuality than there are programmes of education or categories of porn that could accommodate them. Glamour, fantasy and artistic creativity cannot be dismissed too readily, in teaching or in research; post-medium methods enable me to recognise that this is so.

References

Abramson, P R and Pinkerton, S T (2002) *With Pleasure: Thoughts on the nature of human sexuality*. Oxford: Oxford University Press

Atkinson, E (2004) Sexualities and resistance: queer(y)ing identity and discourse in education, in: Satterthwaite, J, Atkinson, E and Martin, W (eds) *Educational Counter-Cultures: Confrontation, images, vision*. Stoke on Trent: Trentham Books: 55 – 68

Bay-Cheng, L Y (2003) The trouble of teen sex, *Sex Education* 3(1): 61-74

Britzman, D P (1998) *Lost Subjects, Contested Objects: Towards a psychoanalytic inquiry of learning*. New York: SUNY

Dance, L J (2002) *Tough Fronts: The impact of street culture on schooling*. New York and London: RoutledgeFalmer

Denzin, N and Lincoln, Y S (2000) (eds) (2nd edn) *Handbook of Qualitative Research*. Thousand Oaks: Sage

De Salvo, D (2002) *Warhol*. Tate Modern, London. 7 Feb – 1 April 2002

Dilley, P (2002) *Queer Man On Campus: A history of non-heterosexual college men, 1945-2000*. New York and London: RoutledgeFalmer

Foucault, M (1990) *The History of Sexuality, Vols 1-3*. New York: Vintage Books

Foucault, M (2001) (ed J Pearson) *Fearless Speech*. Los Angeles: Semiotext(e)

HMSO (2003) *The Future of Higher Education*. White Paper, London: HMSO

Kincheloe, J and Steinberg, S R (1998) *Unauthorised Method: Strategies for critical teaching*. New York and London: RoutledgeFalmer

McCarthy, D (2000) *Pop Art*. London: Tate Gallery

O'Reilly Scanlon, K, Weber, S and Mitchell, C (2004) (eds) *Just Who Do We Think We Are? Methodologies for autobiography and self-study in education*. London: RoutledgeFalmer

Perselli, V (2004a) *Marx and Education: Exploring the teachings of Marx in the context of my role as a school experience liaison tutor in Initial Teacher Education*. [add full book reference later]

Perselli, V (2004b) 'A personal preview': or 'Portraying my professional life in pictures': image and performance as methodology for research in teaching and learning, in: Satterthwaite, J, Atkinson, E and Martin, W (eds) *Educa-*

tional Counter-Cultures: Confrontation, images, vision. Stoke on Trent: Trentham Books: 183-199

Perselli, V (2004c) Teaching for England: five poems, *Cultural Studies, Critical Methodologies* 4(3): 405 – 411

Reardon, V (2004) Constraining bodies: inspection as a form of hygiene, in: Satterthwaite, J, Atkinson, E and Martin, W (eds) *Educational Counter-Cultures: Confrontation, images, vision*. Stoke on Trent: Trentham Books: 103 – 113

Seidman, S (2002) *Beyond the Closet: The transformation of gay and lesbian life*. New York and London: RoutledgeFalmer

Silin, J G (1995) *Sex, Death and the Education of Children: Our passion for ignorance in the age of AIDS*. New York and London: Teachers College Press

Stronach, I (2004) Ending educational research, countering dystopian futures, in: Satterthwaite, J, Atkinson, E and Martin, W (eds) *The Disciplining of Education: new languages of power and resistance*. Stoke on Trent: Trentham Books: 3 – 20

Music References

Harry, D (1991, 1979) Dreaming, from *The Complete Picture: the very best of Deborah Harry and Blondie*. Crysalis Records

No Doubt: (2000, 2003), It's My Life, Bathwater, Excuse Me Mr., Underneath It All, Running, from *No Doubt: the singles 1992-2003*. Interscope Records

Chicago (2003) Miramax Films

Websites

www.hero.ac.uk/rae/
www.nodoubt.com
www.warhol.org
www.warholfoundation.org
www.warholstars.org

Note

1   The Research Assessment Exercise (RAE) is the means by which government funding (from the Higher Education Funding Councils – HEFCs) is allocated to universities in the UK on the basis of the perceived quality of their research. Levels of funding are determined by ranking 'academic areas' within universities on the basis of the RAE panels' assessment of their research activities and output, based on a detailed report submitted to the RAE panel by each academic area in each university.

11

Moving On
A FAAB poem

CATH LAMBERT

Performance cannot be translated; nor can poems. FAAB is the acronym for Feminists Against Academic Bureaucracy; but the FAAB sisters don't advertise this translation of their runes. There is a sense in which we all know what they mean, and what this poem means: a sense which gives us the confidence to understand beyond the words. Beyond the words is the passionate engagement, comic and serious at once, giving us all, performers and readers alike, the courage to 'articulate and perform resistance'.

Introducing some Serious Play

I want to use the reconceptualisation of academic work to ask what becomes possible when our work is intentionally positioned as both within and against other normalised disciplinary convention...what would it mean to create a different space in which to undertake other performances, other thinking, power and pleasures? What would it mean to create new lines of flight, fragments of other possibilities, to experiment differently with meanings, practices, and our own confoundings? (Mary Leach 2000:223)

The poem below, whilst presented here alone, offers one element of a collective work of authorship and performance. It is also, as the poem itself suggests, part of an ongoing process. It was written and performed as part of the FAAB Collective's contribution to *Discourse, Power, Resistance* 2004. The Collective's members are Louise Archer,

Jacky Brine, Valerie Hey, Cath Lambert, Carole Leathwood and Diane Reay, with invaluable support from Analía Meo and Richard Waller. FAAB is not a name or identity owned by us. Rather, FAAB emerged through wider discussions amongst pro/feminist educationalists and, in the spirit of Naomi Klein's (2002) notion of contemporary anti-capitalist struggle as a series of interconnected, creative and fast moving networks or hotlinks, serves as a fluid acronym or identity for any act or series of acts wishing to make use of it.

This particular Collective came together in February 2003 at a British Sociological Association (BSA) Sociology of Education Study Group meeting, where it was suggested that any willing and able members would collaborate on a critical intervention for the forthcoming British Educational Research Association (BERA) annual conference. Some of us met up again. And again. We drank a lot of wine, and laughed a lot. What we all agreed on was that if we were going to try and say something different, we had to say it in a different way. We had to challenge the very form and language that seemed to constrain and regulate our emotional and critical voices. So we talked about songs and dance, poems and satire. We all, in different ways, experienced both excitement and fear at the prospect of exposing our personal and academic selves in what felt like a very risky way – none of us are (or were!) singers or dancers or comedians. However, unified by shared and differentiated feelings of anger, disappointment and frustration at the current state of education and our locations within it, we started on what was to become a collective process of generating ideas and devising and compiling sketches and songs. Individual contributions were thrown into the mix. The process was organic: there were no overarching criteria, and the resulting whole as performed at *Discourse Power Resistance* 2004 consisted of a series of songs, poems, extracts from New Labour educational discourse, and satirical sketches.

One possible reading of this poem (although by no means the only one) is as some articulation of our/my fears and hopes for these collective intentions and the possible interventions that we, and others, might make in terms of challenging and disrupting hegemonic trends in contemporary educational discourse. Drawing on the potentialities of dialogue and laughter (Bakhtin, 1981; McWilliam, 2000) the poem seeks to articulate and perform resistance. We hope that it captures something of the spirit and the process of the wider performance, at times an exhilarating mix of individual and collective struggle as well as a celebration. In the words of Judith Butler (1990:x) we would argue that, 'Without a doubt, feminism continues to require its own forms of serious play'. Serious play offers, we believe, some hope of moving on, and we hope that audiences and readers enjoy what we have put together and are also encouraged to play, seriously.

Moving On

we seek the right words
the right ways to say them
   and they taunt us
   haunt us
as we try to be critical
to seek a politics that does not have us turning at night
   this way and that
how do we find the right words
free our language
free our texts
from the litany of best practice excellence inclusion

how can we reclaim   renew   create
   new ways to narrate
new stories

here we try something different
for there is nothing linear about life
as our lives shift back and forth
through memory
   and dreaming
   and hoping
and yet we pretend
our fine linear texts
   chronological structures
   holding back our resources and
censoring our collective dreams

we are not in isolation
our social existence is born through others
shared language and the necessity of reciprocity
lest our stories echo in a void

so why   oh why
do we think and write and struggle
alone   by the flicker of the screen
seeking answers from within
and angry with the disillusion that we find there
working   to produce little gods

this is not accusatory
we all know why
we comply
we know that which holds us back
    makes us serious
makes us respect and enforce
a norm we do not create
or endorse

there is a fear of laughter   or worse   silence
but when we stop smiling
we have lost
thus into the listening void
we throw a smile   for they are tricky to resist

we seek out cracks
where the sticky fingers of the market
where the breath down our backs
of neo-liberal greed
has not seeped into our practice
our minds   our teaching   writing   thinking

we shout   we care about social justice
    we feel strung out
    crucified on a straight crossed line
between the just   and the success we
must prove
    to remain in the game

but we   the inclusive we
cannot be wished away
wished out of pedagogic spaces
    corridors
texts
spaces must be made   we cry
    we insist
for every landscape shifts

in play we resist
there are new geographies

we seek a new position
and we remember that compliance and resistance
do not sit in opposition

we offer this stance
as a brief respite
    a slip of hope
though there is not one answer
it is not carnival   or protest   or ethical research
it is all of these and more

we open to the floor
in disguise   poor disguise as masquerade
this is a heartfelt struggle
pressing at boundaries
and feeling the sickening liberatory fear of transgression
which takes our longing and makes it public
flinging us from the secret intimacies of what we feel and practice
into a dialogue with the social
    the economic
the political

                            and back again and back again
    caught in the wind of a dialogic freedom
    furrowing the tracks of resistance
digging tracks
digging tracks

here   we do not end
we capture somewhere in the middle
    and then let go

and in this parting we are optimistic   are we
can our optimism sit with the pain of recognition
that the small and large injustices
are all part of the same horrendous game

but the state we are in is process
and we are not standing still

References

Bakhtin, M (1981) 'Epic and Novel: Towards a Methodology for the Study of the Novel' in Holquist, M (ed) *The Dialogic Imagination*. Texas: University of Texas Press

Butler, J (1990) *Gender Trouble: Feminism and the Subversion of Identity*. London: Routledge

Klein, N (2002) *Fences and Windows*. London: Flamingo

Leach, M (2000) 'Feminist Figurations: Gossip as a Counterdiscourse' in Elizabeth A St Pierre, E and Pillow, W (eds) *Working the Ruins: Feminist Poststructural Theory and Methods in Education*. New York: Routledge

McWilliam, E (2000) 'Laughing within Reason: On Pleasure, Women and Academic Performance' in St. Pierre, E and Pillow, W (eds) *Working the Ruins: Feminist Poststructuralist Theory and Methods in Education*. New York: Routledge

Contributors

Elizabeth Atkinson is a Reader in Social and Educational Inquiry in the School of Education and Lifelong Learning at the Unversity of Sunderland, UK. Her research interests include equality, diversity and identity and the application of the radical uncertainties of postmodern and poststructuralist thinking to the excessive certainties of contemporary educational policy and practice. She delights in crossing boundaries of all sorts, and for this reason has taken great pleasure in co-editing the four volumes so far in this series.

Gill Boag-Munroe is Visiting Lecturer in Birmingham University's School of Education, having previously worked as Senior Mentor and Head of the English subject area in the English Midlands. Her doctoral thesis aims to answer research questions which arose from the experience of simultaneously inhabiting the two roles.

Sue Clegg is Head of Research in the Learning and Teaching Institute at Sheffield Hallam University and convenes the University's newly formed Higher Education Research Network. Recent publications include work on personal development planning (PDP) and a critique of evidence-based research. She is editor designate of *Teaching in Higher Education*.

Mike Cole is Co-ordinator of the Inclusion and Social Justice Research Group in the School of Education at the University of Brighton. Recent publications include *Education Equality and Human Rights* (2nd edition, 2005); and *Professional Values and Practice for Teachers and Student Teachers*, (2nd edition, 2005). His co-edited book, *Marxism Against Postmodernism in Educational Theory*, won the 2004 American Education Studies Association award for one of the best education books in the USA. He is the author of *Marxism, Postmodernism And Education: Pasts, Presents And Futures*, (forthcoming 2005).

Tamsin Haggis is a lecturer in Lifelong Learning at the Institute of Education, University of Stirling. Her teaching and research interests focus on the different ways that learning is researched and theorised, particularly within the fields of Higher and Further Education. She is interested in the implications of mass higher education for traditional cultures of university learning, and, more generally, in theory, epistemology and method in educational research.

Lisa Isherwood is Professor of Feminist Liberation Theologies at The College of St Mark and St John, Plymouth. She is an executive editor of the international journal 'Feminist Theology' and the author of several books including, *Liberating Christ, The Good News of the Body. Sexual Theology and Feminism* and *Introducing Feminist Christologies*.

Cath Lambert is a Lecturer in Sociology at the University of Warwick, teaching in the areas of gender, sexuality and education. Her current research investigates the construction of teachers' professional identities and her wider interests include the sexual cultures of teachers and young people as well as the development of critical methods for researching and writing.

Peter McLaren is Professor of Urban Education, Graduate School of Education and Information Studies, University of California, Los Angeles. He is the author and editor of over forty books on the political sociology of education, critical pedagogy, and Marxist theory. Professor McLaren lectures worldwide. His writings have been translated into fifteen languages. His recent books include *Che Guevara, Paulo Freire and the Pedagogy of Revolution*; (with co-editors Mike Cole, Dave Hill and Glenn Rikowski) *Marxism Against Postmodernism in Educational theory*; (with co-author Ramin Farahmandpur) *Teaching Against Globalization and the New Imperialism*; (with co-editors Gustavo Fischman, Heinz Sunker and Colin Lankshear) *Critical Theories, Radical Pedagogies and Global Conflicts*; *Red Seminars*; and *Capitalists and Conquerors*.

Ros Ollin is Principal Lecturer in Education at the University of Huddersfield. She has been involved in post-compulsory education for the past 30 years, both as a practitioner and as a teacher educator. Her research interests are teacher identity; international education; teachers' conceptions and uses of silence.

Victoria Perselli is a Senior Lecturer in Education at Kingston University, UK, where she teaches courses in qualitative research methods, inclusive education, equity and diversity. She is the holder of a HEFCE Promising Researcher fellowship, and in 2005 will begin a writing project, *Diversity and Method*, with Mary Manke at the University of Wisconsin, River Falls. Her current interests include the rereading of European high theory, also the use of narrative and performance arts media as forms of representation and interpretation in qualitative research.

William F. Pinar teaches curriculum theory at Louisiana State University, where he serves as the St. Bernard Parish Alumni Endowed Professor. He has also served as the Frank Talbott Professor at the University of Virginia and the A. Lindsay O'Connor Professor of American Institutions at Colgate University. Pinar is the author, most recently, of *What Is Curriculum Theory?*

Index

9/11: 25, 26, 57, 65, 79, 81, 83, 84, 93, 94
accountability 31, 133, 145, 152, 157
action research 119, 121, 130, 135
activism 36, 124, 126, 160
activity theory 131, 132, 136, 138
Afghanistan 79, 83, 84, 88-90, 93
agency 21, 86, 152, 154, 156, 180
Al-Quaida 8, 67, 82, 89, 90, 94
assertiveness 163-169, 171-172, 180
audit 115, 120, 134
autobiography, autobiographical 26, 31, 34
autonomy, autonomous 18, 19, 25, 28, 37, 114, 134, 135, 143, 146, 148, 157, 159

binary, binaries 90, 98, 99, 154, 156, 169

capitalism 4, 5, 11-20, 49, 53, 56, 59, 65-77, 81, 164, 167, 180
Christ, Christic, christological 69, 70, 73-77
Christian, Christianity xvi, 3, 8, 65-77

civilization 82, 88, 89
class 3-23, 32, 39, 47-63, 91, 104, 106, 108, 122, 133, 168, 169
colour 14-17, 60, 63
common sense 48-49, 134
complexity theory 98, 104, 108
compliance xvii, 119-120, 134, 145, 155, 159, 187
conflict 32, 49, 55, 71-72, 76, 89-90, 94, 156, 175
consumerism 3, 71, 76
creativity xiv-xv, 28, 36, 158, 181
critical discourse analysis 131, 138, 140
critical pedagogy 3, 13-21, 62, 116, 121-124
critique x, xi, xii, 14-18, 45, 55, 73, 79, 98, 102, 113-127, 130, 163, 189
culture xv, 13, 25-29, 33-39, 49-50, 58-59, 67, 72, 75, 77, 81, 87-88, 99, 103, 106, 111, 117, 120, 133, 151, 159, 166, 167, 170, 176
curriculum xv, 4, 25-42, 45, 47-50, 58-59, 63, 120, 133, 137, 142, 146, 167

democracy 5-6, 11-12, 18, 20-21, 28-29, 41, 66, 68, 88
desire 70-75, 170, 180
difference 14-15, 36, 40, 72, 80, 83, 85, 86, 102-105, 108, 168, 176
discipline xiii, 30, 32, 101, 120-122, 130
division of labour 15, 50, 136-138, 146-148
dualism, duality 68, 72, 74, 153
dynamic systems theory 97, 102

élitism 126, 133
empathy, empathic 145, 148
epistemology, epistemological xiii, xvi, 97, 100, 103, 105, 114-117, 119, 121, 125, 127, 152
eros 71-72
evidence-based practice 114-119, 127

fantasy 34, 53, 169-170, 177, 181
female 33, 163-173, 180-181
feminism, feminine, feminist 98, 100-102, 114, 122, 124-127, 167, 170, 176, 179, 183-185

193

Index

postmodern,
postmodernism xi, 13,
20, 47, 53-56, 59, 80-
82, 98, 100-102, 164,
poverty 4, 51, 68
practitioner xvi, 115-120,
135, 156, 157
praxis 19, 20, 65, 67, 71,
74, 75, 95, 122, 125
professional,
professionalism,
professional practice
xii, xvi, 25, 27, 28,
30, 33-35, 38, 41, 97,
115, 118, 131, 134,
135, 140, 141, 151-
162, 173, 175
progress files 116, 118, 119
psychoanalysis,
psychoanalytic 25, 30,
31

quantitative research 97-
112, 117

race 10, 12, 15, 18, 47-63,
169, 177
racialisation, racialised 15,
31-33, 47-63, 122,
167
redemption 65-77
reflective practice, reflective
practitioner 121, 135
reform, reformer xii, 11-13,
16, 25-45, 131, 168

refusal, refuse xvii, 124,
126, 158, 180
rights 6, 19, 31, 52, 53, 58,
66, 67, 71, 152
risk, risky 19, 75, 76, 165,
184
rules 11, 132, 136-140,
145-148, 154

schooling 31, 58, 63, 131-
150
self xiii, xiv, 16-19, 25-45,
65-77, 90, 91, 102,
105, 106, 135, 157,
158, 163-182
September 11th 2001/9/11
5, 25, 26, 57, 65-77,
79-94, 81, 82, 87
sexuality 34, 163-182
silence, silencing, silenced
18, 67, 68, 70, 80,
81, 103, 123, 126,
135, 186
socialism 3-23
standardisation,
standardised 26, 28,
85, 88, 118
standards 131-150, 167,
173
structure xiii, 15, 17, 21,
332, 42, 101, 123,
153, 165, 172, 185
subversion, subversive xvii,
38, 151-162

tactics, tactical 9, 33, 83,
88, 151-162
teacher training, initial
teacher training 131-
150
terror, terrorism, terrorist 1,
3-23, 54, 59, 65-77,
79-94
test, testing xi, 13, 28, 34,
36, 37, 45, 133, 137
transgression, transgressive,
transgress xvii, 74,
75, 168, 179, 187

victim, victimhood xv, 5,
13, 16, 31, 51, 151-
162, 180
vision xvii, 20, 21, 50, 54,
59, 75, 110, 160, 163
voice, voices xi, xiii, 18, 67,
74, 113-116, 122,
123, 125, 140, 145,
148, 156, 179, 184
vulnerability, vulnerable 19,
39, 56, 65-77, 165

xeno-racism 59, 63